Meher Bhoot is Associate Professor and Head at the Department of German, University of Mumbai. Her areas of specialization are German Literature with a focus on Literature of the German Minorities, Postcolonial Studies and Culture Studies, and her areas of interest are European Cultural History and European History of Art. She is an active member of the German Institute's Partnership with the Universities of Göttingen and Freiburg in Germany. Under the aegis of this partnership she has been a Guest Professor at the Department of Intercultural German Studies, University of Göttingen. She is a DAAD Fellow since 2004 and has also been a recipient of the Rotary Cultural and Ambassadorial Scholarship (1997-98). She is also the Member Secretary of the Women's Development Cell and member of the Internal Committee at the University of Mumbai. Apart from articles published, some of her co-edited volumes include *Revisiting Günter Grass, Voices from India and Germany, Interkulturelle Momente, Einfach menschlich.* She has also co-edited textbooks for the short courses for teaching Marathi to non-native speakers.

Rajesh Kharat is Founder Director, School of International Relations and Strategic Studies, University of Mumbai and Dean, Faculty of Humanities, University of Mumbai (on Deputation), and Professor and former Chairperson, Centre for South Asian Studies, School of International Studies, JNU, New Delhi. He has an MA in Political Science from the University of Poona, and has completed his M.Phil. and PhD from CSAS, SIS, JNU, New Delhi. He began his teaching career at the University of Mumbai in 1991 and taught at JNU for 30 years. He has published five books and more than 30 research articles in international and national journals and edited volumes on various themes of contemporary South Asia.

Satishchandra Kumar is Professor and Head of the Department of Applied Psychology & Counselling Centre at the University of Mumbai. He is also the Coordinator of the Mahatma Gandhi Peace Centre. He is the recipient of the Summer Fellowship from the Albert

Ellis Institute, New York. He was awarded a Research Fellowship by the Indian Council of Social Science Research (ICSSR), New Delhi. He has published in international peer-reviewed journals like *Journal of Personality and Social Psychology, Psychological Science, British Journal of Guidance and Counselling,* and also contributed to the Sage volume of *Eminent Indian Psychologists: 100 Years of Psychology in India.* He has published five books and more than 40 research papers in national and international journals, and many students have done doctorate degrees under his guidance. His area of research is Industrial/Organizational Psychology, which includes positive psychology, engagement at the workplace, stress and coping at the workplace. He is also a member of many academic bodies and regularly advises corporates. He is also the co-editor of *Sambhashan,* the journal of the University of Mumbai.

Kanchana Mahadevan is Professor and Head at the Department of Philosophy, University of Mumbai. She teaches and researches in feminist philosophy, continental thought, critical theory and political philosophy. She also works in the interdisciplinary areas of aesthetics and film. Her book *Between Femininity and Feminism: Colonial and Postcolonial Perspectives on Care* examines the relevance of Western feminist philosophy in the Indian context, while bringing Western feminism into dialogue with its Indian counterpart. Her publications on Ambedkar explore his rearticulation of democracy from the Indian perspective. In her recently published research papers on care ethics, she has engaged with its critical potential in relation to health work and the cosmopolitan character of care. She is specifically interested in exploring the comparative and decolonizing dimensions of philosophy. She is currently working on a monograph on the relationship between the secular and the post-secular in the context of gender.

GANDHI THEN AND NOW

AUTOBIOGRAPHIES AND CONVERSATIONS

Edited by

Satishchandra Kumar

Kanchana Mahadevan

Meher Bhoot

Rajesh Kharat

Foreword by

Bhikhu Parekh

in association with

University of Mumbai

SPEAKING TIGER BOOKS LLP
125A, Ground Floor, Shahpur Jat, near Asiad Village,
New Delhi 110049

First published by Speaking Tiger Books 2022

ISBN: 978-93-5447-262-6
eISBN: 978-93-5447-263-3

10 9 8 7 6 5 4 3 2 1

Typeset in Crimson by SÜRYA, New Delhi
Printed at Shree Maitrey Printech Pvt. Ltd., Noida

CONTENTS

ACKNOWLEDGEMENTS

This book is the outcome of a collaboration between the University of Mumbai's *Sambhashan* (an online, interdisciplinary open access humanities journal) and the Mahatma Gandhi Peace Centre on two journal issues dedicated to Mohandas Karamchand Gandhi's 151st birth anniversary. Some of the essays from the October 2020 Gandhi issue of the journal have been included in this collection, with a few additional ones. Our dhanyavad to the authors who have contributed to this book with their thought-provoking essays. Thank you also to our peer reviewers for their timely responses. We thank the consulting editor and the members of the advisory boards of the journal for their inputs. Our debt of gratitude to *Sambhashan*'s assistant editors for their timely help. Shukriyaan to Valenie Lopes and Ayush Srivastava for their help with copyediting. We are obliged to Ravi Singh and his team for their support and assistance.

FOREWORD

Bhikhu Parekh

There are many unresolved puzzles about Gandhi's corpus of writings. He wrote most of his books in his native Gujarati and then translated them himself or got them translated into English. He could have written at least some of these books or booklets directly in English himself, the language in which he was just as, or even more, proficient. Again, he wrote an autobiography, but said inconsistently and oddly on several occasions that he never intended to write one and had, in fact, not written one. He translated several books or their chapters into English such as Plato's *Apology*, Ruskin's *Unto This Last*, and Salter's *Ethical Religion*. He translated Irving's *Life of Prophet Mohammed* but could not publish more than a couple of chapters because of Muslim protest. It is not clear why he did so much translation. To educate the Indian masses? To expose them to new ways of thinking? And if so, why limit it to Gujaratis who were not particularly keen on his central ideas? Again, Gandhi was quite keen to ensure that his comments and activities were properly and accurately recorded, the task initially discharged by Mahadev Desai, and later in a different form, by Manu Gandhi whose diary Gandhi read and signed every night.

Gandhi's reasons for this, however, are not entirely clear. Perhaps he had an eye on history, or he wanted posterity to know his innermost thoughts on a wide range of issues, or he was simply concerned to make sure that nothing he said or did was kept in the dark. These and related puzzles go to the heart of Gandhi's thought and reflect his deepest motivations, concerns, and approach to life. Several chapters in this excellent collection deal with some of these puzzles in one form or another. It would be useful in this Foreword to concentrate on one of them, namely Gandhi's autobiography and his idea of experiments with truth.

Gandhi was above all a great social reformer. India, a once vibrant civilization, had become inert, inward looking, and degenerate and needed to revitalize itself. It had to open itself up to the influence of others, take a critical look at itself, and borrow from other cultures what it found valuable and could assimilate. No culture, no civilization, no religion, no human creation is or could be perfect and had much to learn from others. It also, however, had its own identity, integrity, insights, and needed to learn from others in such a way that these were enriched and not obliterated. How to remain true to oneself and also to the larger truth lying beyond it was an area of Gandhi's central concern. He applied this to different areas of life, including writing an autobiography.

While biography has a longer history, autobiography as a non-confessional and distinct genre of writing began to appear in Europe in the 18th century when its cultural presuppositions became available, such as making major choices affecting one's life, seeing oneself as the author of one's life, and understanding life as a narrative marked by both continuity and discontinuity. The term autobiography itself seems to have been first used in Germany in 1796 from where it travelled to other countries, including England. In India, it did not make an appearance until much later. Since autobiography appeared in a context where biography had long existed, it was initially seen as a form or species of biography, a self-biography, a biography of the author written by the author himself. Not surprisingly the term autobiography was hyphenated, and spelt as auto-biography to indicate its derivative or parasitic character.

Autobiography was largely meant to be written by persons of eminence who had great achievements to their credit and wished to write about them. Not surprisingly, Gandhi felt ambivalent about this. It involved invading the privacy of one's family and friends, selective narration of one's experiences with its inevitable untruthfulness, a measure of boastfulness, and an explicit or implicit assumption of one's greatness. The idea of writing an autobiography was originally not his, but pressed upon him by his close associates. Even then some of them were unhappy and one of them, a 'nirmal' or pure-hearted colleague, warned him against it. It was a Western practice and no-one in the East was known to have written one. Furthermore, given Gandhi's stature, his autobiography was likely to be taken as authoritative, a model to emulate, and that would create problems when Gandhi changed his mind on particular issues. These and other arguments had a measure of influence on Gandhi, but he said he had a way of dealing with these and other objections. He said he was not going to write an autobiography, but rather a story of his experiments with truth. As his whole life was bound up with these experiments, the resulting story would certainly resemble an autobiography, but that was neither his intention nor a necessary outcome. Autobiography was jivanvritant, a story of the details of one's life with the self at its centre. Gandhi was not writing a jivanvritant but a story of his experiments with truth. If his autobiography was to be nothing more than a story of his experiments, it would be morally 'innocent' and free from the vices to which autobiography was prone. Gandhi said that his life had been defined by and exhausted in his experiments and he was going to write about them 'in the name of' or 'under the pretext of' writing an autobiography. He was not concerned with the self but rather with the soul, the self appearing incidentally as a background. To make this point clear Gandhi said he had decided to put 'Experiments with Truth' first and the term 'autobiography' after it in the title of the book.

It is unfortunate that many of his commentators have missed Gandhi's unease and chosen to call the book Gandhi's autobiography. To some extent Gandhi himself must accept responsibility for this. He could have called the book 'Satyana Prayogo' without adding the word autobiography. The fact that he added it indicates that a simple history of moral and spiritual experiments with no reference to the details of one's life could also be an autobiography. Gandhi seems to oscillate between two senses of autobiography. The first refers to the conventional and far more common story of one's life with all its imperfections and impurities; the other to a morally innocent story of oneself as told through one's experiments. In the first sense Gandhi had not written an autobiography, in the second he had.

The important point at issue here is not merely semantic. It relates to Gandhi's style of reform and intercultural borrowing. As we saw earlier, autobiography was to him and others a Western practice. For reasons we cannot discuss here but are of great significance nevertheless, Gandhi liked it and wished to borrow it. He was, however, uneasy about its morally unacceptable associations, such as boastfulness, invading the privacy of one's family and friends, and so on. He wanted to borrow the practice but purge it of its impurities and develop its morally acceptable form. The latter bore some resemblance to the original but was also substantially different. To call it by the same name (autobiography) was to refer to its Western origins. To call it by a different name (Satyana Prayogo), which was just as valid, was to refer to what the Indians had done with it.

For Gandhi, his moral and spiritual experiments were to be the basis of his autobiography. Right at the beginning he asserts his scientific credentials and his determination to conduct the experiments with 'a scrupulous regard for rules' and 'a keen eye for details' that was expected of a scientist. He conducted several types of experiments throughout his life. He discovered that he could not dedicate himself to the active service of mankind without conquering sexuality, which led to the loss of 'vital energy' and built up a world of private loyalties and attachments. He conducted a number of experiments in this direction and concluded that such things as a diet of fresh fruits and nuts, periodic fasting, and absorption in useful social work were most helpful. He also carried out satyagrahas in different areas of life and learned from his mistakes how not to involve the masses in collective action without prior preparation.

In his professional life as a lawyer he decided that he would never lie to or mislead a judge, tutor his clients, plead a false case, or try to outwit his opponent. He concluded that it was not only possible to be a wholly truthful lawyer but also that it cut down a good deal of unnecessary litigation, avoided miscarriages of justice, and raised the moral level of all involved. In his political life Gandhi experimented with the method of satyagraha and concluded that it was possible to convert and win over even the fiercest opponent by means of love.

In the course of conducting these and other experiments Gandhi discovered that living a life of truth and rigourous self-discipline was extremely arduous and liable to lapses. Accordingly he experimented with the practice of taking and adhering to vows at all cost and concluded that they were indispensable for moral growth. He discovered also that all areas of life were closely connected and none could be mastered in isolation. One could not, for example, practice total celibacy unless one also controlled one's diet, habits, and pattern of life. He also discovered that the first step on the road to self-discipline was always the most difficult. After that each subsequent step generated new strength and 'relish' and made the moral journey that much more exciting and enjoyable.

As a story of these and other experiments, Gandhi's autobiography makes fascinating reading. His struggles are clearly and honestly stated and his failures described with great humility. Some of his experiments were unique, such as the satyagraha, others were more common. Some involved his personal life and his relations with his wife and children, others dealt with political leaders of equal stature. From time to time he felt compelled to say things about his associates that appeared necessary but were also improper. He then wondered what to do and even thought of abandoning the writing of the autobiography. By and large the spirit of moral innocence permeates the book and makes it a moving work of great wisdom and humility.

While all this is deeply instructive and provides guidance to those interested in conducting such experiments, as was his intention, it raises several important questions. It is worth noting that with the qualified exception of satyagraha, few of his experiments generated new moral and political truths or led to conclusions much different from the conventional beliefs of a middle class Hindu. Most of the truths he discovered, for example the importance of vows, truthfulness, and the control of the senses have long been an important part of the Hindu moral tradition. As for his satyagraha experiments, they were certainly original but did not warrant his large conclusions. They did not always work against the British and had to be supplemented by such methods as economic boycott and fasting to death.

Gandhi's experiments often ended up endorsing many of the traditional Hindu beliefs for several reasons. First, although he said otherwise, he was not so much experimenting with new truths as with living according to already accepted truths. He didn't try out different ways of life or values and make a comparative assessment. Rather he was only concerned to live by one set of values and his experiments were designed to ascertain if he could do so and what difficulties he would encounter. Secondly, many of his experiments were not properly designed or planned, did not allow for the intervention of unanticipated factors and took things as they came. They were hardly experiments in the proper sense of the term. Thirdly, some of Gandhi's experiments were not only limited and rather conservative, they were also born out of and circumscribed by his religious faith. Take for example his satyagraha experiments. A few of them succeeded but others failed. When the latter happened he did not reconsider them but blamed himself for not being sufficiently pure. He assured the Jews that if they practised satyagraha against Hitler the latter would be won over. Hitler may initially slaughter a few thousand Jews but was eventually bound to give in. If the Jews had followed Gandhi's advice and failed, he would most likely have said that the number of dead was not large enough or sufficiently pure. When challenged, he said that 'absolute efficacy' of non-violence was a 'necessary hypothesis' on which he and others had to act in order to ensure that they acted in full faith and total commitment. He did not say whether the hypothesis should be realistic, when it could be said to have been proved true or false, and what kind of faith in non-violence was expected by it. Gandhi's claims far exceeded his experiments.

As Gandhi said, his Satyana Prayogo inevitably involved references to the details of his life, and the story of his soul could not be disjoined from that of his self. The line between the two could not be maintained, or even drawn, as clearly and as sharply as he thought. From time to time the book digresses into narrating personal details in no way connected with any of his experiments, and even has touches of self-importance. Gandhi was sometimes aware of this and despaired of writing a wholly morally innocent autobiography. On other occasions he was more confident. It is a measure of his greatness that he should be sensitive to both. As always he was a blend of hope and despair and was his own best critic.

INTRODUCTION

Satishchandra Kumar, Meher Bhoot, Rajesh Kharat, Kanchana Mahadevan

As is well known, Gandhi's autobiography is a story of his 'experiments with truth' (2018). However, in an age of absolutism, binary divisions, and credulousness—often spawned by corporatized social media—what is not so obvious is that it portrays his search for knowledge grounded in the labour of inquiry, experimentation and exploration. Instead of lazily asserting a claim, one experiments with it to get past gullibility, and the whims and fancies emanating from subjective caprice. According to Gandhi, 'a votary of truth must exercise the greatest caution' (2018, 469). He upheld an ideal of living in which the fallibility of the self was accepted, along with that of doctrinal truth. In questioning the latter, one questions the tyranny and violence both in the individual and the social domains. Thus, overcoming violence requires a process of deep introspection and self-criticism in a space that is between the public and private. For Gandhi, experimenting is an alternative to social engineering of identities, propagation of fake news and manufacture of thought. Experimentation requires freedom, imagination and creativity. It neither adheres to a set of ideas nor inflicts them on others, but instead enables self-transformation and even social change. Thus, for Gandhi it is possible to resist the 'brute force' (2010, 75) of violence through the 'soul-force' (2010, 74) of love. But the latter is not given and has to be cultivated through an arduous process of penance, prayer, self-reflection, self-correction and self-discipline. Gandhi began his practices of austerity and introspection in his ashram, blurring the space between the personal and the public.

Gandhi's entangled space between the private and the public is reflected in his account of the seven social sins (Gandhi 1925). He enlists them as wealth without work, pleasure without conscience, knowledge without character, commerce without morality, science without humanity, religion without sacrifice and politics without principles. These seven social sins reflect the relationship between personal development and social growth, since the individual's path to becoming moral is socially relevant. Gandhi's account of the self was one that affected the whole of India eventually with his swaraj-based resistance to British imperialism. It spread globally after his assassination in 1948. As the papers in this book reveal, Gandhi's autobiographies and dialogues with his contemporaries show that the search for the self is never isolated, but always linked to others. Hence, the search for oneself is also a form of self-transcendence leading to conversations with others. The latter reveal that differences are not closures, but provocations to engage, critique, reconstruct and be critiqued in return.

Gandhi's life was both deeply personal and yet open to the world. He reflected on his personal experiences and wrote about them to make them public. Consequently, his life fuelled myriad dialogues and critiques. Gandhi's commitment to publicity has a Kantian tone where it is regarded as the foundation of peace, against the violent underpinnings of secrecy. Hence, 'All actions relating to the right of other human beings are wrong if their maxim is incompatible with publicity' (Kant 1903). But Gandhi goes beyond Kant in his commitment to the non-violent dimension of publicity, as it is a necessary feature of the personal itself. Since the self is enmeshed with others, both through its impact on others and inheriting their influences, it cannot be kept a secret. Gandhi's willingness to share his autobiography led him to conversations with contemporaries, both within India and outside. His conversations were not homogeneous. Tolstoy and Gandhi used to share a commonality of non-violence. But he had his share of disagreements with Tagore with whom he was in constant correspondence. This brings to light the importance of respecting differences not only in thought, but also in practice.

Gandhi presents a daunting hermeneutic challenge in the 21st century. Much ink has been spent on discussing his relevance and his significance, in the course of reading his texts and engaging with the applications of his thoughts in diverse domains. Gandhi has his zealous admirers. To mention just a few whom he influenced, Ela Bhatt, Martin Luther King, Nelson Mandela. King professed to be inspired by Gandhian ideals of non-violence after spending a night in Mani Bhavan in Bombay in the year 1959 (Frayer 2019). Yet, years later Obádélé Kambon has critiqued Gandhi's problematic relationship to race (Kambon 2018). Gandhi's critics have posed questions regarding his relation to caste following B.R. Ambedkar or nationalism following Rabindranath Tagore. These criticisms open up the need for autobiographies being self-critical so as to participate in dialogues and pedagogies. These complex and conflictual perspectives show that one cannot adopt a reductionist and uncritical attitude in the continuous attempts to rethink Gandhi. The 'hermeneutics of suspicion' (Ricoeur 1977) towards Gandhi, demonstrate that his thought is always in the plural and shaped by the readers who interpret him. Perhaps this is the meaning of contemporaneity. They also show how the hermeneutics of the self (reflected in autobiographies) are also hermeneutics of others, given the inextricable relationship between the self and the other. The 'contradictory resolve' (1977, 38) of Ricoeur's hermeneutics, entailing both a willingness to listen, as well as suspect, is at work in reinterpreting Gandhi, both then and now.

The foreword to this collection of essays is by Bhikhu Parekh, an alumnus of the University of Mumbai. He sheds light on several puzzles that go to the heart of Gandhi's autobiographical writing and reflects on the multiple motivations that underlie them. The two sections of the book, 'Politics of Lived Experience' and 'Conversations with Contemporaries' reveal Gandhi's relevance in the 21st century. They highlight Gandhi's experiences, experimentation and dialogue with his contemporaries which were left as a legacy from Mohandas Karamchand Gandhi to Mahatma Gandhi.

'Politics of Lived Experience' tracks Gandhi's influences in its explorations of the complex trajectories of his autobiographies. Kirti Nakhare and Aarushi Sharma underline both eastern and western influences on Gandhi's life and expound on how they culminated in satyagraha, ahimsa, self-reliance and many other principles that led to Gandhi acquiring the title of the Mahatma. Indu Prakash Pandey elucidates the influence of Gandhi in his life while acquainting readers with the continuity of Gandhian ideas across generations. Siby George reflects on the rigour of ascetic practices of citizenship that emerge in Gandhi's writings and practices while raising thought-provoking questions emanating from moral individualism. Margaret McLaren explores how several aspects of Gandhian philosophy like non-violence or ahimsa, self-reliance or swadeshi, and satyagraha have transformed women's lives. She argues that this is especially so in the context of marginalized groups who are more vulnerable to several social evils and may receive the short end of the stick in terms of social, economic or political equality. Shweta Sachdeva Jha draws attention to the complex use of visual iconography and multiple narratives in recent children's publishing on Gandhi. She suggests that parents, teachers and writers of children's literature can draw upon Gandhi to address the need for a non-wasteful lifestyle in the environmentally fragile world of today. Faisal Devji sheds light on the role of silence in democracy (emerging from autobiographies of austerity) in the context of the primacy of communication in politics

The second section, 'Conversations with Contemporaries', explores Gandhi's relationships with several of his contemporaries with an emphasis on how those interactions shaped his thoughts and beliefs. Prem Anand Mishra's essay examines the themes of the self and the other, the notion of responsibility in social and political life, and the relationship between freedom and responsibility by investigating Gandhi's original writings as primary sources. Madhavi Nikam delves into French Nobel Laureate, art historian and mystic Romain Rolland's pioneering biography on Gandhi. She attempts to reassess Gandhi as a philosopher and revolutionary in the context of his correspondence with Romain Rolland (during 1923-24). Uday Narayana Singh's article throws light on the relationship between Rabindranath Tagore and Gandhi through the letters exchanged between them from 1915 to 1941. Singh seeks to explore the beliefs, policies, actions and movements initiated by Mahatma Gandhi through the eyes of Tagore. Aakash Singh Rathore explores the relationship between two of the most renowned historical social influencers in India, Gandhi and Babasaheb Ambedkar. His essay reconnoitres their philosophies and ideas by examining the life of Gandhi through his written work, and analyzing his experiments for their internal validity through inconsistencies. Rathore also highlights the impact of Ambedkar's ideas on the philosophy, beliefs and actions of Gandhi. Nikhil Katara delves into Gandhi's philosophy of non-violence and Subhash Chandra Bose's militaristic means to attain freedom. His essay explores their fraught relationship through their correspondence, speeches and conversations with their living family members. Katara evaluates whether their ideologies had a meeting ground and whether their differences are exaggerated. Indrani Bhattacharjee presents an interesting juxtaposition of ideas by exploring the concept of love emerging from a basic commitment to Advaita Vedānta. Her essay also delves into concepts of the self, suffering, freedom and bondage and elucidates the differences in the views of Gandhi and his contemporary, Rabindranath Tagore.

References

Gandhi, M.K. 1925. Young India (22-10-1925). *The Collected Works of Mahatma Gandhi.* Vol 33: 133–134. https://www.gandhiashramsevagram.org/gandhi-literature/mahatma-gandhi-collected-works-volume-33.pdf (accessed on August 2, 2021).

Gandhi, M.K. 2010. *Hind Swaraj: A Critical Edition,* eds. Sudesh Sharma and Tridip Suhrud. Hyderabad: Orient Blackswan.

Gandhi, M.K. 2018. *An Autobiography or The Story of My Experiments with Truth: A Critical Edition,* translated by Mahadev Desai and edited by Tridip Suhrud. New Delhi: Penguin Random House.

Frayer, Lauren. 2019. Gandhi is deeply revered, but his attitudes on race and sex are under scrutiny. https://www.npr.org/2019/10/02/766083651/gandhi-is-deeply-revered-but-his-attitudes-on-race-and-sex-are-under-scrutiny (accessed on September 5, 2020).

Kambon, Obádélé. 2018. Ram Guha is wrong. Gandhi went from a racist young man to a racist middle-aged man. *The Print,* December 24. https://theprint.in/opinion/ramachandra-guha-is-wrong-a-middle-aged-gandhi-was-racist-and-no-mahatma/168222/ (accessed on December 20, 2020).

Kant, Immanuel. (1903) 2016. *Perpetual Peace: A Philosophical Essay,* trans. Mary Campbell Smith. https://www.gutenberg.org/files/50922/50922-h/50922-h.htm#Page_184 (accessed on September 20, 2020).

Ricoeur, Paul. 1977. *Freud and Philosophy: An Essay on Interpretation,* translated by Denis Savage. New Haven: Yale University Press.

Part One

POLITICS OF LIVED EXPERIENCE

A JOURNEY IN THE LABORATORY OF LIFE

A Study of *My Experiments with Truth—An Autobiography*

Kirti Nakhare and Arushi Sharma

'[...] and you will know the truth, and the truth will make you free.' John viii.32. NRSV (1999,101)

These words from the Bible capture the life mission of Mahatma Gandhi. The quest for truth was the ultimate goal of Gandhi's life, which led him to Mahatma-hood. Viktor Frankl in *Yes to Life In Spite of Everything* has drawn attention to the 'fundamental truth'—'being human is nothing other than being conscious and being responsible' (Frankl 2019, 47). Mohandas Karamchand Gandhi's life was driven by the consciousness of responsibility towards attaining truth. The consistent pursuit of truth and the resultant impact on various spheres of his life have been a matter of many scholarly discussions. It would be appropriate to quote Gandhi (2017,12) in this context: 'But for me, truth is the sovereign principle, which includes numerous other principles. This truth is not only truthfulness in word, but truthfulness in thought also, and not only the relative truth of our conceptions, but the Absolute Truth, the eternal principle, that is God.'

This paper is an attempt to study Gandhi's autobiography and delineate the influences which transformed him into the 'Hindu mystic'.[1]

Early Impressions

Born into a staunch Vaishnava household, Gandhi was deeply influenced by his mother who was religious and would abstain from food till her daily prayers were accomplished. The foundations of fasting and restraint can be traced here. Gandhi describes his mother as one who took 'the hardest of vows and she kept them without flinching. Illness was no excuse for relaxing them' (Gandhi 2017, 18). Mythological characters like Shravana from the play, *Shravana Pitri Bhakti,* extolled for his dedicated services to his parents, and the eternally truthful Harishchandra, were the earliest influences. The play about Shravana, Gandhi read with intense interest. 'Here is an example for you to copy,' he said to himself (2017, 20). 'Why should not all be truthful like Harishchandra?' was the question the young Gandhi asked himself often (2017, 21). In fact, Shravana and Harishchandra became living realities for him. The roots of selfless service and the unflinching insistence on truth can be traced to these outwardly insignificant influences, which were subconsciously chiselling the young mind.

Early Betrothal and Marriage vis-à-vis Ahimsa and Brahmacharya

Betrothed at the age of seven and married at the age of thirteen, Gandhi had his own share of trials with conjugal

---

[1] Webb Miller, a long-time admirer of Thoreau and an American journalist, referred to Gandhi as one.

love. The jealousy and possessiveness that characterized the newly formed relationship, and the overpowering lust, which eventually matured into a pure marital bond, are very candidly penned in his autobiography. It's essential to mention this, as we witness Gandhi's growth, from being a possessive husband, thus: 'If I should be pledged to be faithful to my wife, she also should be pledged to be faithful to me [...] The thought made me a jealous husband. Her duty was easily converted into my right to exact faithfulness from her, and if it had to be exacted, I should be watchfully tenacious of the right' (2017, 24).

There is a progression from being a possessive husband to the seeker on the path of self-realisation, who, as part of the process, understood ahimsa in all its aspects, with the 'canker of suspicion (being) rooted out' (Gandhi 2017, 36). Adopting brahmacharya as acceptable conduct made him realize that the wife was not the bonded slave of the husband, but an equal partner in all joys and sorrows, who had her own freedom and choices. Eventually, he realized, the path of attaining celibacy was filled with its own set of trials, but was one of the paths to attaining Truth.

At this juncture it would be appropriate to refer to Ruby Singh's essay on the genre of autobiography. Singh has thrown light on the earliest written autobiography of Saint Augustine titled *Confessions* in Latin, written in CE 397. According to her, autobiography is traditionally a Western genre drawing on the Catholic ritual of confessions and the classical autobiographical genre based on introspection of the self, confessions of sins, expressions of remorse and guilt, which is indeed very theological in letter and spirit (Singh 2015).

Addressed to God, Saint Augustine's autobiography traces

those moments and incidents of his life that mark and shape his spiritual development. Singh further elaborates by stating that Saint Augustine expressed the confessions of sins or evil as ways that lead to their cleansing and how he (the sinner Augustine) ultimately turned into a saint, resonances of which can be found in Gandhi's autobiography.

The confessions of Augustine, states Singh, starting with his initial lack of faith in Christ, stealing fruit as a child, fornication and arrogance of youth, may evoke an ironic smile in the contemporary world, but they have to be understood in the context of early Christianity (2015, 76) Gandhi's autobiography seems to register similar kinds of troughs and peaks, which transformed him into a Mahatma.

Exercise and Good Handwriting

Coming back to Gandhi's work, where he attempted to delve deeply into every aspect of life, in order to achieve perfection and a cleansing, he professed a preference for long walks in the open air, which helped him build a fairly hardy constitution. These walks later paved the path for the long marches that were undertaken in the bid for independence. Besides believing in the power of regular exercise, he believed in good handwriting being a necessary part of education, to develop which children should learn to draw before learning to write. He expresses his views thus: 'Let the child learn his letters by observation as he does different objects, such as flowers, birds, etc., and let him learn handwriting only after he has learnt to draw objects. He will then write a beautifully formed hand' (2017, 29).

Meat Eating and Addictions: Lessons in Ahimsa

Amongst his many experiments were acceptance and denial of beliefs. One of them was hiding the unacceptable deed of meat eating from his Vaishnava parents, which was initially not perceived as departing from truth, as meat eating was an act that he undertook out of the spirit of bringing about a reform, under the influence of a friend. It was also partly the influence of the Gujarati poet Narmad, who held sway over schoolboys then. The poet expressed the might of the Englishman through his doggerel, thus (Gandhi 2017, 33):

> Behold the mighty Englishman
> He rules the Indian small,
> Because being a meat-eater
> He is five cubits tall.

Gandhi eventually overcame this line of thought, as he believed that food reform and eating meat were essential, but deceiving one's parents was not the right way to achieve reforms. Around that time, in fact, even before, Gandhi and his relative became fond of smoking, fancying the clouds emitted by the act. In order to purchase Indian cigarettes, money was stolen from a servant's pocket money. He eventually overcame this addiction.

Along with this, the young Mohandas stole money on various occasions and the ultimate theft was clipping a part of his brother's gold armlet, which was utilised to clear the brother's debt of twenty-five rupees. After clearing the debt, he resolved to never ever steal again. He confessed through a note written to his father, asking for an appropriate punishment. He expected violence, but when he saw tears flow down his agonised father's cheeks, that was an object lesson in ahimsa and the power of love. It was possible only when the confession came from a pure and repentant heart.

Gandhi was thus convinced about the all-embracing power of ahimsa which transformed everything it touched.

Self-realization after a wrong deed suggests evolution, and growth towards the better self; only an individual who has set out to seek Truth will reach there. In this context it would be fitting to mention Tolstoy, another important influence on Gandhi, who has succinctly encapsulated this idea. 'But man is not stationary in regard to truth, but every individual man as he passes through life, and humanity as a whole in the same way, is continually learning to know a greater and greater degree of truth, and growing more and more free from error' (Tolstoy 2005, 183).

Ramanama and Other Influences

Religion was construed as knowledge of self in the broadest sense for Gandhi. He received the lesson to repeat the Ramanama to allay his fear of ghosts from his nurse Rambha, at a tender age. Ramanama was presented as an infallible remedy. Gandhi was exposed to his father's friends of all religions, who would discuss about their faiths. This gave him an early grounding in religious tolerance. The *Manusmriti* did not entice Gandhi due to its propagation of violence and meat eating. Amidst all these influences, Gandhi believed in morality as being the basis of all things and truth being the substance of it. Thus, the pursuit of truth became his sole objective.

At the same time, Gandhi could not accept Christianity as perfect or the greatest of all religions, neither was he convinced that Hinduism was, either, with its scourge of untouchability and its divisions into so many sects and castes. Also, he questioned that if the Vedas were inspired by the word of God, why not the Bible or the Koran? Young Gandhi was thus evolving into a rational thinker. Another interesting influence was a didactic stanza from Gujarati (Gandhi 2017, 45), which became his guiding principle, that professed returning good for evil:

> For a bowl of water give a goodly meal;
> For a kindly greeting bow down with zeal;
> For a simple penny pay thou back with gold;
> If thy life be rescued, life do not withhold;
> Thus, the words and the actions of the wise regard;
> Every little service tenfold they reward.
> But the truly noble know all men as one,
> And return with gladness good for evil done.

These influences slowly but surely laid the foundation for the principles of ahimsa and satyagraha.

The Vow and Departure to England

After clearing the matriculation examination in 1887, it was unanimously decided that Gandhi should pursue the profession of a Barrister, and in accordance he was sent to England, but not before being administered three vows by the family adviser: to not touch wine, woman and meat. Following this, he was permitted to set off for England. Once in England, procuring vegetarian food was a challenge. After reading the book *Salt's Plea for Vegetarianism*, he became a confirmed vegetarian by choice. Being a vegetarian was in the interests of truth and the vow he had taken; however, after reading the book, the spread of vegetarianism became his mission.

The experiments in dietetics followed this choice and helped him search deeper and, accordingly, an inward and outward change ensued. His experiments in leading a simple life, that was lived frugally, harmonised his inward and outward life. This modification made his life more truthful and added joy.

The moral reform followed the change in diet. Gandhi started a vegetarian club which was dissolved later. These associations helped him develop his persona and helped him slowly and steadily improve on the skills of public speaking. However, he never could get over the hesitancy in speech and later, he grew to find this to be a pleasure. 'Experience has taught me that silence is part of the spiritual discipline of a votary of truth [...] My shyness has been in reality my shield and buckler. It has allowed me to grow. It has helped me in my discernment of truth (2017, 70).

The Role of the *Gita* and its Comparison with the Bible

In the second year of his stay in England, Gandhi came under the influence of two Theosophist brothers, who had read the translation of the *Gita* by Sir Edwin Arnold. The verses from the second chapter discussed the impact of the world of 'maya', the materialistic world, on the purpose of life and on the mind, due to which man could be completely undone. He considered the *Gita* as the best resource for seeking the knowledge of truth. At the same time the 'Sermon on the Mount' from the *New Testament* had a different impact, which he compared with the *Gita*. The Bible verses, 'But I say unto you, that ye resist not evil; but whosoever shall smite thee on thy right cheek, turn to him the other also' and 'If any man takes away thy coat, let him have thy cloak too' influenced Gandhi. He compared this with Shamal Bhatt's 'For a bowl of water, give a goodly meal' (Gandhi 2017, 75).

Assimilating the teachings of the *Gita*, the *Light of Asia* and the 'Sermon on the Mount', the fact that 'renunciation was the highest form of religion' appealed to Gandhi immensely (2017, 75).

It would be pertinent to draw attention to Tolstoy's influence on Gandhi's thought processes. Through his book, *The Kingdom of God is Within You,* Tolstoy expresses, 'Not without good reason was Christ's only harsh and threatening reproof directed against hypocrites and hypocrisy. It is not theft nor robbery nor murder nor fornication, but falsehood, the special falsehood of hypocrisy, which corrupts men, brutalizes them and makes them vindictive, destroys all distinction between right and wrong in their conscience, deprives them of what is the true meaning of all real human life, and debars them from all progress toward perfection.' (Tolstoy 2005, 177-178) This work of Tolstoy impacted the understanding of truth and its many aspects. In his autobiography, Gandhi describes the book as one that promotes independent thinking, and is profoundly moral and truthful.

Three Moderns

Gandhi was influenced by three moderns: 'Raychandbhai as his living contact; Tolstoy through his book, *The Kingdom of God is Within You*; and Ruskin through his *Unto this Last.*' (Gandhi 2017, 93)

The teachings of Ruskin, from the above text, that influenced Gandhi, were as follows:

1. The good of an individual is contained within the good of all.
2. The value of a lawyer's work is the same as that of a barber's, in that all have the same right to earn from their work.

3. The life of labour, i.e. the life of the handicraftsman and the tiller of the soil, is the life worth living (Gandhi 2017,273. Our paraphrasing of the points).

Gandhi was much influenced by these principles and ready to put them to practice. The influence of Ruskin was irresistible to Gandhi; so much so that he translated Ruskin's *Unto the Last* into Gujarati, and named it *Sarvodaya*.

Life and Struggle in South Africa

Kicked, shoved and pushed in South Africa, it was no country for self-respecting Indians. Asiatics in South Africa were regulated and their free movement controlled. Gandhi was known as a 'coolie barrister' there; 'coolie' was a common appellation for all Indians. To salvage his self-respect, Gandhi traded the Indian turban for an English hat, as being forced to take off the Indian turban would be construed as an insult.

The Natal Indian Congress fought for the rights of Indians in Natal. Gandhi was Bhai for the indentured labourers in South Africa, who were mostly South Indian. Balasundaram, an indentured Indian labourer who entered Gandhi's office with headgear in hand, was one of the many individuals for whom Gandhi stood up. Balasundaram was severely beaten by his European master, who lost self-control, which resulted in breaking two of his teeth. Gandhi fought for the transfer of the indenture of Balasundaram to somebody else. Gandhi was present in Natal to espouse his cause. When Balasundaram visited Gandhi, he did so with his headgear in his hand. The practice of removing one's headgear in the presence of a European was common; a salute with both hands was not sufficient. Gandhi asked him to tie up his scarf. Balasundaram did so with a little bit of hesitation, but a great deal of pleasure on his face. This ill-treatment of one human being at the hands of another made Gandhi wonder thus:

'It has always been a mystery to me how men can feel themselves honoured by the humiliation of their fellow-beings.' (2017, 149)

Gandhi knew which causes needed his energies. The Mahatma, who insisted on wearing Indian headgear in the District Magistrate's court in South Africa, on the other hand, took it off in obedience of the order of the Supreme Court in South Africa, as he wanted to reserve his strength for fighting bigger battles. His skills were to be used for better causes. The pursuit of truth taught him to appreciate the role of compromise. This spirit, as he saw later in life, was an essential part of Satyagraha. This insistence entailed endangering his life and inviting the displeasure of friends. 'But truth was as hard as adamant and tender as a blossom' (2017,144).

Gaining popularity as the messiah of the Indians in South Africa, Gandhi was perceived as a threat by the Natal whites. When he brought his wife and children to settle in Natal, false charges were pressed against him and as a result, all the passengers on the ship were quarantined for an uncertain number of days, under the pretext of preventing the spread of the plague. However, at the end of twenty-four days, the passengers were allowed to enter the harbour. This surely reminds us that times have not changed even in 2020; quarantining people who might prove to be a threat to those in power still holds true!

Finalizing Brahmacharya in 1906

Gandhi realized, 'in order to serve society, he had to relinquish the desire for children and wealth and live the life of a *vanaprastha*—of one retired from household cares' (2017, 194). To attain brahmacharya, control of the palate was a prerequisite. The brahmachari's food should be 'satvik' and 'it should be limited, simple, spiceless, and, if possible, uncooked' (2017, 196). Brahmacharya thus entailed control of the senses in thought, word and deed. Gandhi began leading a simple life by cutting down unnecessary expenses, doing his laundry himself, throwing away dependence on the barber. These were the extreme forms in which his passion for self-help and simplicity expressed itself.

He believed that fasting of the physical self was not adequate. It was one of the means to the end of self-restraint, but that was not all, and it had to be accompanied by mental fasting, else it was bound to end in hypocrisy and disaster. 'Passion in man is generally co-existent with a hankering after the pleasures of the palate' (2017, 291). As always, the *Gita* influenced Gandhi in pursuing this thought process:

> For a man who is fasting his senses
> Outwardly, the sense-objects disappear,
> Leaving the yearning behind; but when
> He has seen the Highest,
> Even the yearning disappears (*Gita* quoted in Gandhi 2017, 302).

The vow of brahmacharya was sealed in the middle of 1906, this was a preparatory step, part of the self-purification exercise undertaken by Gandhi, to pave the path for the movement which was adopted by Gandhi: Satyagraha. The term is comprised of Satya i.e. Truth and Agraha i.e. firmness; it was to be the mainstay of the Indian freedom struggle.

Service and Truth

Incessantly serving the Indians in South Africa revealed to Gandhi new implications of Truth at every stage. Truth, he opined, 'was like a vast tree, which yielded more and more fruit, the more you nurtured it. The deeper the search in the mine of truth, the richer the discovery of the gems buried there, in the shape of openings for an ever-greater variety of service' (2017, 204).

The Phoenix Settlement was twenty acres of land near Durban railway station, established in 1904. Gandhi set up his little village with nearly half a dozen industrious people and their families and the *Indian Opinion* press was set up on the same land. Inmates of Phoenix and Tolstoy Farm and the Sabarmati Ashram co-existed as one large family, who did their own tasks, including scavenging, cleaning, cooking, etc. Living together was a lesson in religious tolerance, as also an exercise in self-reliance.

The influence of Thoreau on Gandhi cannot be denied. George Hendrick in his essay studying Thoreau's influence on Gandhi (1956) writes that Gandhi may have read *Walden* as early as in 1906; it is evident that before the first Satyagraha movement, he dispensed with servants, acted as his own scavenger, and attempted to be independent of machinery. His views were seemingly influenced by *Walden*.

Also, readers of *Indian Opinion* were frequently reminded of Thoreau's essay on Civil Disobedience. 'Thoreau had opposed the enslavement of man; Indians, being enslaved themselves, needed encouragement in their struggle. The Indian community was openly defying the registration act, and the resistances of Thoreau, Tolstoy, Jesus, and Socrates seemed vital confirmations to Gandhi' (Hendrick 1956, 467).

More on the Work in South Africa and the Influence of the *Gita*

After having worked for the cause of Indians in South Africa, Gandhi enrolled with the Transvaal Supreme Court and set up office in Johannesburg. He was influenced by the Theosophists and their belief in universal brotherhood, the *Gita,* which he had fairly memorized and was his spiritual guide all through his life at all times. 'I turned to this (*Gita*) dictionary of conduct for a ready solution of all my troubles and trials' (2017, 244). These influences were steadily preparing Gandhi for the non-violent war for the nation. The qualities of non-possession and equality pre-supposed a change of heart and a change of attitude.

'Hate the sin and not the sinner' was a precept that is as easy to understand as it is rare to practise. Gandhi believed staunchly in this and in ahimsa: '*Ahimsa* is the basis of the search for truth. I am realizing every day that the search is vain unless it is founded on *ahimsa* as the basis. [...] For we are all tarred with the same brush, and children of one and the same Creator, and as such the divine powers within us are infinite. To slight a single human being is to slight those divine powers, and thus to harm not only that being, but with him the whole world' (2017, 253). He thus cultivated consciously the virtues of ahimsa, brahmacharya, aparigraha and other cardinal virtues. Gandhi believed that the search for Truth should be based on ahimsa. Seeing the divine in every living being and the violation of another fellow being is the violation of oneself and the divine powers that rest in one.

On the Act of Writing the Autobiography

In the midst of the act of writing his autobiography, Gandhi introspects. 'I am not writing the autobiography to please critics. Writing it is itself one of the experiments with truth. One of its objects is certainly to provide some comfort and food for reflection for my co-workers' (2017, 257).

It would be interesting to once again refer to Rosy Singh's essay on the genre of autobiography, where she has discussed whether autobiography as a genre can be classified as fiction or non-fiction. Singh opines that Gandhiji's autobiography can be defined as the life-story of a Being; it cannot be termed fiction. Some critics therefore call it literary or creative non-fiction. Others who are more distrusting assert that autobiographies are more often than not works of fiction for they invariably 'construct' a positive image of the self (Wagner-Egelhaaf 2000 quoted in Singh 2005, 80).

Thus, writing about Gandhi's autobiography, Singh mentions that Gandhi cleverly tried to make his autobiography sound sincere by giving it the title *The Story of My Experiments with Truth* (1927) with emphasis on 'truth' and on the scientific nature of his 'experiments'. He further emphasizes his point in the introduction: 'I hope to acquaint the reader fully with all my faults and errors. My purpose is to describe experiments in the science of Satyagraha, not to say how good I am. In judging myself I shall try to be as harsh as truth, as I want others also to be' (Singh 2005, 80).

Singh's critique is aimed at warning the reader to read autobiographies with a pinch of salt, and look through the personal biases that could possibly seep in. The reader should not turn a blind eye to these biases and erroneously take every word at face value.

Experiments in India

Coming back to Gandhi's experiments with truth in India, the Champaran inquiry was a bold experiment in truth and ahimsa. Due to the efforts of Gandhi, the planters in Champaran were asked to refund a portion of exactions made by them and the tinkathia system[2] which had been in existence for about a century was abolished. The ryots, who had been crushed so far, came somewhat into their own, and the stain of indigo was washed out. Gandhi's ideas were slowly and steadily gaining a strong foothold. To quote Tolstoy once again in this context would be appropriate:

> Just as a single shock may be sufficient, when a liquid is saturated with some salt to precipitate it at once in crystals, a slight effort may be perhaps all that is needed now that the truth already revealed to many men may gain mastery over hundreds, thousands, millions of men, that a public opinion consistent with conscience may be established, and through this change of public opinion the whole order of life may be transformed. And it depends upon us to make this effort (Tolstoy 2005, 185).

Gandhi had garnered the might, through incessant work both in South Africa and in India and was a force whose slightest effort brought about a change in the lives of several Indians. The benevolent father to the inmates of Phoenix, Tolstoy Farm and Sabarmati Ashram, Gandhi fought for the mill hands in Ahmedabad and also reached a peaceful

[2] Tinkathia System: The Champaran tenant was bound by law to plant three out of every twenty parts of his land with indigo for his landlord. This system was known as the tinkathia system, as three kathas out of twenty (which make one acre) had to be planted with indigo.

settlement for the Patidars in Kheda, who due to failure of their crops wanted exemption from the annual assessment. Gandhi was the driving force behind the adoption of the resolutions supporting Hindu-Muslim unity, the removal of untouchability, and uniting India with khadi.

Conclusion

Barring a few exceptions like the Chauri Chaura incident, where people went out of control and defied the principles of ahimsa laid down by Gandhi in letter and spirit, Gandhi's experiments in attaining independence, by following non-violence, satyagraha and self-reliance proved to be successful. Towards the conclusion of his autobiography, Gandhi claims that ahimsa is the extreme extent of humility and it should be followed completely. He concludes his autobiography thus: 'My uniform experience has convinced me that there is no other God than Truth [...] that a perfect vision of Truth can only follow a complete realisation of *Ahimsa*' (2017, 451-452).

Tolstoy opines, 'The sole meaning of life is to serve humanity by contributing to the establishment of the kingdom of God, which can only be done by the recognition and profession of the truth by every man' (2005, 190). Gandhi was a living example, who established the kingdom of God in the hearts of Indians by being a relentless votary of truth all through his life.

On a final note, the malleability and timelessness of Gandhi's teachings can be reckoned by the fact that the mainstream Hindi film industry could entice cinephiles with films based on Gandhian ideology. The box office successes of *Munna Bhai MBBS* (2003) and its sequel *Lage Raho Munna Bhai* (2006) based on Gandhian thought stand testimony to this fact.

Interestingly, the pursuit of 'truth' has always been at the core of parallel cinema. The insistence on truth is taken to its extreme and most of the time to its logical conclusion. This can be witnessed through films like *Aankhon Dekhi* (2013) which stars the versatile actor Sanjay Mishra, who essays the role of a middle-class individual and decides to believe 'only' in the version of 'truth' which he experiences first-hand. He pays dearly for this experiment with his life, as a result of the insistence on this belief. He takes the idea to the extreme, by embarking on the experience of 'flying'. He sets out on the venture and reaches the ultimate destination of mortal beings, leaving the audience awestruck, with questions, groping for answers.

References

Frankl, Viktor E. 2019. *Yes, to Life In spite of Everything*. Penguin Random House: London.

Gandhi, M.K. (1925) 2017. *My Experiments with Truth: An Autobiography*. India Book Distributors: Delhi.

George, Hendrick. 1956. The Influence of Thoreau's 'Civil Disobedience' on Gandhi's Satyagraha. *The New England Quarterly* 29 (4): 462-471. https://www.jstor.org/stable/362139.

The Holy Bible, 1999. Catholic Edition. Theological Publications in India: New Delhi.

Singh, Rosy. 2015. On the Genre of Autobiography: Typology and Evolution. *The Delhi University Journal of the Humanities & the Social Sciences* 2: 76-86.

Tolstoy, Leo. (1894) 2005. *The Kingdom of God is Within You*. Stilwell, KS: Digireads.com Publishing

GANDHIJI IN MY LIFE

Indu Prakash Pandey

(formerly) South Asia Institute, Heidelberg, Germany

(Translated by Dr. Bhagyashree S. Varma, Associate Professor, Dept. of English, University of Mumbai)

From the very early times which I recall of my childhood and the age of learning the lessons of life, I remember five great personalities that influenced the shaping and growth of my mind. Rajaji, (Rajagopalachari), who was a pure intellectual with a futuristic vision, Azad (Maulana Abul Kalam Azad), who had a great impact on me through his impartial and firm stance, and who also created profound faith in me. Jawaharlal Nehru's handsome and attractive face with his ever-expressive enthusiasm, Subhash Babu (Subhash Chandra Bose) whose magnificent visage, with round spectacles that enhanced his thoughtful eyes, invited excitement and cheer by his quest for freedom. And Gandhiji, whose idealism in ethics, spiritual conscience, simplicity in lifestyle and endless zeal for action that inspired my mind always to do something, as he had done for all thinking minds. In those times, it was impossible to think indifferently.

Gandhiji had included all dimensions of life in his activities in such a way that he was completely dedicated to the rise of our nation. This whole-hearted dedication of his life spread hope and faith among all. Many others who followed Gandhiji participated in the mission to liberate our nation, together. He had such great impact even on the minds of illiterate, poor. and helpless farmers from remote villages, that his decision to not pay the tax was doubtlessly supported by all the farmers. His impact was thus powerful on the minds of the educated as well as the illiterate masses. I was not meant to escape the same. I learnt the lesson of Swaraj from him, and I could create self-reliance to some extent in my life. In 1937, Subhash Babu on his tour of UP during the elections, had come to Raebareli. His speech at the station was attended by a huge crowd, including me.

His miraculous personality had so deep an influence on my mind, exciting my patriotic spirit, that I was tempted to join him at that very moment and move onward with him. But I was just a boy studying in the seventh standard at that time. His pure white, loosely-tied dhoti of Khadi, loose kurta, round glasses, and high, crossed Gandhi cap on his head made Subhash Babu look so handsome and grand. My mind was intensely exited by the very sight of this man, this freedom fighter with a mission. In 1931, at Kasganj, we had moved around the central streets of the town, shouting slogans like 'तोडी बच्चा हाय-हाय, लाल पगड़ी हाय-हाय-हाय,' which showed open hatred toward the slayers of Bhagat Singh, and we burned so fiercely for the cause at that time that Kasganj itself looked like Bhagat Singh's assassination spot.

There was this building, Tilak Bhavan, opposite our primary school in Kasganj, that the leaders of Kasganj used to visit often. I had frequently seen a person there in Khadi clothing. He walked with his head held high towards the skies. I tried to mimic his walking style once in pride, and wounded my foot on the stony, bumpy road. I felt wounded even mentally. I was under the impression that Mohandas Gandhiji was our classmate when he had refused to correct the error in his notebook. It was under the influence of Gandhi's ethos that my mother had started spinning cotton on the spinning wheel.

She wove carpets and rugs at home. I used to help her with these tasks. So, the whole of our home, inside and outside, was occupied by Gandhi. In the winter of 1939-40, I participated for the first time in a procession. My friend, the elder brother of Vindhyeshwari Prasad Singh, was elected as the Satyagrahi leader of the Congress, to individually display our opposition to the government. Gandhiji had started the opposition to the British government with Vinoba Bhave at the same time. The British had not taken into consideration any national leader's opinions while including India in the Second World War. The only party leading the nation at that time was the Congress. Gandhiji took it as an insult to the nation and started his Satyagraha to oppose the government. In this Satyagraha, he did not call upon the common masses but selected specific leading workers and planned their rebellious lectures on particular dates. Each leader who followed this had to inform the government where and when he would arrange his rebellious lecture.

The stages were prepared, the roads were opened, and like the Satyagrahi the information-leaking individuals too would reach there with the police and they would arrest the speaker as soon as he started his speech. The common people also would gather to shout slogans, 'Bharat Mata ki Jai, Mahatma Gandhi ki Jai. Inqilab Zindabad' which meant, Hail Mother India, Hail Mahatma Gandhiji, Long live the Revolution!

The police walked ahead with the arrested leaders while

the masses followed them to the police station, loudly shouting the slogans and then returning wearily to their homes. We too went on the crowded path when Bhaisahab was arrested and chatted about the possibilities, sleeping late at night. I started wearing clothes of Khadi at that time. I started wearing Khadi kurta and dhoti or pyjama. When Gandhi haunted my mind like this, I threw away my old clothes and shoes. Now, I got a pair of shoes made by the local cobbler, from lamb's skin, for just one and a half rupees. We too were the followers of Swaraj now. Swaraj was grounded in our minds like an obvious mission. As an effect of this, I started visiting the central building in the city, Tilak Bhavan. Many leaders used to meet us there. I was much younger than them, like a child to them. I was not happy to be seen as a child. My discipline had its own demands.

The first was that I would not fall short in my studies, and I would not accept any hindrance in my routine of exercise or even my sports. My leadership did not help me change my routine. That is how I remained three in one, a student, a sportsman and a follower of Swaraj. The leaders arrested in the individual Satyagraha Revolt were gradually released from the jails. Gandhiji was engaged in creative work even at that point of time. For freedom, Gandhiji had created two major fronts in fighting with the British.

One was the straight war of Non-violence and the second, when no direct action was followed, multiple social actions to be creatively executed in pursuit of adult education, Hindu-Muslim unity, the annihilation of untouchability, rural development and so on. Volunteers were working on around sixteen different plans. This work was done both inside and outside the ashrams. These were all works of social reformation. In the absence of anything else, the work of spinning on the spinning wheel and weaving cloth was a permanent protest. Much was yet to be done in the area of rural development. But finally, Gandhiji decided to confront the British directly through war to gain freedom. How long could we be cheated by them! At that time, the Congress launched the Quit India movement at Bombay under Gandhiji's leadership, on 8th August 1942. The government urgently arrested all the leaders at night. Consequently, there was havoc in the whole country and we all marched forward on the battlefield prompted by Gandhiji's slogan 'Do or Die'. I left my studies and joined the battleground.

This was the last year of my high school. I was studying at Sir Raja Rampal Singh Hindu High school at Raebareli in UP, and had been staying in the hostel with my two younger brothers since the sixth class. This was the fifth and last year for me. In those five years, I had created a lot of pressure in school and the city. Mostly through my fame as a football, volleyball and hockey player and in the last two years as a leader too. The leadership had made the secret police keep watch on me. Cripp's mission had failed. Gandhiji had rejected the proposal of that mission as 'a post-dated cheque on a defunct bank.' In 1935, the Act of provincial autonomy declared the victory of the Congress in the elections of seven states. The Muslim League had been defeated badly and was not included in the making of the new government. The Muslim minorities were hurt by this failure and their anger had taken the form of revolt. Sikandar Hayat tried to form the government in Punjab. But these governments did not work properly due to the reluctance between Hindus and Muslims. The Congress was committed to its struggle for complete autonomy. The British government had stated that autonomous power could not be granted till all the communities came together unanimously. One third of Muslims were not ready for this. How would the kings and emperors be ready? Hence the Muslim league and Communist Party too was reluctant. Hitler and Stalin finalized their pact at that time and the Communist Party was supporting the fascists.

So, when the Quit India revolt was beginning, the Muslim League, the Communist Party, and the nominated kings did not participate. And I did observe that all my Muslim friends were staying out of the march. The Communist Party was not functional in our small town. A few landlords and owners of estates were trying to participate, yet, it was a huge surprise for me to see the fourteen-year-old son of the director of Defence India Rule helping me in legalities during my arrest. And he was a Musalman.

The procession of revolutionaries was moving forward across the court with slogans hailing Gandhiji. When we reached near the government high school we invited the schoolboys to join us. Not a single child from that school came to us, which was really shocking. The message of Gandhiji remained limited to our private schools. But we were not to be discouraged. We moved ahead towards the city till, further on the way, a group walking with the police inspector stopped and warned us to withdraw and return from there. They threatened us, raising their sticks, and scared us with the threat of arrest but we were charged with such passion that such threats did not affect us at all.

So, the four leading boys in front were tied with a rope: me, Shrikant Singh, Radha Raman, and Mahesh Dutt. The police started pushing us towards the court. The noise increased. The crowd in procession raised its slogans to a higher volume. We were sent in the vehicle to the court and then they locked us in a room. The room was suffocating. We were feeling choked in the heat of the closed room. I tried to console my friends with the couplet, 'this is only a beginning, of the passion you love, in place of crying, just watch what is yet to come.' Whatever was to come, we had to pay some price for freedom. At that very moment, the Muslim boy entered like a breeze. 'If you need anything tell me,' he said. He asked for cold water for us and signalled us to go. We tried to sympathise that if he got into trouble because of helping us, his father may struggle to free him, but we did not know what was the scene outside as we were locked up in custody. The same evening, we were brought out and the police vehicle took us to be dropped at some unknown destination.

That destination was R Central Jail. They took whatever little money we had in our pockets and deposited that in the office of the jailor. What rough treatment my companions were given, I do not know, but I was taken to a small closet-like bathroom and locked in there. There was no furniture, no rug, not even a rag there! It was utterly vacant. Within a few minutes my head started spinning because of the stinky smell from the urinals around. Standing or sitting was impossible. My breath was choking and my feet were aching due to standing for so long. I sat down on the dirty, half-cemented floor and my mind was so upset that I could not even think what to do. How was this nation going to get its freedom, where are my companions, are they also locked in dungeons like me, what must they be thinking...I had no answers. There was no way to get any answers. My mind was anxious and my head was heavy. Those narrow walls had brought my breath to a lifeless state and my heart was trying its best to keep beating in this damage to my freedom for the sake of national freedom. How to entertain myself, how to keep the mind engaged, I asked myself and recalled a doha which said, 'do not lose your mind, keep offering prayer.' To find some solace, I also uttered the lines my mother used to often teach me, 'Say Ram, do your work, don't be afraid, you are in alien town,' but my mind was not calmed. I was not really afraid, yet, my eyes filled with tears, regretful of how I was trapped and had taken more people with me; they may be cursing me, I thought. It's quite possible that they will prove braver than me.

The darkness increased and the night fell. Where would I sleep, would they provide food or not? In that gloomy moment someone opened the lock like an angel, one was a policeman and the other was a jailed person who looked like a criminal.

The confidential prisoners become pakka in a few years and they are called 'pakka'. He said, 'You are a lucky man, now they will keep you in B class.' And they took us to a huge open yard, and locked us there. There was a big hall, two rows of cemented benches and rugs placed on those. 'Now, you enjoy,' said Pakka, moving away with the guard. In the same manner, the other prisoners were brought gradually one after the other.

The sparrow twitters too much while she is building her nest, and in the same way, we all were creating noise. No end of talking, as if we had gained freedom. The food was ready and we were so hungry. The kitchen was large and I spread my rug and sat on that. The other prisoners of the jail were assigned to serve the A and B classes. They were all working here, doing something or the other. The cook served food in a brass plate with neat and clean hands. They had given us daal, one vegetable with gravy and one dry, rice and chapatis. Even ghee, prepared in the jail, was added to the daal. The food was so good that I forgot my issues of the whole day. And, receiving one full glass of milk at bedtime, we forgot that we were in jail. We were not actually getting this much even at home. Later I came to know that seventeen rupees were spent at seventeen anna per person's meals, while we gave five rupees for the whole month's food at the hostel and in a day, the jail was spending two rupees on each of us.

So, we were really lucky. A-class people also got fruits and flowers. In the same yard we also had good rooms with bathrooms. We were getting old books to read from the library of the jail. All the things were accessible to us, except newspapers. No news from the outside world could reach us. The empty space in this yard was too large. It was the beginning of August. The monsoon had already commenced. The Naag Panchami festival of worshipping snakes was nearing. We played in the yard and the joy was immediately shared by playing there. Sometimes we met Laalsaheb, the king of Semary, Kedarnath Pandey from Laalganj and a Maulana with a long beard, whose name I don't remember, and we used to sit together and chat for hours. We argued on various matters. The main point recurringly discussed was leaving school after primary education, and whether everyone should join active politics. Except for me, everyone agreed that we had plunged into this battle for freedom on the basis of calls by Gandhiji and we could return to education afterwards when we got our freedom. The free country would certainly need educated citizens.

The country needs to be educated to move ahead. Among the illiterate masses, who will do the work for the country? In the matter of education, I was firmly decided. But presently we were in lock up. Sometimes we used to shout slogans and hail Gandhiji. Who knew when we would be free? Even

Gandhiji was imprisoned with thousands of leaders. Sometimes we heard a few rumours. Gunshots, people dying, army spreading terror all over, and so on. The good food on that day would taste bitter. We used to keep fasting to console our own sense of guilt. Our impotence was expressed in our closed fists and teeth ground in silence. Around three months passed like that and one fine morning there came an order saying, leave, all youngsters. Yes, we were youngsters only. Returning all our things and money, they drove us out of the jail. Where should we go? What to do? The uncertainty took us toward the city. Nobody knew we had been released from the jail. No one would come to receive us. Who would welcome us with flowers or garlands? In Raibareli I had stayed in the hostel, so we went there. The next day we went to the school and met the headmaster. He said, 'Your rustication orders have been prepared and sent to us. If you apologize to the commissioner, he may allow you to come back to school any time. I tried to make you understand that these movements are not for you. But you were haunted by Gandhiji at that time.' I had not imagined this state. He liked me so much. He loved me, in fact. He used to invite me to his place. I thought he approved of me even more as I had taken part in the freedom movement.

After I left the school, he gave me a very good character certificate which still lies preserved with me. My friends tried to apologize and got scolded by him. 'How shameless you are, you don't feel ashamed to apologize. You and your revolution have taken the lives of so many people. Many lost their homes. Now, you go and educate yourself to become a good human being.'

I had already told the headmaster that I would not apologize even if Gandhiji came to tell me to say sorry.

Now, I did not feel the need to contact the commissioner. The case was taken a few days later to the court but we all declined when the question of forgiveness was raised. We were charged ten rupees each and those who could not pay would be put in jail. Someone paid that fine for us at that time. We were released. There was a lot of hush-hush outside the court. And when we came out, the skies were filled with the slogans of the crowd, 'Gandhiji ki Jai!' We entered the school. A few months were left for the final exams of the high school. Somehow, I prepared and appeared for the exams but missed getting a first class by four marks.

I was a sportsperson as well as a very bright student. The headmaster expected a lot from me but those hopes were nothing in comparison to the need of our country. After being released from jail I wondered where my younger brothers had been, all these days. Did they return to our village, did they have any money? I don't know till now. Those were days of extreme madness. We had no sense of being conscious. The headmaster called my father by sending a letter. He took us back forcefully like the ones captured. We went in the night to Lalganj on camels, and later walked nearly ten miles towards Shivpuri.

The vehicles had no access to our village. There was utter silence everywhere and the atmosphere was sensational. We did not talk for a long time. Afterwards at home we were equally quiet. At home, pushing me towards my mother, my father said, 'See, here is your great son. Take him.' And I don't know how and when, much later, my mother told me, 'You are getting married on 14th June.' I jumped out of shock, cried, shouted, kept showing my reluctance saying, 'no, no, no.' 'When father comes back from the camp, show the same drama to him,' she said. We used to speak Awadhi. I could not utter a single word when father came. I kept crying and telling my chacha to stop it. He could not do anything. The marriage was already fixed when I was in prison. All the family members thought that the only way to tie me was to the pole of marriage. I felt like my hands were tied with handcuffs earlier but now even my feet were chained. In this way, I was imprisoned for a lifetime.

A drum was hung around my neck. Whether I played or not, nobody would hear. This imprisonment was not to be eased even by Gandhiji. The father of my intimate friend, Trambakeshwar Prasad, who was a landlord and the honourary magistrate, advised me that I should run away from home. My twin questions were, where shall I go if I run away, and what will happen to this innocent, unknown, illiterate girl who is tied to me. How does she know that her marriage was performed with a revolutionary rebellious youth; she must have believed dreamily that her father had found a suitable groom for her. Her father might have tried to find such a groom from his point of view. I was lost in serious thought. What a trap indeed. She must be dreaming of a happy home, a handsome groom, the unknown and unseen house of her in-laws! And I was thinking how to earn bread, how to provide her with basic needs of clothes and shelter. I was already away from Gandhiji's frenzy and was chained in the web of married life. Sweet were the fruits of desire. So now I had to walk like that cow whose neck bears the burden of living. If I walk faster, my feet will ache, no other way to find out. I could not see any other option. My feet heavy with chains of marriage and my hands tied to the mission of Gandhiji. This country got freedom but what about my freedom, would I be free?

I lost my first child who would have been 75 today, if

it had survived. This country has been independent for 72 years, and I am turning 95, but the question of what is right and what is not right keeps haunting me even now. What is good and are all the good works right? And are all the right things good? How to understand this dichotomy? Is there a way out? Two years went by. I continued my education firmly. My parents have married me off so they have to look after us, I thought. Hence, I stayed with my parents in Kanpur for two years. My mother often called my wife from her maternal home. She wanted to trap me in temptation. I was trapped for a while. Staying in Kanpur I could not do any task for Gandhiji.

I read a lot of books and studied a lot in those two years. I studied the literature of the saints, reading all the books of Vivekanand, Swami Ramteerth, Dayanand and whatever other books were available. How much I could perceive only God knows. In Bengal the masses were dying of the drought at that time. The reports mentioned that around three lac million people died. Calcutta was attacked by the Japanese forces. What Gandhiji said was hard to believe now. He had said that we would be able to protect ourselves after the British left our country. My mind was not at rest. I tried to express my impotent anger in the outbursts of fruitless poetic writing. Fruitless as no periodical would print my poems. I was restless and wandering from village to village to do Gandhiji's work. Nobody listened to my talks and the people who heard me did not do anything. I was so frustrated that I tried to practice some spirituality. All the leaders and Gandhiji were imprisoned. Subhash Babu was hidden somewhere and was preparing the Azad Hind Sena while the battle was going on up to the borders of Imphal.

The British government had started training sessions for

Air Raid Precaution. They had built around two-metre-high brick walls on both sides of the roads. The factories were cheerily working to prepare weapons for the army forces. Even at that time our leaders were all imprisoned. The Communist Party and the Muslim League were active while Jinnah Saheb was terrifying the nation by adamantly putting forward his demand for Pakistan. The Communist Party was supporting them and they were also helping the British in the war. Even before Rajaji they were keenly opposing the Quit India movement. He had also thought up a formula to emphasize his demand for Pakistan. 1941 to 1942 was such a bad time, when all the things were opposing the Congress and Gandhiji.

In 1942, the train tracks, bridges and poles were being destroyed. It was chaos all around. Some people also visited me with ropes and axes but I refused to team up with them and tried fruitlessly to convince them to follow the lessons of non-violence. They argued with me, saying that Gandhiji said this chaos was spread by the British but we are okay with chaos. In 1940 Jinnah had already convinced the president of the League to accept his proposal of Pakistan. There were protests mounted everywhere for Pakistan. In 1945 when Gandhiji was released from jail, he conducted multiple meetings with Jinnah and tried to convert him, to ensure the country was not divided. But Jinnah Saheb did not change an inch. And Gandhiji also did not move from his firm standing on the principles of Hindu-Muslim unity and till his last breath he kept fighting for the same goal. He endangered his own life again and again to protect his ideal of Hindu-Muslim unity.

I often wonder about the relationship of Jinnah and Gandhiji and the question that comes to my mind is how was it possible that Jinnah, who as the secretary of the Congress in 1916 convinced the Muslim League to sign the pact of Hindu-Muslim unity (the Lucknow Pact) was the same Jinnah who was not ready to listen to a single word of Gandhiji now? Gandhiji talked to Jinnah as per the formula of Rajaji and directed that the Muslim-inhabited zones would be taken to plebiscite in the western regions and more such matters which Gandhiji actually did not approve of. In fact, Jinnah Saheb was envious of Gandhiji and his populist politics and his grip on the masses. After his return from South Africa, Gandhiji had attained huge popularity in his Kheda and Champaran protests (1918). He had influenced the Congress to the extent of his domination in it and from 1922-23 all the power was in the hands of Gandhiji. One has to notice that Jinnah was already a well-established lawyer at that time. He was well known and very impressed by the parliamentary membership of Dadabhai Nauroji. He was ambitious about gaining fame also in the area of politics. He was also successful in his ambition despite his father's lack of support for him. After the entry of Gandhiji in the Congress, he had been reduced to just a member. He was a very important lawyer and an impactful and rich man at that time. I guess he was disappointed and lost his space because of Gandhiji's presence.

So, with a sense of defeat, he became an opponent of Gandhiji. Once he even escaped to London for a while and isolated himself from the politics of India. It was in 1930 that Liyaqat Ali Khan somehow convinced him to return as a member of the Muslim League. He accepted this on the condition that the League would accept his plan of Pakistan and obey his commands. He was also offered the title of Qaid-e-Azam which meant the king of law. So, it was impossible for him now to accept any kind of defeat at the hands of Gandhiji. Thus in 1940 and again in 1942 at the procession in

Lahore he announced the formation of Pakistan. The British and the Communists supported him. At that time, Gandhiji and the leaders of our freedom struggle were all imprisoned and reading or writing books in jail. I think Jinnah had taken this revenge on Gandhiji. This is totally my observation, it may be a wild guess.

The fourth decade of the last century was the most terrifying and painful time for our nation. If the time of gaining independence was the greatest triumph and victory for our nation, it was also the toughest time of penance and ordeal for Gandhiji. Cruelty was at its peak, reflected in mass riots, assassinations of innocent people and the unsettling of millions of people in the country. How ironical a time it was, on the one hand, the celebrations of our freedom were enjoyed like festivals through crackers and lights and on the other hand, Gandhiji was the only man trying to console the lost people through his compassion.

He was fasting in Calcutta. At the time of election for the minister of Sohravardi, thousands of people were being killed, and Gandhiji returned from Bihar, after his efforts to quieten the chaotic conditions there, and within six months, three gunshots of Godse sent him to heaven. How and when all this happened, we all know very well. It is not easy to talk about it as we take pride in 15th August 1947, Independence Day. I was fasting in my room on that day, as I had often kept fast on Sunday with my mother and later, following Gandhiji, I added speech fasting on Sundays. So, I kept Maun Vrata till 12 noon. Every day, I also used to spend at least an hour in spinning cotton on the spinning wheel. I could weave around 300 metres of cloth in an hour on Yervadachakra, and through practice I could produce 40-50 count thin cotton easily. It was not that easy to weave the cloth so by covering various objects, I would make dolls and after collecting many a doll, I offered them to the Khadi Bhandar in exchange for some more cotton to weave.

I could weave enough cloth to make a couple of pyjamas, two shirts and two pullovers. In my neighbourhood, there was a student named Katariya who was as gentle as me. He too was under the influence of Gandhiji. Even Gopinath, the next-door neighbour, was of the same thought so we three used to read Gandhiji's books and writings together and used to discuss them freely. Narayan Dutt Tiwari used to stay in the same hostel as Vimal Mehrotra. Both of them were followers of socialist thinking. With them as well the ideas about Gandhiji were discussed frequently. I had established a creative congregation which met every Sunday at two in the afternoon in the union hall. One hour was spent in weaving cloth on the spinning wheel and half an hour was further spent by us in the discussion about the current political updates and movements. In these discussions, Sadik Bhai, Shankar Rao Dev, Kaka Kripalani, Prof. Mahesh Dutt Mishra and many such people participated.

I went to the professor of Physics from Kashi University, Prof. Uddhav Asrani, to get some lessons on the method of working and I tried to understand the ways of activism from him. He was propagating Gandhian thought there in Kashi in the Nandkishor Lodge. I tried very hard to run such an organization in Allahabad but this was not granted to me as I was merely a student. To work on the principles of Gandhiji, I also stayed in the Sevapuri Gandhi Ashram for many months and learnt all those works which I was intending to do further in my life. I stayed in the wise company of people like Karna Bhai, Vichitra Bhai, and Bhai Mazumdar (Ude). I learnt the political philosophy of Gandhiji from Prof. Dhawan and Gandhian Economics from J.C. Kumarappa. I roamed around in the villages to spread adult education as a part of my social experience.

I used to grind nearly two kilos of flour each morning, getting up early. In the Ashram, I used to wash the utensils, mine and those of other people. I also visited the popular leaders of Allahabad, Vishwambharnath Pandey and Purushottamdas Tandon. The son of Tandonji who was a professor of Chemistry used to stay in the backyard of our hostel. Some good books brought were very useful to turn the younger generation towards the thoughts of Gandhiji. I was only a student and such activities, I thought, were not good for me. Yet, I had been walking on this road, with some promises to fulfil. But I got very little time for my studies. So, I used to get up at midnight and write my notes. During the day, I used to attend classes like all, and used to make extensive notes like those of the lecturers. Now, all the playing was stopped but I was still the captain of my hostel volleyball team. In 1945 when the prisoners of 1942 were released for the Quit India movement, one of those prisoners, Hemwati Nandan Bahuguna, after three years of his jail life, came to me. He started staying with me in my room. He did not have enough clothes for himself. He was a student of Allahabad University. So where should he go? Before finding a place to go to, he came to me. I do not know why he came to me when he could have gone to anyone.

He went also but that was much later. He was a politician and I was only a Gandhian worker. He was not like Narayan Dutt Tiwari, an open-minded person. He was a very efficient orator and a very sociable, impactful and brilliant person. Both these persons came like a breeze into my life and disappeared, too, like the same. Yet, he was not out of my sight. Sometimes by chance we used to meet and greet each other warmly. Their activities too were controversial. All know how many traumas were spread in India during 1945 to 1950. The great Calcutta killing happened in the Hindu-Muslim riots as well as open assassinations in Sohrawardi, Hindu-Muslim riots in Bihar, the direct action of Jinnah.

Amid the riots and massacres in the whole nation, the absurd transactions of British missions coming here and going, finally, the partition of India and independence to Pakistan was granted on 14th August and to India on 15th August. And at that time nothing like the huge massacre that took place had ever been seen. Gandhiji kept trying to calm things till his last breath. To stop this painful accident and trauma he told Nehru and Patel that Jinnah should be made the prime minister of the country and with his cooperation the indivisible India could survive as it is. At that moment both the great leaders were taken aback and questioned him, Bapu, what are you saying? And despite the resistance of Bapu, this nation was partitioned. Nehru became the prime minister of independent India, and Sardar Vallabhbhai Patel became his home minister. This time Gandhiji felt let down by his own people. Anyone who does not get defeated by the enemy can be defeated always by his own people. Gandhiji continued to firmly extend his faith in Hindu-Muslim unity. A brother may separate in anger but does not become an enemy. We are like an elder brother.

With love a younger brother can be convinced. Gandhiji recommended that 55 crore rupees be given to Pakistan for restructuring the mosques that were destroyed. For this he undertook a fast till death. Nehru and Patel had to do the same although later only Gandhiji was blamed for this often and again. (In Bombay, the speech was delivered by Patel).

Because of all these reasons the masses in the nation were weary of Gandhiji. His popularity was much declined despite people being still respectful and affectionate to him.

And they were weary of his love for Muslims.

On this my respect for Gandhiji mounted higher. But I was not his worshipper. I was never able to worship any hero. Even then I was prepared to accompany those few Gandhi-followers to convince Muslims to bring them back to India. Kripalaniji, Karmaveer Bhai Sunderlal, and many other disciples of Gandhian thought had the idea of going to Pakistan and returning to India. Sunderlalji also had gone but he had to return. The Kashmir matter was hot on the plate. Even six months had not passed and a young man called Nathuram Godse assassinated Gandhiji, shooting him with a gun. What a horrifying tragedy! This news unsettled the whole country. The natives may have been weary of Gandhiji's Hindu-Muslim unity approach but they really loved him.

This sorrowful accident disturbed me thoroughly. And that very moment Gadreji came to my room and started crying, sitting near me. He wept more intensely as he told me how he was a Brahmin from the rigid area of Sadashivpeth in Pune, opposing Gandhi always, yet, he never wanted Gandhiji to be assassinated. That too at the hands of some so-called sacred Brahmin person. He wanted to lessen his sense of guilt by lamenting with me. Whatever the sense, he was always with me and remained my lifetime friend.

The third day, the cortege of Gandhiji arrived with all small and big leaders.

The slowly marching procession moved from Allahabad station and reached the Sangam, the fusion point, around two o'clock in the afternoon, via Civil Lines road, at a respectful pace. The Ramdhun, Song of Ram, was played. On the big military tank, the body was covered with flowers and they carried it till they disappeared into the January fog. From the station I kept running, across the fusion point of the Ganga. A huge frenzy was in my mind. After returning, I kept brooding in my room with my mind crying on the riotous and woeful conditions in our country.

My MA Previous exams were a couple of months away. So once again my studies were stopped and my examination was escaped on account of Gandhiji. Had I been superstitious, I would have thought that Gandhiji was not in favour of my wasting time in education instead of using that time for our nation. But I truly believed only educated people could work and help the nation progress and carry our life forward. With the same intention I started concentrating on my studies again. In the academic year 1948-49, I was elected unanimously as the president of the hostel union.

At that time, I invited Lal Bahadur Shastri for a speech in the union and Karmaveer Bhai Sunderlalji also came to address our union. He used to speak a lot, and while speaking his eyes would fill with tears. In Hindi he used such tiny phrases while speaking softly in stylized conversation, that a deep impact was created in the minds of his listeners. That was actually his own style. All the students listened to his speech carefully. In the same period, Jinnah Saheb died of tuberculosis in September. Before his death he had started sending his Kashmiri Kabalies to protect his army and he wanted to merge Kashmir in Pakistan. That did not happen but he passed away. Being a Gandhian disciple I called the union meeting to express our condolences for Jinnah Saheb. All came but when I was trying to express the condolence proposal, they started chit-chatting. I was so disturbed that I declared my reluctance to continue the membership of such a union wherein people could not even sympathize with a dead person at least to send a formal letter of condolence. I resigned from the president's post. O.P. Bhatnagar, the superintendent of the hostel, liked me a lot. He, in fact, was very affectionate to me. He came to my room and tried to convince me that I should withdraw my resignation. But I refused to agree with him. Not even if the condolence proposal were revised and forwarded again. Then I left everything except my habit of spinning cotton. A sacrificial sense occupied my mind so deeply that everything else seemed absurd. At the same time my two-and-a-half-year-old son suddenly passed away. I had not known till then the true feeling of being a father. My mind was lost in speechlessness. When the bad news was received by my wife she started lamenting loudly. I was watching it with my wide open eyes. In place of Gandhiji's work, now only his spinning wheel and his thoughts were my companions. When I left India in June 1963, the spinning wheel too was left behind on Indian soil and in place of Khadi, English clothing came with me.

Now the memories of the martyr, the disappointed Gandhi, remained with me. They passed away and became martyrs. I was left behind in my body like a living corpse. Whatever happens, we have to be there and so we are, witnessing everything. Watching with wide open eyes.

Where was Gandhiji and where am I?

We did not ever meet and he did not even know me. There were basic differences which existed between us. He was firm in his creed and faith in God. And I had always been a disbeliever. I could never ground my faith in such a God that does all good to His worshippers. Yet, I admired the innocent worshippers. I liked the devotional engagement of the worshippers in worshipping God. That devotion is admirable indeed. Even if I was willing, I could never be a worshipper. That is why I adore them. Gandhiji was a radical activist. He used to confront any matter any time for the sake of truth. I was too scared to call a thief a thief. He regarded non-violence as his religion. Non-violence for him, in fact, was the only path to arrive at the truth. Non-violence was the only religion he believed in. Love thy enemy. I may like to follow him on this point but my non-violence is without any courage. Out of fear though, I am a true follower of non-violence. In today's violent world I am also a propagator of non-violence.

I was afraid of Gandhiji's moral rigidity. In any way, I never dared to go near him. I went to his ashram only when he was absent. I visited Sabarmati and Sewagram like a pilgrimage destination with all the others. I also visited the ashram of Vinobaji, and had the pleasure of seeing him but he was on a speech fast. I had adored him greatly for his land donation movement. Even then I could not gather the courage to walk with him on his mission of Journey on Foot. Dada Dharmadhikari always used to tell Gandhiji that your words are an order for us Bapu, you need not explain. So, even today we can narrate the miraculous stories of Gandhiji's courage and soul power. And whatever was expected to happen could not happen without Gandhiji.

Anna Hazare came forward but was caught in the Lokpal bill. I was willing to participate in his mission, leaving all, but not merely for the Lokpal bill. Had he started the protest to express the mass opposition to the all-pervading corruption, I might have. It is not only a few officials and ministers who are corrupt in our government, but the whole society around is corrupt. We have to reform the society in our nation. But they soon came to a compromise. Life is to be lived, finally;

how much can we go on fighting and with how many people, how many times? They disappointed me more. One possibility then is kindled through Gandhiji. One infinite possibility.

To some extent like Gandhiji, by being aware and awakened all the time and living with a sense of fearlessness so that we will never be exploited. Each generation has to bring its own revolution and carry the cross of its own progress.

For Peace and Truth, the only path is that of non-violence which Gandhiji proved to us by his martyrdom.

> In this simple way I made life easier
> Asked for apologies from the one
> and offered forgiveness to the other.

This couplet of Ghalib may make life easier, but not justified, and the unjustified cannot reach the truth. For the real attainment of Truth and Peace constant working with non-violence is essential.

GANDHI'S AUTOBIOGRAPHICAL SOCIAL PROGRAMME

Siby George

The Gandhian political ethic of frugality and equality resonates well with contemporary ecological and socio-political critique. The potential of Gandhian ethics for understanding and stimulating social action, leading to social change, is the subject of this paper.

First, I shall argue that a careful scrutiny of Gandhi's life and writings will unambiguously reveal a strong conception of moral individualism as the underlying moral ontology of the Gandhian ideal of the ascetic, moral citizen-subject. Gandhian moral individualism means that for an action to be moral it must be a free moral choice of the individual on the basis of culturally sanctioned morality with which she/he relates rationally in a minimal sense. Gandhi distances himself from the economistic ideal of the self-interested, rational choice-maker, inherent in modernity, and embraces the ideal of the free moral agent. Gandhi's invitation to Indians to become ascetic, moral citizen-subjects has an autobiographical slant because the evocative example that forms the basis of his narrative is his own life.

Second, referring to the writings and the social

programme of Gandhi, I shall argue that as a prism for analyzing, understanding and galvanizing social change, the autobiographical, self-referential rationale of moral individualism is inadequate. Gandhian moral individualism considers privileged individuals in general as morally capable of voluntarily choosing to reform unjust social systems, which are conditioned on their privilege. Gandhi's social programme is autobiographical because his own experiments with the principle of non-violence and the non-violent movement form the basis of his claim about the moral citizen-subject, who can bring about social change. In the Gandhian scheme of social action, social change is neither a matter of the individual's claims concerning her rights (the liberal model) nor a matter of structural transformation (the leftist model); it is, rather, a matter of moral choices of individual agents out of their sense of duty towards society, which has basis in a culturally sanctioned morality that they share, and their moral motives, dispositions and rationality.

The Autobiographical Mode of Social Action

In liberal theory, methodological individualism, as distinguished from moral individualism, means that social action must always be explained with reference to the motives and dispositions of individuals, not of social groups (Hanson 2008, 416). Moral individualism has different nuances. It can mean that individuals should be treated not on the basis of their group membership but their individuality (May 2014, 155), and, as in Amartya Sen's capability theory, that only individuals should be the concern of our evaluations and decisions in social policy (Robeyns 2005, 107). It can mean, as in Émile Durkheim, the socially constructed and enforced morality that emphasizes the universal human rights of the individual in general (Cristi 2012, 413).

It can be shown that a strong strand of moral individualism and the consequent ideal of the ascetic, moral citizen-subject permeates Gandhi's writings and the story of his life. Moral individualism in the Gandhian sense amounts to belief in the free individual as the basis of moral choice, although choices themselves have to be broadly in line with and minimally in rational engagement with the morality or the set of duties sanctioned by one's culture or religion. That is, the individual is called upon to make her choices in conscience, but a judgement regarding the goodness or wickedness of the choice made can be done only with reference to a set pattern of social morality with which she must engage rationally in a minimal sense. Therefore, Gandhi's moral individualism implies that discrete individuality should be the animating nucleus of social morality, and the social normal can be transformed only when the individual chooses to act morally in terms of her sense of duty. The stipulation to interpret the moral duties sanctioned by tradition in a minimally rational sense, or the minimal principle of rational interpretation alone can release the Gandhian scheme, if partly, from the vicious circle involving individual moral consciousness and the sense of duty nurtured by tradition. Thus, for Gandhi, it appears, the inalienable moral conscience of the individual self, which is imagined in a spiritual-metaphysical fashion, must be nurtured by tradition, and personal and collective good actions must be undergirded by thus nurtured conscience. Gandhi believed that such conscientious actions will inhibit violence and force exerted on the self from the outside, and social change resulting from social action, even if slow and gradual, would be morally sound only when it finally comes about by means of the voluntary cooperation of moral individuals. I shall defend this interpretation in what follows, and demonstrate the inadequacies of the autobiographical social programme.

We read in *Hind Swaraj* (1909): 'It is Swaraj when we learn to rule ourselves...But such Swaraj has to be experienced, *by each one for himself*. One drowning man will never save another. Slaves ourselves, it would be a mere pretension to think of freeing others' (CWMG 10, 39; added emphasis).[3] Here is a strictly positive idea of liberty, where liberty is defined not as freedom from external interference, but, as Isaiah Berlin argues, freedom from 'the despotism of something which I cannot control' (2002, 185). Not even the expulsion of the English from India (external interference) is necessary when we consider freedom as the experience of the individual from the shackles of her own internal demons. Berlin famously argued that such conceptions of freedom as self-government is perennially in danger of leading to despotism by the wisest, who are eager to reform others *for their own good*.[4] However, theorists of positive freedom defend this view, arguing that as long as self-correction is necessary, help from some outside source or other, at least to call out what is wrong with one's doings and beings, cannot be ruled out (see Taylor 1985, 222-23). *Hind Swaraj* is full of injunctions on controlling the individual's mind and body, and on cultivating the self. A

[3] *The Collected Works of Mahatma Gandhi* will be cited as CWMG with volume number, followed by page number.

[4] John Stuart Mill states in relation to his famous harm principle that 'the only purpose for which power can be rightfully exercised over any member of a civilized community, against his will, is to prevent harm to others. *His own good*, either physical or moral, is not a sufficient warrant' (2015, 13; added emphasis). Unfortunately, Mill goes on to defend the use of force over 'uncivilized' people like 19th-century Indians in the British Colony.

spiritual, personal, and strictly moral sense of freedom must accompany political Swaraj according to Gandhi.

Gandhi's attempt to nurture the Indian as ascetic, moral citizen-subject is compared by Barton Scott (2016) with the cultural goals of the social movement of European Protestantism. He argues that the stage was set for Gandhi and others by the 19th-century critique of the spiritual despotism of priests in India, which helped cultivate the ideal of the self-ruling subject, the worldly householder, disciplined by a rigourous set of ascetic practices of citizenship. Anticolonialism and Hindu reform wouldn't have been possible without the ideal of the ascetic, self-ruling subject. 'Swaraj, for Gandhi, entails something more than the simple transfer of state sovereignty from Britain to India; instead, it requires a radical dissemination of sovereignty as a principle of ascetic 'self-rule'... an ethic of ascetic self-discipline' (Scott 2016, 9). Thus, in Foucauldian parlance, Gandhi was initiating a new disciplining technique or ethic of this-worldly salvation for Indians, predominantly moral-spiritual but political as well. His *Autobiography* consists of many experiments with the relative manifestations of the absolute truth in the world, from which he derived 'such power as I possess for working in the political field,' and since the autobiographical details of his experiments are conducted not in the closet but in the open, they are edifying to the others, for 'what is possible for one is possible for all' (CWMG 39, 3). In Gandhi's gently persuasive rhetoric, his example of the ascetic model of self-rule is a paragon for every Indian to emulate in order to protest against modern civilization and against its avatar in India—the colonial government—and above all to become the new subject of self-reform. His 'special message' for the oppressed blacks of America in 1945, scribbled in reply to the questions of the African American journalist Denton Brooks, was revealing with respect to the autobiographical logic of the Gandhian ideal of the non-violent citizen-subject: 'My life is its own message. If it is not, then nothing I can now write will fulfil the purpose' (CWMG 80, 209).[5]

In the *Autobiography*, the spiritual is the moral; religion concerns itself with 'self-realization and knowledge of the self'. Moral-religious phenomena for Gandhi are matters of the individual self, but they can become edifying to others. Even the most profane realm of realpolitik for Gandhi must be shot through with the spiritual-moral personality of the individual agent. The *Autobiography* bids farewell to the reader emphasizing self-purification, which is infectious and which cleanses whatever the individual touches and lives with. Transformative power emerges out of the morally cultivated individual self and affects whatever she is concerned with, even 'the meanest of creation'. Such a moral individual 'cannot afford to keep out of any field of life. That is why my devotion to Truth has drawn me into the field of politics ... [T]hose who say that religion has nothing to do with politics do not know what religion means' (CWMG 39, 401). The moral individual's transformative connection to all things, even the most profane field of politics, is thus laid out. This is the Gandhian model of self-transforming and morally infectious individuality—the autobiographical social programme—crucial to the reformed and resistant Indian. In Scott's portrayal, Gandhi thus became 'the icon of political asceticism,' and he 'experimented with how religious asceticism could be used to reform the capitalist subject' (2016, 208).

[5] A pithier version of these words to Brooks became the epigraph in front of the Mahatma Gandhi Memorial in Washington, D.C.: 'My life is my message.'

Moral individualism of the Gandhian variety is also noticeable in his emphasis that all developmental indicators of the nation can be measured only with respect to the benefits accrued to each individual. In this, Gandhian moral individualism goes hand in hand with the capability approach's ethical individualism, to which I have referred above. The talisman that Gandhi gave to a co-worker in 1947 is revealing. It has the following counsel for social workers when they are in doubt: 'Recall the face of the poorest and the weakest man whom you may have seen, and ask yourself if the step you contemplate is going to be of any use to him…[W]ill it lead to swaraj for the hungry and spiritually starving millions?' (CWMG 89, 125; see also Weber 2011, 150). Two striking aspects of this statement are the unwavering focus on the individual subject, and the coupling of physical with spiritual starvation.

While Gandhi's views are said to be eclectic and fluctuating, his moral individualism is unflinching. In his 1945 letter to Nehru, clarifying that his notion of future India has not changed from his *Hind Swaraj* vision of 1909, Gandhi writes:

> The sum and substance of what I want to say is that the individual person should have control over the things that are necessary for the sustenance of life. If he cannot have such control the individual cannot survive. Ultimately, the world is made up only of individuals. If there were no drops there would be no ocean (CWMG 81, 320).

This statement follows a highly personal reaffirmation of the credo of *Hind Swaraj*. The deposit of experience since 1909 is only reconfirming his belief in its vision. 'If I were the only one left who believed in it, I would not be sorry. For I can only testify to the truth as I see it' (CWMG 81, 319). This decidedly personalized vision and conviction of the moral individual is also the secret of the charm of Gandhi's *Autobiography*. In his disclaimer about the finality of his experiments with truth in the Introduction to the *Autobiography*, Gandhi nevertheless writes: 'For me they appear to be absolutely correct, and seem for the time being to be final' (CWMG 39, 4).

I now want to clearly distinguish Gandhi's moral individualism, as I have described above, from the methodological individualism of liberalism—the view that social phenomena such as behaviour of the market must be explained on the basis of individual rather than group motives. The 'capitalist subject' in Scott's description or the rational agent who maximises self-interest is the individual of methodological individualism.[6] In his 1924 conversation with his Tamil associate G. Ramachandran, Gandhi insists that he would make intelligent exceptions to his critique of machines such as the Singer sewing machine, which according to him was invented when Singer saw his wife struggling with the mending of clothes. Gandhi concludes: 'The *individual is the one supreme consideration*. The saving of labour of the individual should be the object, and honest humanitarian considerations, and not greed, the motive...[R]eplace greed by love and everything will come right' (CWMG 25, 252; added emphasis). If modern economics assumes the self-interested rational choice-maker, Gandhi assumes the individual who can choose in moral freedom.

---

[6] Kristiina Hellsten argues that liberalism itself is justifiable only when one moves from methodological to moral individualism in the realization that 'liberal identity is not found in the actualization of Western materialist egoism or ethical nihilism, but in the recognition of the metaphysical ideal of moral agency and in one's striving for its actualization in practice, that is, in finding one's moral identity' (1998, 343).

The capitalist subject is disavowed by Gandhi in yet another moral-spiritual sense: in terms of the Advaitic sense of interconnectedness of all beings. Hence, the individual cannot gain spiritually if those who surround her suffer. 'I believe in *Advaita,* I believe in the essential unity of man and for that matter of all that lives. Therefore I believe that if one man gains spiritually, the whole world gains with him and, if one man falls, the whole world falls to that extent (CWMG 25, 390). If one helps one's opponents, Gandhi continues, one helps oneself and one's co-workers. The Advaitic sense of interconnectedness is also said to be the basis of Gandhi's notion of equality. He argues that there is neither inherited nor acquired superiority between persons, and that all are born equal. 'All—whether born in India or in England or America or in any circumstances whatsoever—have the same soul as any other' (CWMG 35, 1). Thus, moral individuality means realizing within one's consciousness the Advaitic sense of no-twoness. Gandhi argues that it is this belief in the equality of persons, grounded in Advaita doctrine, that powers his critique of caste and Brahminical superiority. But he does not begin the argument from the opposite direction: he does not argue for drastic social upheavals that would transform unjust systems of property, caste or gender relations that would finally benefit each individual morally and spiritually. After all, if the whole world gains when one person gains spiritually or morally, it is true even more that the moral gain of the whole world is a superior form of moral change because it would morally benefit all individuals concerned. My contention is that Gandhi does not entertain such a proposition because moral action has meaning for him only when it arises out of discrete individuality, and because politically enforced social change might involve violence towards the individual.

Gandhian moral individualism must be distinguished from liberal individualism also because Gandhi's emphasis is on duties, not rights. The Gandhian individual, unlike in liberalism, is not the bearer of rights. This is why we have defined in this paper Gandhian moral individualism as the view that discrete individuality is the seat of moral choice, and that the individual chooses, however, by engaging in a minimally rational sense with the duties sanctioned by religion. 'Minimally rational' because, as we shall see below, Gandhi did not seem to have employed critical questioning of tradition in a strong sense in his engagements with questions of social morality, although Bhikhu Parekh calls him a critical traditionalist (1999, 93). Judith Brown observes that Gandhi's idea of duty was based on his understanding of Hindu dharma, which is related to the necessity to maintain universal order and balance or *rta* (2000, 89). Again, G.N. Sarma points out that 'Gandhi's individualism is less political and social than ethical and religious' (1980, 216), and details the elements of Hindu dharma that underlie the Gandhian conception of individual duty. The clamour for rights was seen by Gandhi as an evil afflicting society, ensuing from the forgetfulness of duties. His suggestion to H.G. Wells in response to his *The Rights of Man* in 1940 attests to this belief: 'Begin with a charter of the Duties of Man, and I promise the rights will follow as spring follows winter' (CWMG 73, 90). In 1947, as the fundamental rights were being discussed in the Constituent Assembly, Gandhi told an audience during a prayer meeting: 'The zamindar insists on his rights, the peasant on his. But there are no such two classes here that one of them should exercise only rights and the other discharge only duties' (CWMG 88, 231). In the context of the unwillingness of Indian princes to give up their privileges, Gandhi admits that it is the duty of the people to bring them down, but always abiding by non-violent methods. 'The people should fight against him with courtesy, truth and peace. The people should not merely run after rights...When you do your duty the rights will drop into your lap' (CWMG 38, 238). The ideal of individual duty is the focal point also of *Hind Swaraj*. The editor admonishes the eager reader who is ready for action: 'You make a mistake. You and I have *nothing to do with the others*. Let each do his duty. If I do my duty, that is, serve myself, I shall be able to serve others' (CWMG 10, 64; added emphasis). Gandhi's advice to his relative and follower Maganlal Gandhi in 1910 also is a striking example of his emphasis on dutiful, moral self-cultivation: 'Please do not carry unnecessarily on your head the burden of emancipating India. *Emancipate your own self*...In your emancipation is the emancipation of India. All else is make-believe...*You and I need not worry about others.* If we bother about others, we shall forget our own task and lose everything' (CWMG 10: 206-07; added emphasis). This view of a highly personalized, individualized sense of moral duty towards oneself, which must purportedly flow 'naturally' towards all, is central to the Gandhian social programme.

Gandhi's moral individualism, rooted in a strong notion of the conscientious individual self, is deeply indebted to such Western critics as Tolstoy, Ruskin and Thoreau. In this framework, social change must be brought about by the conscientious, free self-transformation of the moral individual. The individual must not be changed by changes in the external conditions of human life as Hegel, Marx and other progressive theorists of positive freedom held. Although indebted to the Western sources, Anthony Parel argues that Gandhi's ideal of self-rule is finally based on the *Gita*-ideal of the person of a controlled mind or *sthithaprajna*, who acts without the desire for reward (*nishkamakarma*). 'Inner change within the individual ought to be the starting point of outer changes in society. Modern social science tends to ignore this principle. Gandhi reinstates it into political philosophy' (Parel 1997, lxi). That is: Gandhian moral individualism goes by the counter social scientific insight that social action to bring about social change must emanate freely from the morally convinced, converted individual citizen-subject. Such would be the Gandhian principle of protection against violent coercion of individuals to participate in social change. *Hind Swaraj* ends by reiterating the principle of self-rule and duty: 'Real home-rule is self-rule or self-control...What we want to do should be done, not because we object to the English or because we want to retaliate but *because it is our duty to do so*' (CWMG 10, 64; added emphasis).

I shall now consider whether the ideal of the moral individual, the acetic and self-ruling citizen-subject, is a sufficient animating nucleus for a cogent social programme.

Questioning Autobiographical Social Programme

Gandhi's autobiographical moral individualism enunciates a model of social thinking that must constantly return to the self and its moral fabric (spiritual tradition) in order for the world to be set right. If his beliefs were staunchly based on the *Gita* and the religious worldview in general as commentators avow (Parel 1997, xlix), his interpretation of the *Gita* is a model of his preoccupation with self-cultivation and self-purification. At the beginning of the commentary on the *Gita*, Gandhi asks the reader to leave aside the question of violence and war, which forms the background of the text, and consider that 'this *dharma-grantha* was written to explain man's duty in this inner strife' (CWMG 32, 95)—a strife of the soul between good and evil. The *Gita*'s philosophy of *nishkamakarma* (selfless action) is the central pillar of his interpretation, which for him comes to mean the work of ahimsa, underpinned by two conditions: 'One is that there should be no element of selfishness in our motive, and the second is that there should be no self-interest of ours in it, that on the contrary it should be for the good and for the benefit of the world' (CWMG 32, 356). Worldly action in this sense is the door to spiritual liberation. In the Introduction to the *Autobiography*, Gandhi declares that the striving of his life is 'self-realization, to see God face-to-face, to attain *moksha*' (CWMG 39, 3). Such is Gandhi's ascetic model of self-discipline and self-rule.

Gandhi thus made profane and worldly the proverbially unworldly life of the serious traditional Hindu. He did so in a very symbolic and dramatic sense, thus inscribing in his body and person an ascetic ideal of self-government for the modern Indian citizen, an ideal of positive freedom of the self, ruled by the moral principles of the dharmic tradition (see Sarma 1980, 226). Gandhi believed that he truly represented every Indian, or at least every Hindu in the context of the Hindu-Muslim question during the freedom struggle, that he represented the former untouchables more than Ambedkar. 'I claim myself in my own person to represent the vast mass of the Untouchables...I claim that I would get, if there was a referendum of the Untouchables, their vote, and that I would top the poll' (cited in Ambedkar 1991, 68). This statement reveals the autobiographical social programme without dissimulation. Scott remarks that Gandhi's 'highly publicized flesh' came to symbolize the ethic of ascetic self-rule. He strived to make ascetic self-rule not only an elite practice but a national one. He recruited the masses to non-violent satyagraha and to spinning cotton on the charkha. Scott argues that in these ways Gandhi undercut the abstract individual of liberalism, 'the self-interested citizen-subject'. Instead, 'Gandhi set out to reduce the self to "zero", in the belief that such a renunciation of self would establish non-violence as the basis of politics' (Scott 2016, 11). Scott also reads the Gandhian political saga as a mode of undermining the capitalist subject: 'by exercising greater control over their consumer desires, he suggested, Indians could staunch the flow of mass-produced British goods into India' (9).

In the Gandhian perspective of the moral citizen-subject, social action begins from the moral resources of the self, and its attractiveness lies in the self's direction, responsibility and decision concerning what is happening outside it. There is no blaming the outside, others and the world for what one lacks, a right that one does not possess, a privilege that one does not have, a desire that one cannot fulfil. In the least, as Parel points out, the Gandhian model of social engagement reminds the individual that 'the project of outer transformation ought to begin with the inner transformation of the moral agent' (1997: lxi). Parel's point is really that the Gandhian model is a rectification of the prevalent model in the social sciences that external or structural changes are necessary for the transformation of subjectivity and the personal sense of wellbeing. There is a specifically Indian angle, David Hardiman argues, to Gandhi's disavowal of social change considered as structural transformation, and the avowal of social change taken to be individual-initiated. In a society where community and caste sanctions were unscrupulously deployed to ensure solidarity, where people in general were not considered as moral individuals in distinction from their community, 'Gandhi was demanding that swaraj be rooted in a very different modality of power, that of individual conscience' (Hardiman 2003, 57). Hardiman cites Rammanohar Lohia's view that Gandhi gave the masses self-confidence in the individual to resist oppression and injustice even without any social support. He also cites Gandhi's argument in *Hind Swaraj* that all reform is initiated by the minority against the will of the majority. Thoreau and Tolstoy condemned the corrupting influence of mass mobilization. Instead, Gandhi made 'the right of individual dissent' a tool for mass mobilization and protest. That is, the conscientious individual makes a moral choice to protest against and change unjust social systems. But this valorisation of individual moral agency, while inspiring and motivational, is completely blind to the systemic and structural social logic of power, privilege and marginalization. It does not pay sufficient attention to critical examination of social organization. Individual agency is thoroughly embedded in the discursive shape of the world of the individual, and so the social weight of marginalization cannot be considered as the sole responsibility of the individual, whether sufferer or aggressor. What is imperative is to rectify systems, structures and the world that shape individual consciousness. Individual and especially collective agency of the marginalized must be deployed against traditional seats of power in order to neutralize and change them. It is, therefore, more accurate to say that radical social change would transform individual agency rather to say that individual moral decision would transform the social world.

I now want to consider the counter-perspective to the Gandhian model of individual-initiated social change. It is well-known that contemporary ontologies of the self, whether poststructuralist, Marxist or communitarian, challenge the liberal ontology of the discrete individual. The self is, rather, a discursive being-in-the-world, a dialectical relation to the spirit of the times or a dialogically engaging member of the community. Gandhian non-violent agitation and the power Gandhi exercised through such technologies as his proverbial fasts in fact attest to the effect of performativity or discursive force upon the affective sensibilities of individuals. There is no given individual moral subject of unsullied conscience; one's moral consciousness is formed in dialogue with the world outside. The Gandhian conception of subjectivity is distanced from this contemporary philosophical ontology of subjectivity. It is true that Gandhi is unconcerned about the liberal notion of the abstract, self-obsessed individuality. However, he still enunciates a different notion of discrete individuality: a predominantly spiritual or moral self, detached from the world, who can thereby morally assess for herself worldly affairs, social and political matters, decide on them and rectify them morally. What differentiates the liberal notion of selfhood from the Gandhian one seems to be self-interest and economistic choice-making rationality. A discrete individuality, capable of disinterested moral decision-making and morally-attested voluntary social action, seems to be the Gandhian ideal. The autobiographical logic in this ideal, needless to say, is unmissable. While Gandhian moral individualism presupposes tradition as the ground of individual moral consciousness, it does not sufficiently interrogate this presupposition in relation to the ideal. As we shall see, tradition is the invisible ground of the moral individual's social action that makes the Gandhian social programme gradualist and diffident with respect to such thorny issues as caste and redistribution of property.

Let me now ask whether the above Gandhian narrative about individual moral agency and its power to bring about social change had any real effect on the public life of the nascent Indian nation that he ruled rather unchallenged for about three decades. If it is true that various kinds of subjectivities develop in line with the discursive formations of different epochs of history, as poststructuralists like Foucault argue, the moral citizen-subject of Gandhi was itself a powerful discourse that governed Indian subjectivity at the nascent juncture of the new nation. Not that there is a given, discrete self that directs moral action; this is ontologically impossible. But there can surely be a historical discourse of the ascetic, self-ruling subject that can gradually usher in the newfound awareness of a disciplined, moral citizen-subject. At the same time, the newfound moral citizen-subject of Gandhi is embedded strongly in the morality (dharma) of tradition. The conscience of the Gandhian moral individual is circumscribed by tradition to a great extent. This is the paradox, the double bind: pure moral individuality backed by tradition. Since Gandhi was a foundational personality, a significant event of rupture and transformation in the life of the new nation, several aspects of the Gandhian framework crept into the fibre of the nation at its incipient moments. One of these was gradualism and another was the idea of agential moral individualism. According to the second, human beings can and must morally decide to enter into schemes of social cooperation (trusteeship) and can voluntarily overcome centuries-old hierarchies of caste, gender and wealth inequality. The slow moral awakening of the individual is central to gradual, non-violent social change. The world or governmental technologies cannot revolutionize the self; the individual moral self will transform the world in the fullness of time. Non-coercive social change must be the rule because the first moral principle is uninfringeable non-violence, which is self-evident at least for the moral citizen-subject of the dharmic tradition.

The above Gandhian ideal had to confront bitter criticism. Gandhi's severest critic, Ambedkar, saw in Gandhian gradualism and agential moral individualism, which alone can initiate social action, an eagerness to protect the status quo. Analyzing the Gandhian critique of the modern technological civilization, Ambedkar argues that the evils wrought by machinery are a product of erroneous social organization, which sanctifies private property and profiteering as absolute. 'If machinery and civilization have not benefited everybody the remedy is not to condemn machinery and civilization but to alter the organization of society so that the benefits will not be usurped by the few but will accrue to all' (1991, 283). Ambedkar calls Gandhism 'conservatism in excelsis' because 'its philosophy helps those who have, to keep what they have and to prevent those who have not from getting what they have a right to get' (291). If social change must be left to the voluntary decision and autobiographical resources of the moral individual, even if she/he is part of the privileged traditional social sections and discourses that perpetuate oppressive systems, Ambedkar's criticism is inescapable. In his final speech in the Constituent Assembly on 25th November 1949, Ambedkar exhorted Indians to give up hero-worship or bhakti in socio-political matters—a call to shun, in the pursuit of liberty and justice, the tendency to gratefully cling to the biographical details of great leaders like Gandhi.

The Gandhian social programme is autobiographical not only because the figure of Gandhi and Gandhism is its moving spirit. It is autobiographical also because of the uncritical play of auto-affection: the sameness of the discrete self of the individual behind moral conscience without carefully considering how the self is formed and operates in terms of a heterogeneous relation to tradition. In Gandhi, it is tradition considered in a minimally rational sense that determines the morality of the decision, although this remains an unacknowledged assumption. This minimal critical engagement with tradition is the essential problem of the Gandhian autobiographical social programme.

Gandhi's ideal was, Judith Brown argues, moral regeneration of every Indian; political self-government was for him a minor instrumental aim. Gandhi hoped to morally and spiritually persuade the privileged and the powerful to realize their moral duty towards others. Brown remarks that conservative Congressmen, who feared socioeconomic revolutions, loved the Gandhian programme because he was 'definitely not attempting to organize movements for the pursuits of "rights" or the forcible reordering of the distribution of power and resources' (2000, 97). One can routinely notice Gandhians, who abide by caste norms and a feudal worldview, while adhering to the strictest of moral codes concerning honesty and politeness in social interactions.[7] Studying Gandhi's *Delhi Diaries* of the period after independence, Sarma observes that Gandhi's concept of satyagraha was formed under the negative conditions of a foreign rule, and he found its reckless use in free India disillusioning. It goes without saying that in the Indian context the 'reckless' use of satyagraha would first of all mean assertion of marginalized Indians in order to revolutionize unequal social structures. Sarma's diagnosis

[7] About the paradoxical coexistence of polite social interactions and caste prejudice, Suryakant Waghmore writes that in the Marathwada villages he studied recently, this contradiction 'mostly translates into couching disgust and caste hubris under new forms of politeness' (2018, 121).

is that extending moral individualism to the political arena is likely to cultivate hypocrisy and selfish motives in human relations. 'The pursuit of power and profit would become easier when it is done in the name of morality, whereas under a secular and unpretending ethic which takes note of human frailty, motivations and the essentially external nature of political action, lapse in public conduct and standards may be more easy to recognize and expose' (Sarma 1980, 231). Political action is 'essentially external' because it is about new forms of social organization that can inaugurate new forms of subject formation. Most significantly, it must be noted that subjectivity is formed in pre-reflective rather than deliberate relation to the outside world of action, consent and dispute, be it subjectivity of the Gandhian moral individual. The autobiographical is the worldly.

As we have seen, the moral principle of non-violence is ultimate and absolute for Gandhian political practice. This is problematic because the political ethic and culture of non-violence can make invisible a great deal of social violence, perpetuated systemically in the ordinariness of everyday life. Violence certainly cannot be unethical only when it is employed to rectify injustice and revolutionize social structures; unjust social systems themselves are violent more effectively. The famed Gandhian gradualism was undergirded by the fetishism of non-violence. In 1924, Gandhi advised the former untouchables not to violently wrest their rights as Westerners would do. His advice to them is forbearance until the aggressors are won over by argument and the victim's good conduct. 'So long as they are converted, I can only ask you to put up with your lot with patience' (CWMG 25, 514). He believed that the Nazis could be won over by *satyagraha* (Brown 2000, 95). Such Gandhian conundrums show why uninfringeable moral principles could become a moral obstruction in the actual pursuit of justice.

Many instantiations of the problems relating to the Gandhian autobiographical social programme or the ideal of the moral individual's voluntary initiation of social change can be pinpointed. One example is the Gandhian doctrine of trusteeship. Gandhi's mobilization of the peasantry virtually deterred the Indian have-nots from acting assertively to set things right. In 1934, Gandhi was speaking to a group of zamindars (traditional landowners), who were worried that the new offshoot of the Congress, the Socialist Party, would dispossess them of their landed property. Gandhi's discussion with the zamindars emphasizes the following: (i) class war will not be permitted as it does not fit with the ideal of non-violence and the 'essential genius of India'; (ii) the envisaged Ramrajya would ensure the 'rights alike of prince and pauper'; (iii) the zamindars are trustees of the land; (iv) class war will become unnecessary if landowners develop a familial sense of kinship with their ryots (tenants), providing for their security and wellbeing, rather than indulging in extravagant living; and (iv) this would help India develop 'an indigenous socialism of the purest type' based on moral grounds different from the Western socialist/communist assumption of the essential selfishness of human beings. This remarkable conversation assures the zamindars that the whole weight of the personal influence of Gandhi and Nehru would be behind preventing class war for the sake of non-violence. However, 'supposing that there is an attempt unjustly to deprive you of your property, you will find me fighting on your side... Our socialism or communism should therefore be based on non-violence and on the harmonious cooperation of labour and capital and the landlord and the tenant (CWMG 58, 248).

Further: 'The ryots have themselves no greater ambition than to live in peace and freedom and they will never grudge you your possession of property provided you use it for them' (249). Later in the same year, Gandhi agrees in a conversation with the anthropologist Nirmal Kumar Bose that a minimum use of violence by the State may be required if private owners are absolutely unwilling to abide by the spirit of trusteeship. However, Gandhi insists that the violence of private owners is 'less injurious' than State violence, and his biggest worry is that the State 'does the greatest harm to mankind by *destroying individuality,* which lies at the root of all progress. We know of so many cases where men have adopted trusteeship, but none where the State has really lived for the poor' (CWMG 59, 319; added emphasis). To Nehru, who suggested in 1933 in a letter that vested interests in India (the British, the princes and the landowners) must be made to give up their privileges in order to free the masses economically, Gandhi replied that although the existence of the princes and the zamindars depends on 'the exploitation of the masses', their fears and distrust must be assuaged by ensuring 'the innocence of our methods'. 'We do not seek to coerce any. *We seek to convert them.* This method may appear to be *long, perhaps too long,* but I am convinced that it is the shortest' (CWMG 55, 427-28; added emphasis). Ambedkar understandably has harsh words for the doctrine of trusteeship because, according to him, it deceives the victims with the hope that 'a little dose of moral rearmament to the propertied classes...will recondition them to such an extent that they will be able to withstand the temptation to misuse the tremendous powers which the class structure gives them over servile classes' (1991, 286). That is, Gandhi was unable to appreciate how the moral consciousness of privileged classes generally supports, justifies and reinforces privilege rather than disrupts it.

The role of non-violent struggle and Gandhism in modern Indian history is sometimes interpreted favourably. Mridula Mukherjee claims that even radical communists among the Indian peasantry functioned within the boundaries of non-violence, realizing that 'non-violence itself had enabled a certain kind of mass participation that was not possible otherwise' (2004, 392). However, violence is an inescapable and originary aspect of the human condition inasmuch as we are embodied beings, dependent on others to become a self in the first place. Unjust social systems are already entrenched in violence, visible and invisible. We can only reduce and negotiate violence; we can strategize non-violence, not because violence against injustice is ethically nonsensical, but especially because the domination of the oppressor is founded precisely on superior and craftier use of violence. Gandhi's answer to the question of property redistribution in the about-to-be independent nation was trusteeship. Sandipto Dasgupta remarks about the Gandhian programme: 'A more equitable property regime had to come about through moral and voluntary action on the part of the property owners—charity and renunciation, not land reform' (Dasgupta 2017, 651). The question of drastic redistribution and land reform were, thus, foreclosed from the political horizon of independent India; it became a matter of the privileged individual's moral largesse. The Land Ceiling Act still remains an unfulfilled dream in India, and land not with the tiller but traditional landowners. Writing about the fate of the Gandhian movement of satyagraha in independent India, Bhikhu Parekh observes that Vinoba Bhave 'obligingly redefined it to exclude all forms of conflict and to mean nothing more than gentle moral appeals to the government and vested interests' (1999, 324). According to Bipin Chandra, the Congress leadership, including Gandhi, 'opposed all anti-landlord actions of the peasantry in the name of non-violence and the unity of the anti-imperialist struggle' (1981, 66). This also means that, Chandra remarks, the class and political consciousness of agricultural labourers and poor peasantry remained the same as that of the landlords. Thus, an unequivocal aspect of the Gandhian autobiographical social programme was the interdict against the deployment of force or revolutionary legislation to transform the feudal, caste-ridden, agrarian socio-economic order—for force, even revolutionary legislation, is violence.

Gandhi's attitude towards the social organization of caste is well-known. His campaign against caste, Christophe Jaffrelot contends, was mainly religious (temple entry) and moral (personal), but not political.[8] He vehemently opposed the radical political step of a separate electorate for the former untouchables. During his famous 1932 fast, Gandhi told an interviewer: 'I would accept any pact that has not a tinge of

[8] Nishikant Kolge (2017) argues the case that in personal practice Gandhi was impeccably non-discriminatory. To a journalist's question in 1945 whether he still adhered to the views on caste expressed in his writings, Gandhi's reply was the following: 'I do not need to refer to my past writings to say what I believe today, because only what I believe today counts. I wish to say that the caste system as it exists today in Hinduism is an anachronism. It is one of those ugly things which will certainly hinder the growth of true religion. It must go if both Hinduism and India are to live and grow from day to day. The way to do it is for all Hindus to become their own scavengers and treat the so-called hereditary Bhangis as their own brothers' (CWMG 79, 384). In this paper, my argument has not been that Gandhi personally adhered to caste practices and beliefs, or that his views did not evolve over time. Instead, my argument has been that Gandhian moral individualism and inadequate moral ontology does not help visualize a radical social programme, but one that emphasizes the conversion of hearts of the privileged.

separate electorate about it. I would, with utmost reluctance, tolerate reservation of seats under a joint electorate scheme. But I should insist upon what is to me the vital part of the pact, the social and religious reform' (CWMG 51, 126). Thus, progressive legislation favouring the erstwhile untouchable castes in India (reservation of seats in education, employment and electoral politics) came to force despite Gandhi. Jaffrelot maintains that Gandhi did not demand social equality for Dalits, and 'did not imply the eradication of caste as a social unit' (2005, 63). In her recent chronicle of the events of the Vaikom Satyagraha (a temple entry movement led by Gandhi in today's Kerala in 1925), Mary King observes that Gandhi's strategy of aiming at the moral conversion of hearts of the upper caste Hindus did not succeed in Vaikom. She argues directly against considering conversion of hearts as a mechanism for social change, although non-violent agitation for her is a democratic method of civil resistance to influence political opinion and to effectively enforce change. Conversion, she contends, 'remains exceedingly infrequent' and considering the suffering of protestors as a strategy to convert the hearts of perpetrators is 'a dangerous basis for planning [civil resistance] strategy' (King 2015, 301). On the individual-centred Gandhian approach, Mark Juergensmeyer writes in his review of several central works on Gandhi: 'Most of those who write about Gandhi in both India and the West are content to envisage change on a much more *individual level*, and they see Gandhi's main significance as an inspirational and easily understandable model for personal piety and virtue' (1984, 297; added emphasis). The internationally loved Gandhi (of Louis Fisher and Richard Attenborough) is, Juergensmeyer remarks, 'a lone moral individual', who triumphs over all odds, although there is always an 'implicit social dimension' in Gandhi. I have argued that the social dimension of the Gandhian programme, autobiographical in essence, however, is problematic, when we carefully consider Gandhi's moral individualism and his views on social change.

Conclusion: Beyond the Autobiographical

Gandhi's autobiographically evocative moral individualism came in the way of his social programme, although he made many prophetic diagnoses and contributions: his method of non-violent protest or civil disobedience, his analysis of the ills of modern technological civilization, his galvanization of the Indian masses for freedom, his national sensitization of the evil of untouchability, his public enactment of religious amity—more significantly than any major founding figure of the nation—in declaring free India a home of both Hindus and Muslims alike. I have argued in this paper that the man who mobilized the masses unlike no other Indian, asking them to be self-ruling moral individuals like he was, always went by a self-referential, autobiographical moral logic even in his social programme. What convinced him about the moral conversion of the privileged was his own conversion. The masses must reform themselves, re-enacting the morals of the self-story, and the self-story they must relive is one of self-reliance, self-rule and self-sacrifice. The privileged will, thus, self-consciously give up their privilege; the oppressed will self-effusively resist their temptation to fight for their rights. The autobiographical social programme must preserve the social order and reproduce harmony and peace rather than violence and chaos, although a minimal and gradualist model of rational engagement with tradition is envisaged. India has not unshackled itself from the Gandhian vision of the autobiographical social programme of ascetic self-rule in terms of duties fulfilled for the sake of order.

It seems to me that the Gandhian programme of non-violent social change, based on the good will of the moral individual, can only be a small part of the moral narrative concerning social change, for social action must be primarily conceived and marshalled socially and politically. For revolutionary social change to occur, the moral subject must be socially pressurized and persuaded through discursive formations in the world of politics, social policies, religious movements, legislative transformations, critique of oppressive traditions, courageous legal applications, governmental technologies, social mobilizations, civil society activism and, most importantly, earnest, unashamed demand for their rights by the oppressed. These social upheavals in the world and the metamorphoses they initiate are the affective phenomena that move or must move the hearts of the moral individual to make moral choices. Self-formation of the moral individual, located within unchanging tradition, and her moral decision, instead, reproduces the moral status quo.

In socio-political matters, the two dimensions of the autobiographical figure of the moral citizen—reference to the exemplary life of Gandhi himself and to the individual subject's moral resources—can finally mean only *the ethical response of the person* to the ethical logic enunciated in the public sphere. There ought to be a subjective ethical response of the person to a public ethical discussion. Everything depends on how one responds to a new ethical argument being posed in the public sphere—a questioning of historically protected privilege, for example—which moves away from and challenges one's cherished moral sensibilities, backed by tradition. If one is able to read the world only with reference to the self's historical horizon and the moral logic of that horizon, there is a moral deadlock and lack of moral development of consciousness. I have shown how some aspects of the Gandhian social programme, such as its response to questions of redistribution and caste, accentuate this failure. However, the upshot of my analysis is not this failure. Gandhism as a social programme is still alive and its repercussions still reverberate in India's socio-political life. Gandhism will benefit from a more robust moral and social ontology of the person. The takeaway from this discussion of the Gandhian autobiographical social programme is the moral subject's ability to assess new ethical arguments and demands in the public sphere in terms of the questions they pose and in dialogue with others rather than with reference merely to the self's moral sensibilities backed by tradition. In this sense, the Gandhian moral citizen-subject is a searcher beyond the precincts of the autobiography of the self.

References

Ambedkar, B.R. 1991. *Dr. Babasaheb Ambedkar: Writings and Speeches*, Vol. 9, edited by Vasant Moon. Bombay: Education Department of the Government of Maharashtra.

Berlin, Isaiah. 2002. Two Concepts of Liberty. In *Liberty*, edited by Henry Hardy, 166–217. Oxford: Oxford University Press.

Brown, Judith M. 2000. Gandhi and Human Rights: In Search of True Humanity. In *Gandhi, Freedom, and Self-Rule*, edited by Anthony Parel, 87–102. Lanham, MD: Lexington Books.

Chandra, Bipin. 1981. The Peasants and the Project for National Integration in Contemporary India. In *Peasantry and National Integration*, edited by Celma Agüero, 51–82. Mexico: Colegio de Mexico.

Cristi, Marcela. 2012. Durkheim on Moral Individualism, Social Justice and Rights: A Gendered Construction of Rights. *Canadian Journal of Sociology* 37 (4): 409–438. https://doi.org/10.29173/cjs12253

Dasgupta, Sandipto. 2017. Gandhi's Failure: Anticolonial Movements and Postcolonial Futures. *Perspectives on Politics* 15 (3): 647–662. https://doi.org/10.1017/S1537592717000883

Gandhi, M.K. 1969–1994. *The Collected Works of Mahatma Gandhi* (100 Volumes). New Delhi: The Publications Division of the Ministry of Information and Broadcasting, Government of India. https://www.gandhiheritageportal.org

Hanson, F. Allan. 2008. The Anachronism of Moral Individualism and the Responsibility of Extended Agency. *Phenomenology and the Cognitive Sciences* 7 (3): 415–424. https://doi.org/10.1007/s11097-008-9098-y

Hardiman, David. 2003. *Gandhi in His Time and Ours*. Delhi: Permanent Black.

Hellsten, Sirkku Kristiina. 1998. Moral Individualism and the Justification of Liberal Democracy. *Ratio Juris* 11 (4): 320–45. https://doi.org/10.1111/1467-9337.00094

Jaffrelot, Christophe. 2005. *Dr. Ambedkar and Untouchability: Analysing and Fighting Caste*. Delhi: Permanent Black.

Juergensmeyer, Mark. 1984. The Gandhi Revival: A Review Article. *The Journal of Asian Studies* 43 (2): 293–298. https://www.jstor.org/stable/2055315

King, Mary Elizabeth. 2015. *Gandhian Non-violent Struggle and Untouchability in South India: The 1924-25 Vykom Satyagraha and the Mechanisms of Change*. Oxford: Oxford University Press.

Kolge, Nishikant. 2017. *Gandhi Against Caste*. New Delhi: Oxford University Press.

May, Todd. 2014. Moral Individualism, Moral Relationalism, and Obligations to Non-human Animals. *Journal of Applied Philosophy* 31 (2): 155–168. https://doi.org/10.1111/japp.12055

Mill, John Stuart. 2015. On Liberty. In *On Liberty, Utilitarianism and Other Essays*, edited by Mark Philp and Frederick Rosen, 1–112. Oxford: Oxford University Press.

Mukherjee, Mridula. 2004. *Peasants in India's Non-violent Revolution: Practice and Theory*. New Delhi: Sage.

Parekh, Bhikhu. 1999. *Colonialism, Tradition and Reform: An Analysis of Gandhi's Political Discourse*, Revised Edition. Thousand Oaks, CA: Sage.

Parel, Anthony. 1997. Editor's Introduction. In *Hind Swaraj and Other Writings*, edited by Anthony Parel, xiii–lxii. Cambridge: Cambridge University Press.

Robeyns, Ingrid. 2005. The Capability Approach: A Theoretical Survey. *Journal of Human Development* 6 (1): 93–117. https://doi.org/10.1080/146498805200034266

Sarma, G.N. 1980. Gandhi's Concept of Duty. *The Indian Journal of Political Science* 41 (2): 214–231. http://www.jstor.com/stable/41855023

Scott, Barton J. 2016. *Spiritual Despots: Modern Hinduism and the Genealogies of Self-rule.* Chicago, IL: The University of Chicago Press.

Taylor, Charles. 1985. What's Wrong with Negative Liberty. In *Philosophy and the Human Sciences: Philosophical Papers 2*, 211–229. Cambridge: Cambridge University Press.

Waghmore, Suryakant. 2018. From Hierarchy to Hindu Politeness: Caste Atrocities and Dalit Protest in Rural Marathwada. In *Contested Hierarchies, Persisting Influence: Caste and Power in Twenty-first Century India*, edited by Surinder S. Jodhka and James Manor, 111–139. New Delhi: Orient Blackswan.

Weber, Thomas. 2011. Gandhi's Moral Economics: The Sins of Wealth without Work and Commerce without Morality. In *The Cambridge Companion to Gandhi*, edited by Judith M. Brown, and Anthony Parel, 135–153. Cambridge: Cambridge University Press.

BEING THE CHANGE

Women's Activism in India

Margaret A. McLaren, Rollins College, USA

Gandhi's well-known phrase: 'Be the change you wish to see in the world' indicates that his philosophy is meant to be viewed as a practice, an active engagement with the world. Gandhi's philosophy and life have influenced struggles for national sovereignty, actions of civil disobedience, non-violent protests, and movements for social equality and economic justice. The central ideas of Gandhi's philosophy: ahimsa (non-violence), swaraj (self-rule), swadeshi (self-reliance), satyagraha (soul-force), sarvodaya (welfare of all) and sarvadharma (the equality of all religions) reinforce one another as a philosophy equipped to understand and challenge oppression, that values equality and interdependence, and that recognizes the importance of material circumstances and economic justice.

This article discusses the ways that some contemporary grassroots women's organizations in India embody Gandhi's philosophy through their activism.[9] First, I draw connections

---

[9] In this article I draw upon some ideas from my forthcoming chapter in *Routledge History of Indian Ethics: Gender, Justice, Ecology*, (Ed. Purushottama Bilmoria, Routledge, 2022) and from my recently published book, Women's Activism, Feminism and Social Justice (Oxford University Press, 2019).

between the mode of Gandhi's philosophy and feminism in relation to the theme of autobiography. Next, I discuss aspects of Gandhi's philosophy and how they lead us to understand that activism and social and economic justice are integral to his overall philosophy. I provide contemporary examples of women's organizations in India that carry on Gandhi's legacy through their activism and service. I focus on the Self-Employed Women's Association (SEWA) because it is based explicitly on Gandhian principles; I also include two other examples of organizations that embody Gandhian principles, MarketPlace India and AVANI. I conclude that the legacy of Gandhi's philosophy is evidenced through contemporary women's activism for social justice as well as organizations that work for the welfare of all by challenging economic and social barriers to equality and working with those who are historically marginalized, exploited, and disenfranchised.

Gandhi is most well-known for his campaign for national independence for India, yet, his writings and ideas touch on many aspects of human existence. Here I want to note that one characteristic of Gandhi's philosophy is the way he presented his ideas. His autobiography, *My Experiments with Truth* is a key text not only for learning about his life, but also for insight into his philosophy of life. While reading about his early childhood years when he experimented with his diet, and his adulthood when he fought against the colour line in South Africa and helped to organize worker campaigns in India, we see that Gandhi embodied his philosophy. For him, life was an expression of his philosophy exemplified by his tireless work for social justice achieved through non-violent methods.

Being the Change: Connections between the Personal and Political

Before discussing some of the main ideas of Gandhi's philosophy, I want to point out what I see as some commonalities in contemporary feminist approaches to theorizing and making meaning and Gandhi's mode of philosophizing. This chapter is not about what Gandhi says (or does not say) about women in his work, nor about his relationships with women during his lifetime; it is not even about whether or not Gandhi could be called a feminist retrospectively. Instead, I focus on how his ideas—especially about social justice and non-violence—can be used to advance feminist aims through women's activism in India. In this section, I draw connections between Gandhi's expression and embodiment of his philosophy and some aspects of feminist approaches. At least since the 1980s, feminists have viewed autobiography as a valuable method for using personal stories to convey larger social or political realities (Personal Narratives Group 1989). The validation of autobiography as a legitimate form of theorizing is particularly important for marginalized groups such as women; autobiographical narrative gives voice to those who may have been silenced or ignored. At the same time, autobiography can communicate philosophical concepts and criticize dominant social relations. Though autobiography covers a wide and differentiated genre of writing it holds a special place for feminists: 'There has always been a strong feminist interest in the autobiographical, beginning with the attempt to connect the "personal" with the "political"' (Coslett, Lury and Summerfield 2000, 2).

Gandhi's philosophy, too, connected the personal with the political; he famously stated: 'My life is my message.' For

Gandhi, acting on his principles was important both in his personal life and in his public actions and political work. In his philosophy there is not a sharp division between ethics and politics: you speak your truth, act on your truth, and work for the manifestation of it in public life. His commitment to non-violence permeated everything he did, from the way he interacted with others in his personal relationships to his vision of a world that embraced diversity and social equality. He saw the harmful effect of unjust social policies on those of the lowest caste and on women and he realized that in order for individual dignity to be realized for all, social systems and structures would need to change. In terms of diversity, not only did he welcome people from every walk of life, ethnicity and caste, he also advocated acceptance of a plurality of religions, viewing each as contributing to the same goal of reaching Truth.

Gandhi's philosophical approach exemplifies how a commitment to fundamental principles is reflected in the way that one lives one's life. In what follows I discuss how some contemporary organizations working for social justice in India continue Gandhi's legacy by enacting the core commitments of his philosophy.

Core Concepts of Gandhi's Philosophy

Ahimsa (non-violence) holds a central place in Gandhi's philosophy. Non-violence is commonly associated with refraining from physical violence even in the face of attack; this proved to be effective as part of the movement for India's national independence as well as in movements for racial justice in South Africa. Yet, it was not simply politically strategic on Gandhi's part, he was deeply committed to non-violence, seeing it as an ethical principle to live by. Ahimsa is not simply refraining from harming others; it is an active and positive force of love. Ahimsa should infuse our daily lives; it 'must shine through your speech, your action, your general behaviour' (Gandhi 1968, 143). And, it is also the underlying principle of a well-constructed society: 'All well-constructed societies are based on the Law of Non-Violence...Only under that law would a well-ordered society be intelligible and life worth living' (Gandhi 1968, 135).

While ahimsa is a powerful force, himsa (violence) is part of Nature; it is up to humans to counter this violence. According to Gandhi, violence can be active or passive. Active violence is generally physical violence or force. Passive violence can include not standing up to injustice, wasting resources, and poverty (A. Gandhi 2017). According to Ela Bhatt, a Gandhian and the founder of the Self-Employed Women's Association (SEWA), 'poverty is wrong because it is violent; it does not respect human labour, [it] strips a person of his or her humanity, and [it] takes away their freedom' (Bhatt, 8). Poverty is a form of structural injustice, that is, it results from the systemic injustices in economic, social, and political systems that discriminate against and marginalize people, often severely curtailing their life chances. Gandhi explicitly links economics with non-violence when he says: 'Economic equality is the master key to non-violent independence' (Gandhi 1962, 37). The organizations that I discuss work with poor women to help them get out of poverty and also to challenge systems of social and economic injustice that perpetuate poverty.

One of the methods for achieving non-violence is satyagraha (soul-force) (Gandhi 1968, 154-155). Satyagraha involves opposing unjust laws and being willing to accept the consequences for civil disobedience in opposition to those laws. Standing up for justice against injustice takes courage and is a non-violent method to work for social change. Satyagrahis must incorporate non-violence into their personal life and behaviour as well as in their political action. Satyagraha depends upon a commitment to non-violence: 'Satyagraha excludes the use of violence in any shape or form, whether in thought, speech, or deed' (Gandhi 1968, 159).

Swaraj, or self-rule, is mainly associated with Gandhi's struggle against British colonialism; indeed, national independence is a significant aspect of swaraj. But swaraj also means self-rule on an individual level, the ability to control one's desires and to be able to make meaningful choices. Swaraj can also refer to the organization of communities or villages as functioning units based on cooperation to meet basic needs. Gandhi envisioned village swaraj as 'a complete republic, independent of its neighbours for its own vital wants, and yet interdependent for many others in which dependence is a necessity' (Gandhi 1962, 31). He felt that India's villages held the key to a sustainable future for India and also recognized the importance of economic and social programmes, which he called 'constructive programmes', that would allow rural areas to thrive and to meet their basic needs. Organization of villages on his plan would operate on principles of non-violence; all activities would take place on a cooperative basis, and there would be no caste system (Gandhi 1962, 31). Gandhi sees the ability to meet one's basic needs through dignified labour as essential for individuals' moral and spiritual growth. In keeping with his advocacy of the importance of constructive programmes, he viewed economic equality as central to social justice and a decent life: 'True economics, on the other hand, stands for social justice, it promotes the good of all equally including the weakest, and is indispensable for a decent life' (Gandhi 1962, 37).

Swadeshi, or self-reliance, encapsulates a holistic approach to economic, social and environmental issues. The concept of swadeshi has four aspects: political, economic, dharma and moral welfare. The religious aspect of dharma reminds us that we should pursue Truth, the aspect of moral welfare reinforces a commitment to love and non-violence, the political and economic aspects relate to the idea of village swaraj. As far as possible, political and economic systems should be decentralized, that is, villages should be self-ruled and organized so that food, water, clothing, and other basic necessities are produced locally. This allows for fuller employment and also supports environmental sustainability. As has become even clearer since Gandhi's lifetime, supply chains for necessities like food that must be transported for long distances contribute to environmental destruction through the use of fossil fuels used in transportation. Movements for 'slow food' and 'local food' have increasingly become part of the overall push for environmental justice in the 21st century. His commitment to local self-reliance also animated his campaign for khadi (homespun cotton cloth) and spinning to produce the cotton fibres used in khadi. Finally, swadeshi values local roots and cultural and religious traditions; Gandhi uses the example of improving one's ancestral religion by ridding it of its defects rather than abandoning it (Gandhi 1962, 54). The organizations I discuss also see value in continuing some local traditions, such as block printing, while criticizing others, such as dowry. Swadeshi can be summed up as: 'That spirit within us which restricts us to the use and service of our immediate surroundings to the exclusion of the more remote' (Gandhi 1962, 54).

The principles of swaraj and swadeshi underlie Gandhi's call for constructive programmes, economic and social programmes that would lift people out of poverty and allow them to become self-reliant. He was especially concerned with the poor in rural villages whose traditional way of life had been eroded by industrialization and the rise of the cities. Gandhi believed that creative, sustainable work is important for human dignity, especially for those who are poor and disenfranchised. Dignified work has both a practical component of economic support, and a moral aspect of self-respect. Self-reliance (swaraj) means not only formal independence, but also cultural and moral autonomy. The organizations that I discuss are also committed to these principles because economic security provides access to the basic goods, such as food, shelter, clothing and health care, that allow people to have decent lives. Note that for Gandhi economics and production should be organized to serve life, not profit. He strongly advocated cooperatives as the best form for all types of production and labour (Gandhi 1962, 65-66).

Lastly, sarvodaya (the welfare of all) and sarvadharma (respecting all religions, all people) play a large role in Gandhi's philosophy and also in the ways that contemporary organizations carry forward his legacy. Gandhi credits his reading of Ruskin's *Unto This Last* with helping him solidify and deepen his own convictions about equality and equal worth. Reading it helped him solidify the three main points that underlie sarvodaya: the good of the individual is contained in the good of all; all work should be equally valued and remunerated, from lawyer to day labourer; and that 'bread labour'—working with one's hands—is a worthy life (Gandhi 1968, 197). In short, honest and productive labour makes life worth living, manual labour is to be respected, and we can only thrive when we work for the good of the entire community. Gandhi puts it beautifully when he discusses his view of sarvodaya: 'Everybody would regard all as equal with oneself and hold them tighter in the silken net of love' (Gandhi 1968, 199).

Sarvadharma, the idea of the equality of religious traditions, aligns with Gandhi's commitment to recognizing the value of great religious traditions. One of the primary commitments that Gandhi held was to an openness to all religions and faiths. He stated: 'I believe in the fundamental truth of all the great religions of the world' (Gandhi 1968, 226). At his ashrams there were often interfaith prayers and in his writings he often discussed the relationships among God, Truth, and morality, claiming that each religion contributes to our understanding of Truth and God. Comparing different religions to different parts of a tree, Gandhi said that great faith traditions were branches and 'various religions were like leaves on a tree. No two leaves were alike, yet there was no antagonism between them or between the branches on which they grew' (Gandhi 1968, 227). The principles of sarvodaya and sarvadharma uphold a commitment to recognizing the equal worth of people of every caste, religion, gender, ethnicity, race, and social status. Social equality and respect for diversity are important to a Gandhian approach.

In what follows, I discuss how these Gandhian principles are enacted through three contemporary organizations: SEWA, MarketPlace India, and AVANI. I focus on SEWA because it is explicitly grounded in Gandhian principles, which are embodied in its many programmes. I also discuss two other contemporary organizations and the ways their practices reflect Gandhian principles and values, MarketPlace India, and AVANI. All three organizations see economic and social equality as connected and central to living a decent life (sarvodaya). And, each organization values and respects diversity, including religious diversity. The Self-Employed Women's Association (SEWA) organizes women working in the informal sector into unions and cooperatives to improve their working conditions and enable them to secure basic goods, such as food, shelter, and healthcare. MarketPlace India (although not specifically founded as a Gandhian organization) is also organized as production cooperatives and is committed to respecting diversity and social equality (sarvodaya and sarvadharma). AVANI: Women and Child Rights in Kolhapur, India (hereafter AVANI) focuses on stopping child labour and providing a variety of services: residential homes for children, for women, and for men, and organizing recyclers, who are mainly women, so that their jobs are safer and easier. AVANI works with those who are socially marginalized and economically impoverished, living out Gandhi's commitment to sarvodaya, the welfare of all. AVANI also uses non-violence to work for political and social change (satyagraha); both in terms of active resistance through collective action to change policy and in terms of a loving approach to those who oppose your goals while working to change their minds.

SEWA

Gandhian ideals both infuse and are exemplified by SEWA, especially his ideas about human dignity, self-reliance, and non-violence. SEWA, founded in 1972 by Ela Bhatt, was originally part of the Textile Labour Association (TLA), a labour union influenced by Gandhi that emphasized mediation and negotiation to resolve disputes between labour and capital. The Gandhian principles that underlay the TLA were also to infuse SEWA, especially his ideas about the dignity of labour, the importance of human values, and non-violence. Taken together, these principles indict poverty in several ways. As discussed, poverty is a form of violence that undermines human dignity, inhibits full human development, and presents an obstacle to freedom. Ela Bhatt calls economic freedom 'the second freedom' (political freedom is the first freedom), viewing it as essential for a full human life. SEWA explicitly adopts a Gandhian approach following 'the principles of satya (truth), ahimsa (non-violence), sarvadharma (integrating all faiths, all people) and khadi (propagation of local employment and self-reliance)' (SEWA website 2020). SEWA's main goal is to organize women workers for full employment, including work security, income security, food security and social security; this ensures that women are able to meet their family's basic needs for food, shelter, health care, and child care.

SEWA organizes women in the informal sector of the economy in India using a feminist model of participation and power sharing characterized by democratic practices and institutions. Informal sector jobs are those that do not provide workers with a written contract, health benefits, paid leave or social security. As of September 2020, jobs in the informal sector comprise over 90% of employment in India, so it is by far the largest part of the economy. Because the vast majority of women working for wages in India are employed in the informal sector (94%), wages and conditions of labour within the informal sector are very much women's issues (SEWA website 2020; Bhatt 2006). Informal labour includes many activities, such as piecework, including tailoring, embroidery, cigarette rolling, and incense making; street vendors; ragpickers/recyclers; gum collectors; salt-makers; and construction workers, but the common feature of informal labour is that there are no benefits and no steady salary. Workers are paid the bare minimum for their labour, almost always less than it takes to survive, and there is no job security. Often women working more than full time in the informal sector do not earn enough to provide for their basic needs, such as housing, food, and healthcare.

SEWA defines itself as a movement not a programme. It is a membership organization where the needs and goals of the members are given priority. The common denominator is each member's desire to earn enough to help provide basic necessities for herself and her family. But SEWA's success lies not only in helping each individual achieve her goal, but also in helping all members realize the power of acting collectively. As a workers' movement, SEWA stays close to its roots by facilitating the formation of cooperatives and unions. Both unions and cooperatives have a democratic, participatory structure that fosters empowerment of individuals within the organization as well as creating solidarity.

As an all-female group SEWA promotes and supports the idea that women are powerful and capable. Women are encouraged to take on positions of leadership, which are not generally available to poor women with limited education. The skills that they learn in these leadership roles—traveling outside their village, collecting information, public speaking, running meetings, and keeping accounts—increases their confidence and their status in the community. Along with these skills, the women benefit from increased security due to their affiliation with SEWA. Membership in SEWA provides the women access to SEWA's Cooperative Bank, healthcare insurance, disaster insurance, childcare, literacy classes, computer classes, transportation for raw materials and finished products, etc. In addition to all these benefits, in many cases women's income and working conditions improve as a direct result of their collective power as members of SEWA.

Following the principle of swadeshi, projects begin locally in neighbourhoods, communities, or villages that have contacted SEWA for support. SEWA begins each campaign or project by doing surveys to find out the issues and the problems of the community. Surveys are invariably an initial step when SEWA begins working on a new issue or in a new community, as the survey provides a deeper understanding from multiple perspectives, and it also helps to identify potential leaders in the community. In this way SEWA exemplifies the community-based, democratic model of leadership advocated by Gandhi and prized by many feminists.

Oftentimes one of the frustrations that the women express in the community meetings is not only the low wage for their work but also the lack of control over their working conditions. Usually the low wage is symptomatic of a lack of resources and choices in general and especially with regard to work. As SEWA's founder Ela Bhatt says, 'To be poor is to be vulnerable. The condition of being poor, of being self-employed, and of being a woman are all distinct yet interrelated states of vulnerability. Poverty makes one the chronic victim of forces beyond one's control' (Bhatt 2006, 23). SEWA's commitment to sarvodaya (the welfare of all), swaraj (self-rule) and swadeshi (self-reliance) leads to their twin goals of full employment and self-reliance, allowing women an improved quality of life and more control over their circumstances.

Because of the vulnerability rendered by poverty, one health crisis or a disaster such as an earthquake, drought or flood, can push an already struggling family deeper into poverty. Even under normal circumstances, poor families must borrow money from moneylenders to make ends meet. The moneylenders charge an exorbitant interest rate, and borrowers find themselves further indebted with each day, and with no way to pay off the interest, let alone the loan. This cycle of poverty is familiar, and barring access to credit for the poor, seemingly inevitable.

This is why banks that lend money to the poor, such as the SEWA Cooperative Bank, are an important part of ending the cycle of poverty. Usually people with no assets and without any credit history cannot borrow money. Other obstacles for the poor include illiteracy, making it difficult to fill out forms; no bank in the area and no transportation; and no safe place to keep money. SEWA Cooperative Bank instituted picture identity cards so that illiterate women could also have access to the bank and has set up local savings groups and mobile banks in villages and some areas of cities. Additionally, the SEWA bank offers a quick turnaround time between applying for and receiving a loan. This is especially important if the loan is going to be used to recover from a disaster, pay for emergency healthcare, or cover funeral expenses. Access to credit, in addition to sustainable and dignified work, moves toward the goal of Gandhi's principle of self-reliance (swadeshi).

So far I have stressed the importance of economic issues and the role that SEWA plays in securing a livelihood for its members. The values of collectivism, solidarity and economic and social justice clearly both ground and arise from SEWA's work. Moreover, the Gandhian principles of respect for human dignity and human equality are explicitly stated as integral to SEWA's mission. The validation the women experience, particularly from their peers when they meet together in small groups to discuss the problems and issues they are facing, is important for establishing a connection among the women, and also fosters feelings of self-respect. The community identifies leaders from within to be organizers and spokeswomen. Once the needs of the members of the community are identified, SEWA works with them to build the capacity to accomplish their goals. For instance, if the women in the community have embroidery skills, but live in a remote rural area where there is no market for embroidery, SEWA helps them organize into groups (cooperatives) and several cooperatives pool their resources to transport their goods to the city. Because each cooperative is an entity with collective resources, someone needs to be trained to keep the accounts of the group and to attend to administrative matters. As the women learn these new skills, their confidence grows.

Gandhian principles of swadeshi and swaraj are also enacted by respecting traditional work systems and by supporting traditional artisan skills such as embroidery, spinning, and weaving as well as textile skills such as batik and block-printing. SEWA provides training, links to markets, and skill building to give women control over more of the process from production to sale. According to Renana Jhabvala, 'The reason we [SEWA] support artisan production is because it is giving employment, and what else do artisans have to do? We want to protect what they have, and we want to increase what they have—their bargaining power, their skill levels' (Rose 1999, 232). One way in which the women workers are given more control is to help them control an entire process of production all the way to the point of sale. 'For example, women block printers had been working on a piece-rate basis for a trader, doing only the one step of the process they knew—the actual stamping of the dye onto the cloth, for very low rates. Once they were trained in how to make dyes, design blocks, prepare the cloth, and make more sophisticated designs and garments, they broke their relationship with the contractor, controlling the entire process and selling through the cooperative' (Rose 1999, 230).

SEWA's organization of work through unions and cooperatives fosters the sense of collective power; this collective power, in turn, may lead to individual empowerment. As one's economic power increases, so does one's status in the family and the community, which often shifts the gendered power dynamics and gender roles. SEWA anchors women's power firmly in a material and economic basis—as bank members, property holders, income earners, policyholders, etc. But this individual empowerment remains inextricably tied to the women's membership in a larger group and their collective power to transform the conditions of their lives. The participatory, collaborative structure of cooperatives combines meeting economic needs with developing the confidence and skills to challenge oppressive social structures. 'The poor women must also be equipped to shed the sense of inferiority because of gender, caste, illiteracy, poverty, by building their organised strength through self-managed, self-owned, viable economic organisations. It is the organised economic strength that helps them exercise their political rights, resist oppressive forces' (Bhatt 2000, 10).

By working together, the women are able to secure a decent livelihood, access to education, healthcare and insurance, childcare, and loans. They recognize that their success relies on the success of their SEWA sisters as they share resources and problem-solve together. Empowerment not only changes individuals' lives, it also transforms social relations in concrete, particular ways. SEWA fosters values of economic and social justice and creates solidarity among poor women. As is true of Gandhi, cooperation is embraced as both a philosophy and an economic model by SEWA: 'Cooperation is a way of life, a philosophy, an approach to human problems, based on the principle of equity and justice. All human beings are equal in their right to live and to develop and can be free only if they are not exploited by others but are independently productive and creative members of society' (Bhatt 1995, 11).

Finally, SEWA exemplifies principles of sarvadharma and sarvodaya through its commitment to inclusiveness, respect, and the human dignity of all. Holding firm to principles of human equality and dignity, caste, ethnicity, religion, and social status pose no barriers to leadership within the organization; in fact, special attention is paid to inclusiveness across these social categories in SEWA's structure. This helps to break down entrenched social and religious hierarchies through forming connections, relationships, and working towards social justice. 'While always honouring a women's religious convictions and the skills imparted through her caste, SEWA has broken away from the traditional organizational hierarchy of the village. Every caste is represented in the union and cooperative leadership...Just as SEWA set the precedent by uniting urban women across community barriers, it deserves immense credit for its ability to organize across caste barriers in its rural work' (Rose 1999, 149).

Held up as a model of diversity, SEWA provides a shared basis for organizing around work and gender across other types of differences such as ethnicity, religion, and caste. In her book-length study of SEWA Kalima Rose notes that 'The spirit and diversity of SEWA would presently be difficult to come by anywhere else...Tribal, Hindu, Harijan, migrant, and Muslim women; tattooed Vaghari women, women in purdah;

sinewed, muscular smiths; sun-darkened cart-pullers and agricultural labourers; young, nimble girl bidi rollers with their mothers and grandmothers, progressively more thin and bent from sitting over their rolling work; street-wise and bawdy vendors alongside of women timidly emerging from homebound communities; all in different dress; speaking different languages and dialects; practising different trades—all are coming together to generate strength' (Rose 1999, 20).

In terms of integrating different religions, SEWA has taken proactive steps not only to be inclusive in its organization, but also to bridge differences and promote non-violence among religious communities. After the Hindu-Muslim riots in Ahmedabad in 1985, SEWA members agonized over the fact that women in the same occupations and neighbourhoods were separated into the relief camps that were segregated by religion, Hindu or Muslim. SEWA members from both religious communities had formed bonds through their struggles to attain better working conditions, so they spearheaded a meeting between the Hindu and Muslim communities in Ahmedabad. This was a first step in reconciliation and peace between the two communities. SEWA leadership also played a role in negotiating with officials to lift curfews, and in bringing the communities together to meet. Building connections and relationships among women of different religious communities helped to restore communication and begin to heal the rift between those communities.

SEWA indeed carries out Gandhi's legacy through its programmes and its adherence to the principles of sarvadharma, sarvodaya, satya, and swadeshi (khadi). The principle of ahimsa weaves through their programmes and activities as well; the organization has worked to change unjust laws and to promote the welfare of all through eradicating the violence of poverty.

MarketPlace India

Consistent with Gandhi's principle of sarvodaya, MarketPlace: Handwork of India (hereafter MarketPlace) began as a non-profit organization intended to provide employment for socially and economically marginalized members of society. Originally founded in Mumbai, India, in 1980 by two sisters, Pushpika Freitas and Lalita Monteiro, MarketPlace is an umbrella organization for a group of 13 cooperatives providing job training, educational programmes, and a centralized structure for marketing goods. MarketPlace defines its mission as 'a pioneering non-profit that empowers women in India to break the cycle of poverty, as they become leaders in their work, their homes, and their neighbourhoods, and effect lasting change in their communities' (MarketPlace India website 2018). In spite of not explicitly endorsing Gandhian principles like SEWA and AVANI, MarketPlace nonetheless carries on a Gandhian legacy through its work to improve the lives of women who are poor and vulnerable (welfare of all), by embracing a cooperative economic model for its production units, and by a conscious commitment to respecting and honouring diversity in all its forms (sarvadharma).

Like SEWA, MarketPlace focuses on economic and social welfare for women through collective organizing. MarketPlace's production units are all organized as cooperatives with member-workers making decisions, taking leadership, and sharing in profits. A spirit of collaboration permeates every aspect of MarketPlace. Although there are educational and class differences between MarketPlace staff and cooperative members, the commitment to a democratic, participatory structure runs throughout the organization. From the beginning, the founders listened to the women and created the organization to respond to the needs that they raised and prioritized: 'This democratic approach would become a bedrock for social action projects that would build greater self-confidence among the women and expand the impact of the work to their communities' (Littrell and Dickson 2010, 57-8). MarketPlace combines gainful employment for marginalized women with social programmes that educate and empower them; this dual focus on economic opportunity and social and gender equality is crucial to its success as an organization committed to social change.

While MarketPlace provides some access to outside programmes, most are developed, modified, and managed by the women themselves. This involvement at every level serves to empower its members. According to one member, Sharda, 'The best part of my training is the education and information I am getting: even if I'm not the smartest person in the room, just the feeling of sitting in that chair and learning makes me feel equal and worthy.' The organization does not seek to control the production and programmes of the various cooperatives; rather, they facilitate the interaction among the various groups and coordinate the marketing of their products. Each piece of clothing or household item produced utilizes hand-printed fabric and incorporates embroidery work; each item is unique and beautiful.

In keeping with a commitment to valuing culturally and historically significant practices, the producers, considered artisans, draw upon artistic cultural traditions such as batik and block-printing. The artisans are involved in decision-making at every level; they help to design the products, and they are trained to check the quality of production at their respective units, as well as do quality control before the products are shipped overseas. The artisans also contribute photographs and stories to the catalogue. This involvement in the overall production process allows artisans to understand the entire production process, fosters a sense of empowerment, and leads to a sense of shared responsibility for the welfare of the whole organization. This realization that the welfare of each person depends on the welfare of all connects to Gandhi's principle of sarvodaya. Moreover, MarketPlace's commitment to social equality in terms of gender, caste, religion, ethnicity, and ability is consistent with Gandhi's vision of unity in diversity and equality for all (sarvadharma).

The products produced by the artisans of MarketPlace India are developed with attention to the needs and skills of the workers. Some of the artisans choose to work at home, while tending to children, cooking and dealing with other household responsibilities so each article made includes some handwork, such as embroidery, crochet, or patchwork that can be done at home. Even the artisans involved in machine-sewing the items enjoy somewhat flexible work schedules depending on their personal situations. Some women bring their children to work with them or leave work to make the big midday meal. Sunanda's son had unexplained seizures and she appreciates being able to bring him to work, 'At first I was scared to leave my sick child at home, but then I was able to bring him to work and he stayed at the crèche.' The artisans' needs are taken into account in other important ways as well. Although every item includes hand stitching, care is taken not to choose small designs that can cause eyestrain, or that the older women cannot do because of arthritis. Members of the co-ops appreciate the fair working conditions and living wage that working with MarketPlace India provides them, as well as the skills and leadership training, and the educational and social programmes. Fair wages, safe and healthy working conditions, and control over decision-making all contribute to the artisans' ability to engage in self-rule through creative, dignified, and sustainable work.

The benefits for members of MarketPlace India go beyond these tangible benefits of better wages and more control over working conditions—virtually everyone I interviewed thought of their co-op as a supportive community, almost like an extended family. Kavita says, 'The co-op is like a family. The first thing that came with the job is self-confidence which I didn't have before because I never left the house and did not take public transportation.' The cooperative model builds social relationships of solidarity that are important for collective political action and social change, and also for support in daily life.

Consistent with a commitment to religious diversity and inclusion, the religious affiliations of MarketPlace members reflect some of the religious diversity in India; three of the major religious traditions are represented among members: sixty-six percent are Hindus, thirty percent are Muslims, and four percent are Christians. Working together brings women from different religious traditions together who likely would not have formed relationships with one another: 'Within the Mumbai slums, while the artisans may reside next door to each other, they formerly limited their daily exchanges to others of similar religious faith. Accordingly, for many women, the MarketPlace workshops provide the first opportunity to talk with and work closely among women with varying spiritual beliefs and viewpoints' (Littrell and Dickson 2010, 90). Respect for religious diversity is encouraged and fostered within MarketPlace.

Religion is an important aspect of life for many, if not most, of the women. Pushpika describes the way that one of the groups incorporated the importance of religion with the respect for religious diversity into their cooperative: 'When I went to the workshop to see what had been done, I saw that they had put up a small altar where they had pictures of different gods and a light there. That's very important in Indian culture. Every home will have a small altar. And I felt very good that here this was part of showing their ownership that they had decided "we want to have this altar because it's like our house" and they are going to represent different religions' (Littrell and Dickson 2010, 64). As Mary Littrell and Marsha Dickson note in their research study of MarketPlace, 'Women...speak fondly of the social bonds of support they establish with other MarketPlace women from different religions and backgrounds' (2010, 85). Moreover, they found that their cooperative workplaces 'provide a critically important psychological refuge where "caste and religion do not matter"' (Littrell and Dickson 2010, 143).

While exposure to other religious traditions happens as a natural result of working alongside women from different backgrounds and communities, MarketPlace includes social programmes that explicitly focus on dialogue and diversity such as the Global Dialogue programme. MarketPlace members choose a current topic that relates to women globally, such as the imposition of the burka by the Taliban in Afghanistan, and discuss it. During the course of their discussion they are able to share different opinions and gain insights into their topics that affect women elsewhere while at the same time discussing their own differing religious beliefs and practices. MarketPlace India values and encourages respect for diversity, and women in the cooperatives often come from different religious, ethnic, caste, and community backgrounds. Forming relationships as co-workers and friends across these differences breaks down long-standing social divisions both within the cooperative group and outside it.

Although not explicitly based on Gandhian principles, MarketPlace India is committed to the welfare of all, the inclusion of and respect for different religions, social equality, cooperation as an economic model and as a philosophy, and in its production of clothing, to a tradition of handwork that fits with Gandhi's ideas of swadeshi and khadi.

AVANI

AVANI: Women and Child Rights is a non-governmental organization established in 2000 and led by the dynamic Anuradha Bhosale. AVANI's work came out of the work that the Verala Development Society (hereafter VDS) had been doing in the area (Kolhapur, Maharashtra) since the 1960s. Focused on community development work, VDS had an initiative to provide housing to homeless women which Bhosale led when she joined the organization. Shortly after she joined VDS in 1996, she spearheaded an initiative to improve the situation of migrant child labourers by stopping child labour. This included not only meeting with employers to ask them to abide by the law and stop exploiting children, but also providing on-site schooling and childcare in the brickyards and cane fields where the parents work. These initiatives are linked—child labourers contribute to the family income and the employer's profits. But even if the children were not working, in the absence of school and childcare, parents had no choice but to bring their children to work. AVANI grew out of this initiative started by the Verela Development Society and became a separate organization in 2000.

AVANI now provides residences for girls and boys who

have lost their parents or whose parents cannot house them due to housing and job insecurity. Just last year, they completed construction of a new residence for girls, the Sunanda Gandhi Home for Daughters, so that they will have more room and sufficient housing for the children. In addition to housing and education, AVANI also provides meals, medical care, and opportunities for children to learn crafts, dancing, and singing. More recently, in response to the effects of the coronavirus pandemic, AVANI began providing meal kits to those in need in the community and sewing and selling masks as an opportunity for poor women to have some income. AVANI's leader, Anuradha Bhosale, is committed to Gandhian principles not only of selfless service but also non-violent resistance to achieve political and social change and non-violence in interpersonal relationships.

Providing essential services and support is at the core of AVANI's work but also important is their commitment to changing government policies and laws to support those who are socially marginalized and excluded, such as the children of migrant workers. For instance, AVANI and Anuradha were instrumental in helping to pass the Right to Education Act: 'In 2007, AVANI led the mobilisation work with other NGOs and approached state and central Governments, with the aim to make policy-makers realise the imperative need for every child to go to school. In 2010, the Right to Education for children between 6-14 years was finally enacted as a law' (Chandra 2015). When the Kolhapur area government did not provide adequate public education after the Right to Education Act was passed, Bhosale led a large group of women and children to Mumbai to meet with legislators. They held a peaceful sit-in in the lobby of the government building until officials met with them and assured them that the resources would be made available to provide public schooling for all children between 6-14 as per the law. Bhosale views education as essential in order for children to make a better life for themselves, and she embraces a Gandhian view of education. 'She [also] believes in education from the Gandhian philosophy: that is, not just education for itself, but education that will make the child into a different person, by learning through heart, head and hands' (MSSO website 2020).

The peaceful protest organized by AVANI and led by Bhosale is an instance of Gandhian satyagraha (soul-force) or non-violent resistance against injustice. In her work with AVANI Bhosale utilizes a Gandhian approach, viewing each person as a potential friend while relentlessly and lovingly championing social justice, whether related to ending child labour, access to public schooling, housing security for women, or food for those suffering economic devastation from the pandemic. AVANI provides many services including housing, schooling, healthcare, and livelihood programmes but just as important as meeting the basic needs of those who are economically deprived and socially excluded is social and political action to change unjust laws, policies and practices. Speaking truth to power, Anuradha Bhosale meets with officials to remind them of children's constitutional rights. 'Anuradha also wants to address the root cause rather than just treating symptoms—she educates factory owners, local police and judges about the laws forbidding child labour in the constitution, yet, they are rarely, if ever, used by ordinary people, and usually there is no one to advocate for them anyway. Anuradha is tireless and fearless about this work. She does the necessary demanding paperwork to bring perpetrators of child labour to court—and in true Gandhian fashion, some of these former enemies are now her strongest supporters!' (MSSO website 2020).

When writing about ahimsa, Gandhi defined it not just as non-violence which is a minimal requirement but as an active force of love: 'Ahimsa is not merely a negative state of harmlessness, but it is the positive state of love, of doing good even to the evil-doer' (Gandhi 1968, 132). It is from this positive and loving place that the most powerful and effective social change can be achieved. Arun Gandhi, M.K. Gandhi's grandson, recounts his grandfather's words: 'I don't consider anyone to be my enemy...They are all my friends. I want to educate them and change their hearts' (A. Gandhi 2017, 32).

Changing minds and hearts is at the core of AVANI's work for social justice for those marginalized and excluded. Operating on the principles of ahimsa and satyagraha, AVANI works toward social change and social equality. Through its services, livelihood projects, and support of education, AVANI carries forward Gandhi's commitment to sarvodaya and swadeshi.

Conclusion

Gandhi's legacy is carried on in all three organizations through their commitments to changing laws and social policies to embrace social equality and economic security for all. Valuing the welfare of all (sarvodaya) is consistent with focusing on the most vulnerable. All of the organizations recognize that women are particularly vulnerable both economically and socially: SEWA is exclusively a women's organization; MarketPlace has primarily women as cooperative members, and AVANI's early initiative was to provide housing security to women, especially those who were widowed or divorced. Gandhi's principles are demonstrated in the work of these organizations, and we see that women's activism through a

Gandhian lens works to realize the ideals of the uplift of all, social equality and respect for diversity. Gandhi's legacy continues through the work of SEWA, MarketPlace and AVANI as they strive to improve people's lives, challenge injustice and make the world a better place.

References

Bhatt, Ela R. 2006. *We Are Poor But So Many: The Story of Self-Employed Women in India.* New Delhi: Oxford University Press.

Bhatt, Ela. 2000. *Towards Second Freedom.* Gujarat, India: Mahila SEWA Trust.

Bhatt, Ela. 1995. *Cooperatives and Empowerment of Women.* Gujarat, India: SEWA Academy, Mahila SEWA Trust.

Chandra, Kavita Kanan. 2015. From a domestic help to a social activist, this Kolhapur woman has come a long way. *The Weekend Leader* 6 (27) 4 July. https://www.theweekendleader.com/Heroism/2206/poverty%E2%80%99s-child.html. Accessed September 29, 2020.

Cosslett, Tess, Celia Lury and Penny Summerfield, Eds. 2000. *Feminism and Autobiography: Texts, Theories, Methods.* London: Routledge.

Gandhi, Arun. 2017. *The Gift of Anger.* New York: Simon & Schuster.

Gandhi, M.K. 1993. *Autobiography, or The Story of My Experiments with Truth.* Boston: Beacon Press.

Gandhi, M.K. 1960. *Village Industries.* Ahmedabad: Navajivan Publishing House.

Gandhi, M.K. 1962. *Village Swaraj.* Ahmedabad: Navajivan Publishing House.

Gandhi, M.K. 1968. *The Selected Works of Mahatma Gandhi, Vol. 5: The Voice of Truth.* Ahmedabad: Navajivan Publishing House.

Littrell, Mary A., and Marsha A. Dickson. 2010. *Artisans and Fair Trade: Crafting Development.* Sterling, VA: Kumarian Press.

Maharashtra Seva Samiti Organization (MSSO) website. https://www.mssoonline.org/projects/msso-supported-projects/avani-project/accessed September 25, 2020.

MarketPlace: Handwork of India website. Mission statement accessed March 2, 2018.

Personal Narratives Group. 1989. *Interpreting Women's Lives: Feminist Theory and Personal Narratives.* Bloomington: Indiana University Press.

Rose, Kalima. 1992. *Where Women Are Leaders: The SEWA Movement in India.* New Delhi: Vistaar Publications.

Self-Employed Women's Association (SEWA) website. http://www.sewa.org/About_Us.asp Accessed September 25, 2020.

LOOKING BACK AT BAPU

Gandhi and Children's Picture Books in Contemporary India

Shweta Sachdeva Jha

(Exploratory research on Children's Picture Books in India was supported by the Delhi University Innovations Grant, 2015–16)

Introduction

Writing on constructivist grounded theory, Kathy Charmaz discusses the need for an interpretive approach to qualitative research in which theory should develop from the researcher's view about an experience (2006). I follow her advice in beginning with a personal note that is the basis of the conceptual framework of this paper. Here Gandhi/Bapu is not a historical figure but rather an experience intertwined with memories of my childhood. I trace the trajectory of Gandhi's visualization in Amar Chitra Katha comic books of the 1980s to the visual representations in picture books written for children today. My recollection of Gandhi is based on the memory of Bapu during my childhood in the 1980s. I do not remember the exact year when I heard the story of 'Gandhi's talisman' from my parents; however, the same text, also known as 'Gandhiji Ka Jantar' in Hindi has continued to be reprinted in books and children's magazines such as the October 2015 issue of *Chakmak* published by Eklavya (2015, 6-8). This note is considered special because it was written in the last year before his assassination on January 30, 1948. In this note, Gandhi said:

> I will give you a talisman. Whenever you are in doubt, or when the self becomes too much with you, apply the following test. Recall the face of the poorest and the weakest man [woman] whom you may have seen, and ask yourself, if the step you contemplate is going to be of any use to him [her]. Will he [she] gain anything by it? Will it restore him [her] to a control over his [her] own life and destiny? In other words, will it lead to swaraj [freedom] for the hungry and spiritually starving millions? Then you will find your doubts and your self melt away (quoted in Nair 1958, 65).

The power of this note lies in the possibility of 'looking' at others as a means to find one's own position and relevance in the world around us. Most textbooks and magazines for children use this to begin a conversation on empathy and our position in relation to others. For me, this note marks a moment in memories of my childhood. Gandhi's talisman worked for me in times of anger and self-doubt throughout my school-going days. However this did not continue when I was a college student; Gandhi's relationship with Kasturba Gandhi and his sons, his debates with Dr. Bhimrao Ambedkar on separate electorates and his views on caste have made it increasingly difficult to agree with his views. Writing about Gandhi, Ashis Nandy famously says:

> I do not care who the real Gandhi was or is. Let academics debate that momentous issue. Contemporary politics is

> not about truths of history; it is about remembered pasts and problems of fashioning a future based on collective memories. For good or for worse, Gandhi seems to have entered that memory (2000, 41).

The key theme in this paper is built on Nandy's formulation that there is more than one Gandhi. I have chosen distinct narratives of Gandhi meant for child readers between five and ten years of age, the period when most read picture books. In each narrative, we come across different Gandhis. The Gandhi I choose to study is one who stands for questioning, empathy, curiousity and change. It is this Gandhi that picture books have begun to recreate or construct in contemporary times that is of significance. As an experience in children's picture books, Gandhi is woven through a complex use of him as an image and as an idea. It is this dual experience of a narrative and a visual presence that make up the Gandhi experience that is the focus of this paper. Beginning in Amar Chitra Katha comics in the late 1980s and then in children's picture books in recent times, I will argue that the transformation in visual aesthetics of Gandhi representations marks a shift from a realistic form to an icon in contemporary narratives. Now, the Mahatma has been replaced by Gandhi as an 'ordinary' man who changed the world.

More recently, Gandhi's grandson Arun Gandhi's recollection (2017) of his grandfather is built on his relationship with Gandhi or Bapuji as he addressed him. In one of his anecdotes he remembers the days spent with Gandhi at Sevagram in the summer of 1944. Arun and his six-year-old sister Ela had left their home in South Africa to spend time with their grandfather at Sevagram where Arun would stay for the coming few years. On their arrival, the children did not like the food they were served and Arun Gandhi recalls:

> (T)he food at Sevagram was (to put it plainly) terrible. Every day we got some version of boiled, unsalted pumpkin. Every meal was as boring and tasteless as the ones before. Ela and I complained to our parents, they hushed us, pointing out that we were guests and needed to follow Bapuji's plan (2017, 37).

Both the children were unhappy about the meals but Arun did not have the courage to say it. However, Ela walked up to her famous grandfather to say that he should change the name of his ashram to 'Kola (Pumpkin) Ashram' since everyone had to always eat pumpkins. Gandhi was surprised by Ela's reaction but he had a sense of humour and enquired about the situation. When he found that the manager was serving pumpkins because they had a big crop of pumpkins, he was quick to advise him to grow more variety on the farm (A. Gandhi 2017, 39-40). The courage with which Ela confronted their grandfather was a lesson to Arun that all should speak their minds, even if it meant questioning Gandhi, the Mahatma. It is in the same spirit that this paper is written. It is an interrogation of how children's picture books construct one type of Gandhi today which is distinct from the Gandhi children read about in the 1970s and 1980s.

Gandhi in Comic Books: The Saint and the Man

In the 1980s, when I was growing up, our first gateway to Indian history were the Amar Chitra Katha (henceforth ACK) comics. Nandini Chandra (2008,1) argues that ACK, these 'serious comics', charted the cultural history of India through a 'potent mix of innocence and naturalness', where the former 'is projected on to its child audience' and the latter is constructed for its adult audience. 'The series used "photographic realism" in its drawings' (Chandra 2008, 6) and their title on Mahatma Gandhi was published in two parts in July and August 1989 while the title on Jawaharlal Nehru was published in November 1991. In ACK, Gandhi was drawn realistically, keeping in mind details of his attire as a young lawyer in South Africa down to his later years when he had a frail physique, walking stick, glasses and an upright posture. His life-history was created using the typical ACK aesthetic which included 'seductively realistic...techniques of western illusionistic painting and mechanical reproduction such as oleography, photography and lithography' (Chandra 2008, 207). The realistic visual representation was accompanied by deft use of elements of hagiographic storytelling. Gandhi's life was traced from the 1820s in Porbandar where his grandfather Uttamchand served as Prime Minister under the Rana of Porbandar. After the Rana's death, Uttamchand goes to Junagadh because he was not given the 'respect due to him' by the Rana's successors. His refusal to serve the Nawab of Junagadh because he has already 'pledged his right hand' and his loyalty to Porbandar symbolizes the first trait that will mark Gandhi as a boy from an honourable family of truth-seekers.

The commentary builds on the 'truthfulness, sense of loyalty and courage' of Uttamchand, the grandfather of M.K. Gandhi and then leaps ahead to the 1870s, Rajkot. Uttamchand's son Karamchand was a minister to Thakore Bavairaj. The Thakore loved to drink wine but when he hears about the arrival of his minister, he quickly tries to hide the wine and opens the windows to make sure there is no smell of alcohol. Karamchand is not one to be fooled easily and chastises the Thakore, warning him against wasting his life. In a dramatic statement, the young readers are told, 'If the ruler could be in such awe of his minister, what kind of man was this minister? He was the father of Mohandas Karamchand' (1989, 3).

Gandhi's lineage is traced in two ways; one asserts his upper-caste origins as the child of a well-to-do family and the other locates him in a tradition of values of honesty, loyalty, courage and truth. These initial few pages of the comic book create a hagiographic narrative that prepares the reader for the coming of the saint or the Mahatma named Gandhi. In ACK, Chandra argues that 'texts on saints and religious leaders, all fall into the hagiographical mode' (2008, 18). Establishing him as a mythological hero in the tradition of earlier bhakti saints like Tukaram, ACK's narrative reaffirms his 'purity' of thought and action. Heidi Pauwels notes that in the process of narrating hagiographies, 'identities are forged, or reforged, announced, communities are created, or consolidated' (2010, 55). ACK begins the story of Gandhi as Mohandas Karamchand who goes on to become the Mahatma. Instead of a history, the comic book offers a hagiography with distinct visual semiotics similar to its earlier narratives on bhakti saints and mythological heroes. Specific events such as the widely known story of the young Gandhi and his brother stealing gold from their house and eating meat on the sly, become significant. These episodes slowly build towards the epiphany—the point of self-realization in Gandhi's life as narrated in his autobiography. Following Gandhi's own storytelling, ACK also focuses on those moments that Gandhi chose to recollect as moments of gross moral misconduct that left him guilt-ridden. These acts of stealing and lying were selected to assert the significance of the confession made in front of his father, leading to his pledge of honesty in the future.

The ACK team always took pride in its narrativization and its selection of material and its research to include lesser known 'secrets' or 'facts' that made their comics stand out. This use of micro-narratives, according to Chandra, was ACK's real secret, their attention to detail, and the deployment of a 'double structure' that moved 'between the macro and the micro, the sacral and the narrative, the icon and the index' (2008, 10).

In the last few panels after the scene of Gandhi's assassination, ACK depicted the loss felt by people through the emotions of a family (a father consoling his young daughter and a shocked saree-clad mother with knitting needles) listening to the radio announcement of Gandhi's death. The hagiographic narrative depicted how the nation imagined the saint and how families mourned their loss through a glimpse into their homes, the radios, and through Nehru's address to parliament on 2nd February 1948. In another panel, a whole mass of people are shown as they gathered to mourn Gandhi's death while moving across the map of India as the pyre burns. This panel then culminated in a sketch of Gandhi which is visually supplemented through the image of a lamp that spreads its light all over.

ACK thus transformed the biography of Gandhi into a hagiography of a saint through its choice of events, its language and its symbolic use of visual motifs. Though packaged as a part of the 'Makers of Modern India' series, ACK reproduced the life-narrative of Gandhi as a patron saint or Father of India. This superimposition of the text of saintliness on to the life-text of Gandhi transformed him into a Mahatma for children. Writing on Gandhi, the well-known historian Shahid Amin writes that, in the 1920s, 'what people thought of the Mahatma were projections of the existing patterns of popular beliefs about...[saints] in rural north India' (1984, 316). He posits that deification of saints is based on some factors which include emphasis on the 'purity' of their lives, and the power to perform miracles. Amin studies how newspapers like *Swadesh* added to the rumours of Gandhi's powers in the 1920s by printing these as news (1984, 335). ACK also borrowed from Hindu mythology and hagiography to create Gandhi as a Mahatma for children as readers. Chandra explains that although ACK was aimed at children, they did not want to 'protect children from depictions of violence or sexuality...for most part, ACKs do not include children in their narratives. Children, if at all presented, are adults read back into their formative years, their childhood inflected with signs of heroism and martyrdom' (2008,18).

But post-liberalization in India in the late 1990s, children's publishing saw a transformation in the kind of books that began to emerge. Foreign and international publishers like Penguin Books, Scholastic and Bloomsbury arrived in India, and this was accompanied by the emergence of independent, regional publishing houses. These publishers included Eklavya (established 1982), Katha Books (1988), Tulika Books (1996), Tara Books (1996), Karadi Tales (1996), Pratham (2004) and many more.

Most of these publishing houses such as Tara Books, Katha and Tulika were established by women publishers. These independent publishers played a key role in rethinking and redefining childhood in the late 20th century as they focused on narratives written and visualized from the perspective of children rather than adults. Women played a key role in rethinking children's literature and promoted children picture books, a genre that emerged only in recent times in India.[10]

Children's Picture Books: Gandhi the Ordinary Man and the Icon

A children's picture book uses both words and pictures to tell a story. It is not the same as an illustrated book where pictures supplement the written word. In praise of John Caldecott, one of the first picture book authors, Maurice Sendak wrote that 'he [Caldecott] devised an ingenious juxtaposition of picture and word, a counterpoint that never happened before. Words are left out—but the picture says it. Pictures are left out—but the words say it. In short, it is the invention of the picture book' (Popova 2012). *My Gandhi Story* (2014) was published by Tulika Books with the Warli painter Rajesh Chaitya Vangad, in collaboration with the academic, animation filmmaker and picture book writer Nina Sabnani and the Dastango performer Ankit Chadha. These three collaborators tell their Gandhi story through distinct perspectives. Using illustrations, Vangad depicts the inquisitive child who asks questions that are sometimes answered by Bapu using quotes from his autobiography or other adults. Vangad uses the Warli art form of the adivasi tribe which belongs to the North Konkan region of Maharashtra, where the pictorial form is drawn using white rice flour paste on red ochre mud walls in village homes.

He begins the narrative by sharing that he chose to draw

---

[10] This argument emerged as part of a research project funded by the Delhi University Innovations Grant (2015-16) on Children's Picture Books in India: Rethinking History, Storytelling and Pedagogy. For more see the blog https://childrenspicturebooksinindia.wordpress.com.

Bapu '[b]ecause he was like us! In our village, we all work very hard. Bapu, too worked hard all his life. He liked to do all his work himself' (Figure 1.1).

The Warli art form uses lines with triangles and dots for figures. Yashodhara Dalmia notes that though the pattern may appear repetitive, it represents a complex world view, where the 'juxtapositioning of squares, circles and triangles provides a perfectly balanced, grand unity of the whole'

(1984, 22). The illustrations of Gandhi are made using lines, squares and triangles with a dhoti, his walking stick and a clock. The symbolic use of triangles, circles and dots is both universal yet culturally specific (Figure 1.2).

The painful and life-changing moment in Gandhi's life when he was thrown out of a first-class train compartment in

South Africa is illustrated using complex and multi-directional scenes made of Warli symbols (Figure 1.3).

Through its use of Warli symbols in non-linear visual narratives which are interspersed with photographs of Gandhi and quotations from his autobiography, this picture book transforms Gandhi's life into a multimodal experience. The young Gandhi is portrayed as a shy boy, who is not lazy but still not the best in studies; for example, he finds multiplication difficult. The sea port of Porbandar is the backdrop where the young boy grows up; he is an ordinary child who is not perfect and is driven by curiousity.

The last dialogue between the curious child and the reader in this book is significant:

> How did one man make the British leave? Bapu *was not alone. He was a great leader and the whole country was behind him.* So the British had to leave and India became free on 15 August 1947 (2013, emphasis added).

Bapu's status is clearly affirmed as a leader, not a saint (Figure 1.4).

The collaborative exercise between storytellers creates a multi-layered narrative that uses creative possibilities of engaging with specific values among children and humanises Gandhi, making him appear as an ordinary child who went on to do great things.

Two more picture books continue this practice of collaborative authorship to tell the story of Gandhi. Their intention is not so much a biography but rather a narrative on what we can learn from Gandhi to handle anger and violence. *My Grandfather Gandhi* (2014) and *Be the Change* (2017) written by Arun Gandhi, Bapu's grandson in collaboration with Bethany Hegedus, an American writer, and the illustrator Evan Turk. The narratives in these two picture books include word and mixed-media illustrations using watercolours, paper collage, cotton fabric and embroidery threads. Both these books were published internationally by Simon & Schuster, which has had a presence in India since the late 1990s.

Perry Nodelman argues that picture books are a complex mode of storytelling where both words and pictures create 'meaningful aspects of visual imagery' to become a 'subtle and complex form of communication' (1989, 22). *My Grandfather Gandhi* (2014) focuses on the emotion of anger, that all of us and not just children struggle with. Arun recalls his struggle as a young Indian boy growing up in the racially divisive society of apartheid-ridden South Africa. He recounts that 'as an Indian child growing up in racially charged South Africa, I was attacked by white children for not being white enough and black children for not being black' (2014). Since he would often get into confrontations, he was sent to stay with his grandfather in Sevagram, where his parents hoped that he would be able to 'understand...inner fury and be better able to cope with it' (2014).

Even at Sevagram, Arun faced a similar situation. One day, while playing soccer, a boy shoved Arun and he fell down. In retaliation, Arun picked up a rock to hit the offender but finally decided to let go of the rock. This episode is shared in the picture book powerfully through the use of expressions like clenched teeth, fingers clawing a rock, entangled threads and tiny paper-cut figures for other boys in the team. When Arun went to meet Bapuji, he felt both the anger against the boy who pushed him as well as the burden of being a Gandhi. These crucial words reveal how Gandhi had become synonymous with non-violence and a calm temperament but it was also a legacy that could be oppressive for a young boy. This tension and stress of not being able to control one's emotions and the acknowledgement of anger as a universal emotion makes this narrative significant in contemporary times. Bapu helped Arun to channelize this anger by telling him that 'anger is like electricity'. It is like lightning that can split a tree into two, 'or it can be channelled, transformed. A switch can be flipped, and it can shed light like a lamp' (Gandhi and Hegedus 2014).

Turk powerfully evokes this through visual motifs of a big spinning wheel in the centre of a double-spread with threads and little human figures made of paper wearing white sarees and dhotis spinning their own wheels. It almost seems as if all people are connected through a complex circuit. Anger needs to be controlled and channelized like electricity, which also motivates us and child readers to think of ways to control our emotions through meditation or other constructive practices. In Arun's case, Bapu advises spinning cotton, another powerful symbol for the Swadeshi movement, but in the picture book it suggests a means to focus and calm oneself. While learning how to manage his anger, Arun recalled that one of the eleven vows of living in Sevagram, that he found hardest to follow, was not to waste.

Waste and Non-violence: Gandhi's Wisdom on Recycle, Reuse and Reduce

Once, while staying with Bapu at Pune, Arun threw a pencil away that he had not completely used. He was reminded by his grandfather to go back and search for it and reuse it. The incident reminds readers to think of each of their actions as connected to each other and with consequences for the people around and the environment. These early lessons in ecological consciousness and the interconnectedness of our lives with the natural world are depicted through an exercise that Arun is taught. He learns to keep notes of how his actions will affect Arun's tree, which he is supposed to draw and maintain. The picture book narrative cleverly makes Arun and the readers realize that each action by an individual has a ripple effect on others and the world around them. Our excess, our hoarding affects others. When we buy more than we need, we affect ourselves, create waste and inequality. This theme of excessive consumption and the need to renew and reuse is captured in the picture book by the illustrator Evan Turk through his deft use of scraps of paper, cloth, and embroidery threads to create multi-layered, mixed media collages.

Again, the picture book narrative successfully manages to weave Gandhian thought on minimizing excessive consumption towards simplicity through visual semiotics as well as the storyline. The need to reuse, recycle and reduce, the three Rs we have become so familiar with today becomes more comprehensible through the clever use of symbolism and art, which emphasizes the need to make connections between our actions, our need to consume more and the violence it wreaks on this planet in terms of the environment or social relationships. Gandhi's life thus becomes an ideal subject to introduce and discuss ecological issues with child readers while providing them a way to think of themselves as individuals and how their actions can have a wide impact to change this world. This rewriting of Gandhi's life through a visual imagery that links him to his child readers as a grandfather simultaneously transforms him into an icon.

In her analysis of the visual representations of Gandhi, Seema Bawa has recently argued that Gandhi is one of the few nationalist leaders who are iconic in the real sense—who can both be reduced to one or two attributes as well as expanded to include landscape and other background features or narratives. He can also be represented by permutations and combinations of symbols and motifs associated with him—a pair of wire-rimmed spectacles and a stick, large ears and a walking stick, or khadaon (wooden slippers) (2018, 54).

According to Bawa, Gandhi became an icon before his martyrdom partially because he was an 'arresting and appealing figure, whose appearance adds to his politics and engages with its philosophical and ideological underpinnings' (2018, 55). Her perceptive analysis explains the changes in representation of Gandhi that are also visible in contemporary children's picture books. For most children, their first interaction with Gandhi begins as an old man, Bapu, who is frail, wears a white dhoti, carries a walking stick, a watch and has a toothless grin. He is not the authoritarian father or grandfather figure for young readers; often he is shown sitting with a charkha spinning away like the monks or old wise men of folk tales.

We can see a clear example of how Gandhi's transformation into an icon has resulted in a form which most would call a cartoon in Brad Meltzer and Christopher Eliopoulos's *I am Gandhi* (2017). This book is part of a series called 'Ordinary People Change the World'. Here, Gandhi is a tiny character, sketched with clear lines into a cartoon. The child readers see themselves in the cartoon when they identify with Gandhi as a tiny man of the same size as children. The book retells the story of Gandhi's life and asserts the 'ordinariness' of his fears and 'gentle ways' which also make him take up bigger challenges. Throughout the narrative, Gandhi remains a tiny figure in a big world. He says, 'In my life, I was the Small one. The skinny one. The poor one. Even the shy one. But I was never the weak one' (2017).

The book belongs to a biography series which aims to inspire all children by saying that all of us can be heroes. In *Understanding Comics,* Scott McCloud perceptively remarks that, as children, 'we are fascinated by cartoons because of universal identification, simplicity and child-like features. The cartoon is a vacuum into which identity and awareness are pulled...We don't just observe a cartoon, we become it' (1997, 36). Gandhi's illustration as a cartoon has to be understood as the final stage of this transformation where the child reader is pulled into the narrative as a protagonist. As articulated by Vangad in his Warli illustrations of Gandhi, Bapu has become 'one of us' today, an experience and an icon which marks the history of the transformation of pictorial representations of Gandhi.

This paper approached Gandhi from a personalized narrative, beginning with my own recollection and my experience during my childhood which was coterminous with the popularity of Amar Chitra Katha comic books. We traced the visual and literary narratives that built his image as a Mahatma to the shift that takes place in contemporary children's picture books where he is more an icon than a historical figure. Debates among Gandhian scholars, Ambedkarite scholars, and others clearly see Gandhi as a contested subject. The recent controversy over Arundhati Roy's introduction to Navayana's edition of Dr. B.R. Ambedkar's *Annihilation of Caste* and Ambedkar Age Collective's criticism of appropriation of Ambedkar's writings reveals the fault lines to be loud and clear (2015). In April 2019, Penguin Books reprinted the controversial introduction, *The Doctor and the Saint*, as a stand-alone text. Roy's text is significant because it addresses the neglect towards Ambedkar's contribution to political thought and a stringent critique of eulogizing Gandhi as a Mahatma. Children's picture book publishers such as Tulika include Ambedkar through stories such as the *Boy Who asked Why?* (2013) compared to ACK which produced hagiographic accounts of the Mahatma. In a witty yet rigourous essay, 'The Gandhi Everyone Loves to Hate', Vinay Lal argues that 'no more profound gift did Gandhi bestow than the gift of being able to live with ambiguity... To enter into Gandhi's world is to come to the awareness that paradoxes leap from every page of his life' (2008, 56). Gandhi was a man who adapted and changed with the times. He appears inconsistent to some while to others, he was a master strategist. In the words of Shashi Tharoor, 'We were not led by a saint with his head in the clouds, but by a master tactician with his feet on the ground' (2013). The Gandhi we come across in children's picture books today is one Gandhi among the many that exist, a subject to be debated, critiqued and studied.

References

Dutt, Gayatri Madan and Souren Ray. 1989. *Mahatma Gandhi: The Early Days.* Mumbai: Amar Chitra Katha Pvt. Ltd.

Amin, Shahid. 1984. Gandhi as Mahatma: Gorakhpur District, Eastern UP, 1921-22. In *Subaltern Studies III: Writings on South Asian History and Society* edited by Ranajit Guha. Delhi: Oxford University Press.

Ambedkar Age Collective. 2015. *Hatred in the Belly: Politics Behind the Appropriation of Dr. Ambedkar's Writings*. Shared Mirror Publishing House.

Bawa, Seema. 2018. Power and Politics of Portraits, Icons and Hagiographic Images of Gandhi. *Economic and Political Weekly*, vol. LIII (5), February 3.

Chadha, Ankit and Nina Sabnani. 2014. *My Gandhi Story*. Chennai: Tulika Publishers.

Chandra, Nandini. 2008. *The Classic Popular: Amar Chitra Katha 1967-2007*. Delhi: Yoda Press.

Charmaz, Kathy. 2006. *Constructing Grounded Theory: A Practical Guide Through Qualitative Analysis*. London: Thousand Oaks, New Delhi: Sage Publications.

Dalmia, Yashodhara. 1984. The Warli Chawk: A World-View. *India International Centre Quarterly* vol. 11 (40) 79-80. http://www.jstor.org/stable/23001706.

Gandhi, Arun. 2017. *The Gift: Ten Spiritual Lessons for the Modern World from My Grandfather, Mahatma Gandhi*. New Delhi: Penguin Books.

Gandhi, Arun and Bethany Hegedus. 2014. *Grandfather Gandhi*. New York: Atheneum Books.

Gandhi, Arun and Bethany Hegedus. 2016. *Be the Change: A Grandfather Gandhi Story*. New York: Atheneum Books.

Gandhi, M. 'Gandhiji Ka Jantar' or 'Gandhi's Talisman'. 2015.

Chakmak, October, 6-8. https://www.eklavya.in/chakmak/magazine/2015/October/files/mobile/index.html#9

Lal, Vinay. 2008. The Gandhi Everyone Loves to Hate. *Economic and Political Weekly* vol. 43 (40) 55–64.

McCloud, Scott. 1997. *Understanding Comics: The Invisible Art*. New York: William Morrow.

Meltzer, Brad and Christopher Eliopoulos. 2017. *I am Gandhi*. New York: Penguin Random House.

Nair, Pyarelal. 1958. *Mahatma Gandhi: The Last Phase*. India: Navajivan Publishing House. https://www.mkgandhi.org/gquots1.htm

Nandy, Ashis. 2000. Gandhi after Gandhi. *The Little Magazine* vol. 1 (1) 38–41. http://vlal.bol.ucla.edu/multiversity/Nandy/Nandy_gandhi.htm Accessed 02 December 2020.

Nodelman, Perry. 1989. *Words about Pictures: The Narrative Art of Children's Picture Books*. Athens, University of Georgia Press.

Pauwels, Heidi. 2010. Hagiography and Community Formation: The Case of a Lost Community of Sixteenth-century Vrindavan. *The Journal of Hindu Studies*, 3 (1) 53–90. https://doi.org/10.1093/jhs/hiq007

Popova, Maria. 2012. A Brief History of Children's Picture Books and the Art of Visual Storytelling. https://www.brainpickings.org/2012/02/24/childrens-picturebooks/

Roy, Arundhati. 2019. *The Doctor and the Saint: The Ambedkar–Gandhi Debate: Caste, Race and Annihilation of Caste*. New Delhi: Penguin Books.

SPEECHLESS POLITICS

Faisal Devji

Democracy is very often linked with voice, speech and communication, just as tyranny is defined by silence and obedience. Yet, silence also lies at the heart of freedom, represented in democratic practice by the secret ballot. As an institutional form the secret ballot is meant to guarantee the voter's anonymity as well as liberty from the undue influence of external forces. But it possesses another dimension as well, one which has to do with the coincidental character of the democratic majority. If such majorities are to reflect anything more than the identity, organization and prejudice of the largest or most powerful social groups, they must be composed of voters who have arrived at their decisions independently and so in silence.

Democratic majorities are constituted by a logic of coincidence, with the general will understood as a statistical average rather than a social identity. Its legitimacy depends upon this will representing the decisions of a range of social identities brought together for a number of sometimes incommensurable reasons. However far the working of elections falls from this logic, it remains the only justification for democracy as a political form. But this means the voice, speech and communication that make democracy possible can also endanger it by unduly influencing voters. Their decisions are then deprived of autonomy and integrity far more insidiously than through bribery or threats, with the elimination or ritualization of silence destroying the individual's very capacity for freedom.

At issue is the character of political debate as a kind of rehearsed conversation, one in which social identities and passions are mobilized to prevent the formation of a statistical average by way of silent, solitary and even ignorant decisions. While under ideal conditions interests are meant to cancel each other out precisely in order to produce such an average, their institutionalization in political parties accomplishes the opposite. It is not social identities that are themselves problematic, but rather the party structure that appropriates them to create collective passions. For the political party produces pre-digested arguments and talking points in which individual reasoning is not only set aside for its voters, but actively forbidden among their representatives as well (Weil 2013).

In his manifesto of 1909 entitled *Hind Swaraj Or Indian Home Rule*, Gandhi inveighed against parliamentary democracy as a system whose cacophony actively subverted the kind of liberty that was premised on the freedom and integrity of voice, speech and deliberation. He sought to describe the way in which parliament operated only with the spur of outside pressure, indifferent as to whether this took the form of popular demands or the blandishments of a wealthy few. At the same time, it was placed under the control of changing masters, in the shape of the prime minister and his cabinet, who bought loyalty by the inducements of wealth, honours and influence. Forced to abide by party discipline, its members were in thrall to these changing leaders, who were themselves concerned solely with the expansion of their power. In such a system, whose stability relied upon the ritualization of conflict along party lines, neither truth, justice, goodness nor indeed the public interest were served except by accident.

As for the voter's freedom of conscience and judgment, whose deliberations were necessarily silent, it was drowned out by a purely partisan political debate in parliament and the press. 'To the English voters their newspaper is their Bible. They take their cue from their newspapers which are often dishonest. The same fact is differently interpreted by different newspapers, according to the party in whose interests they are edited. One newspaper would consider a great Englishman to be a paragon of honesty, another would consider him dishonest. What must be the condition of the people whose newspapers are of this type?' (Gandhi 1921a, 19). The competition set up by parliamentary democracy produced stability at the expense of truth and so freedom, which could only lose meaning without the former.

Instead of seeing the alternation of governments in a democracy as demonstrating the political freedom it promised, Gandhi understood it as an example of inconstancy that was itself mechanical. 'These people change their views frequently. It is said that they change them every seven years. These views swing like the pendulum of a clock and are never steadfast. The people would follow a powerful orator or a man who gives them parties, receptions, etc. As are the people, so is their Parliament.' (Gandhi 1921a, 19-20). Rather than blaming the English for this state of affairs, Gandhi attributed it to the link between parliamentary democracy and industrial capitalism, or what he called modern civilization, whose 'true test lies in the fact that people living in it make bodily welfare the object of life.' (Gandhi 1921a, 21).

But modern civilization failed to satisfy bodily wants, and not only because it was made possible for a few at the expense of the many. Also important was the fact that its desire was insatiable and led to a limitless expansion no different from that which marked the thirst for power in party politics. Indeed, the two were linked in the growth of capital, industry and empire. Gandhi described this desire in the language of addiction, and saw it resulting in the destruction of the subject whose freedom democracy was meant to seek. 'It is eating into the vitals of the English nation. It must be shunned. Parliaments are really emblems of slavery. If you will sufficiently think over this, you will entertain the same opinion and cease to blame the English. They rather deserve our sympathy' (Gandhi 1921a, 25).

In order to protect political voice, speech and deliberation from being drowned out by the noise of parliamentary democracy, Gandhi had recourse to the power of silence instead. Gandhi's withholding of speech in practices like his weekly days of silence have been interpreted in purely religious and nativist terms. But I want to look at his many pronouncements on silence as political statements that had contemporary debates on representation as their context. During the 19th century, for example, the real and potential expansion of the franchise in England gave rise to new anxieties about the independence of voice in political life. It was ostensibly to protect the liberty of this voice that voting rights were restricted to adult males, property owners and the educated. These qualifications made for overlapping but not identical groups, whose eligibility to vote was determined by the gravity of their voices. For it was thought that only such men possessed the requisite investment in, responsibility for and knowledge about their society to be entrusted with its governance.

The reasoning behind such exclusions, in the name of guaranteeing both the freedom and therefore meaningfulness of an individual's political voice, remained the same even when some alteration to these qualifications was made. Thus, men of little or no property and education, or women of greater age would be included in the electoral rolls once they were deemed to have assumed control over their own voices. Like slaves in ancient times, however, and prisoners in some countries even today, those defined as children still cannot have a say in the laws that govern them, and for the same reasons that had once been used to exclude women or the poor, to say nothing of non-white or colonized populations.

But the inclusion of new categories of people into the practices of political representation led to another 19th-century anxiety, which had to do with the possibility of a majority drowning out the dissenting voices and interests of minorities, whether defined by birth, wealth, religion or political views. The prospect of such a tyranny of the majority produced many ideas to have the minority heard, of which John Stuart Mill's proposal in his *Considerations on Representative Government* is one of the most famous (Mill 1861). Mill suggested adding together the votes of constituencies defined not merely by territory but issues, which would allow minorities the chance to represent themselves by their total number.

Both these liberal anxieties, to ensure the independence and meaningfulness of political voice by a process of exclusion, and to allow for the representation of minorities amidst the uncertain passions of a more undifferentiated electorate, achieved perhaps their starkest manifestation in British India. Voting there was severely restricted by all the qualifications described above from the time it became available to Indians early in the 20th century. And while Mill's efforts to represent minorities made little headway in England, the most thorough project ever to do so was launched in India. This was a system of joint and separate electorates that guaranteed the election of Hindu and Muslim legislators in areas where each community comprised a minority.

The debate over political voice in India was defined not so much by the desire to gain or recover as to endow it with meaning. For it was typical of British administrators to dismiss Indian demands for a say in their government as being the unrepresentative claims of self-interested elites, the coerced and irresponsible voices of their ignorant followers or the oppressive desires of a caste or religious majority. Voice in this situation was a mark not of freedom but slavery and the childish immaturity of those not yet ready to govern themselves. In a reversal of conventional thinking, it was often silence that became the sign of political maturity and power in the empire, with voice understood as the womanly expression of powerlessness.

Gandhi's views about voice and silence must be understood in the context of these 19th-century debates, whose terms I want to argue he went on to radicalize rather than reject altogether. The Mahatma's advocacy of silence, in other words, has everything to do with the twin anxieties of voice in the liberal imagination of empire: it had to be meaningful and to stand against the tyranny of the majority. These virtues were nowhere better revealed than in the character of the Englishman as empire-builder. In his essay, *The Intimate Enemy: Loss and Recovery of Self Under Colonialism*, Ashis Nandy describes how British ideas of masculinity were formed in imperialism, and I want to dwell upon some of them here. (Nandy 1988).

The image of a strong and silent hero labouring to do

his duty by those in his care has become a stereotype, one whose imperial context is made clear in locutions like Rudyard Kipling's 'white man's burden'. Important about this figure is the fact that his actions are defined by their silence, not least because they represent a duty that is necessarily unilateral, in that he can have no conversation with those among its objects who are not his equals. The relationship of ruler and ruled in imperialism is silent because it is conceived of as a moral and not a political one, with the former's duty requiring the latter's education but not representation. This is how silence comes to constitute freedom.

A good example of such a character is to be found in Thomas Carlyle's *Past and Present,* itself a forerunner of Gandhi's criticisms of industrial capitalism with its cult of Mammon and utility without moral ideals. In his chapter on 'The English', Carlyle defines his countrymen's national character by their silence: 'Of all the nations in the world at present, we English are the stupidest in speech, the wisest in action' (Carlyle 1843, 215). Comparing the English to the Romans in their love of silence, matched as he thought it was by their building of empires, Carlyle pours scorn on facility of speech as being a sign of powerlessness among the Greeks in ancient times as the French in his own.

It comes as no surprise that a colonized population like Indians serve as the exemplars of voluble impotence: 'Nay, of all animals, the freest of utterance, I should judge, is the genus *Simia*: go into the Indian woods, say all Travelers, and look what a brisk, adroit, unresting Ape-population it is!' (Carlyle 1843, 213). The awkward silence and even stupidity of the stereotyped Englishman, John Bull, is what Carlyle treasures: 'Nature alone knows thee, acknowledges the bulk and strength of thee: thy Epic, unsung in words, is written in huge characters on the face of the Planet—sea moles, cotton-trades, railways, fleets and cities, Indian Empires, Americas, New-Hollands; legible throughout the Solar System!' (Carlyle 1843, 216).

In a chapter titled 'Democracy', Carlyle goes on to argue that only when the heroic duty of deeds done in silence falters, does the politics of institutions take over: 'Hence French Revolutions, Five-Point Charters, Democracies, and a mournful list of *Etceteras*, in these our afflicted times.' (Carlyle 1843, 288). Here, then, is another criticism of parliamentary democracy for which silence is crucial. While Gandhi was partial to Ruskin's and Tolstoy's style of anti-modern radicalism more than to Carlyle's, we shall see how he transformed imperial ideas of silence and freedom, speech and deeds, majority and minority into a quite novel vision of democracy in which the politics of mastery is replaced by the power of renunciation.

Like Carlyle, Gandhi wanted to recover the subject's freedom in non-institutional ways, precisely by foregrounding silence in the making of a moral subject. He placed silence alongside fasting, celibacy and other practices which sought to limit the multiplication of insatiable desires and the ever-growing forms of consumption they promoted. Yet, silence had its own role to play in this menu of renunciations, because it addressed not only the body's integrity and moral agency, but specifically that of the mind or rather its thought and judgement. For Gandhi saw that political speech as it was defined by liberalism only became possible through the mediation of the state and in the shape of an interest.

In *Hind Swaraj*, for example, Gandhi inveighed against doctors and lawyers as, in effect, agents of the colonial State, itself representing the ultimate form of mediation as a neutral third party there to arbitrate between Indians rendered into partisan interests. He described doctors as purveyors of commodities from the pharmaceuticals industry meant to alienate patients from their own bodies in another instance of addiction. Lawyers, for their part, existed not to resolve conflicts but increase the State's power by imposing a peace that needed constant enforcement between the rival interests it relied upon and therefore had to maintain.

Such forms of mediation, of course, represented both the manner in which the colonial State operated as well as its justification, with Gandhi advocating their circumvention in unmediated relations between Indians who should no longer be defined as antagonistic interests to be brought together only by the mediation of the state. The unmediated relations Gandhi sought, however, were not conceived as being either more transparent or authentic, to say nothing of easy and direct. Instead, by removing the medium as a third party, which is the way in which the colonial as also the liberal State worked, he wanted to pause communication and force people to think more seriously about its implications.

Unmediated relations, in other words, meant juxtaposing persons, parties and arguments in such a way as to make them conscious of the violence entailed in voice, speech and language. This is why language played a role in all the instances of mediation I have described, especially the highly technical kind used for legal and medical communication that Gandhi had criticized doctors and lawyers for. But it had also become crucial in certain types of conflict, of which the mounting controversies over proselytizing in the 1920s took pride of place, especially among Hindus and Muslims in North India but also including Christian missionary activity directed against both groups throughout the country.

Rather than seeing these disputes as the problematic inheritance of pre-modern identities, we should understand them as the utterly modern products of liberal politics, which had turned religious communities into interests and therefore constituencies. Proselytizing, in other words, became controversial for the first time in this manner because it was thought to be an attempt at augmenting the electoral or political power of one group over another, in much the same way as parties operated to diminish the real or potential majority of their rivals. Addressing the violence that accompanied accusations from Hindus, Muslims and Christians of predatory missionizing by their religious rivals, Gandhi suggested stopping not conversion itself but its mediation in language.

To be true to the ideals of their own faiths, he argued, missionaries should serve as their best representatives in refusing to lie about, unfairly criticize or run down the religions of others. In doing so, they would also serve humanity by conducting their charitable works in silence and thus drawing converts by the sheer force of their example rather than through unseemly and invariably untruthful polemics. In a 1931 speech to Christian missionaries in London, for example, he said, 'The idea of converting people to one's faith by speech and writings, by appeal to reason and emotion and by suggesting that the faith of his forefathers is a bad faith, in my opinion, limits the possibilities of serving humanity... Religion is like a rose. It throws out the scent which attracts like a magnet and we are drawn to it involuntarily.' (Gandhi 1984, 122).

Speech and indeed language itself, in other words, betrayed religious, like all other truth, by mediating it in argument and collective passion. And while Gandhi was concerned here with missionaries in particular, his criticism held true of persuasion as an important part of political practice more generally. As a fundamental liberal virtue, this kind of argumentation had already come under attack from both the left and the right as a disingenuous form of bourgeois discussion, one incapable of advancing any real change. These ideologues sought to cut liberal debate short by creating facts on the ground either in acts of empire-building, as with Carlyle, or of revolutionary violence as with Lenin. Gandhi, however, reimagined persuasion in sacrificial terms, by offering up the sight and sometimes even spectacle of speechless acts as the most effective demonstration of their truth.

In order to manifest itself, therefore, political as much as moral or religious truth had to disavow voice for action and sound for sight, in a way that was both linked to and yet quite different from a political thinker like Lenin's theorization of revolutionary action as a force for change. While privileging the visible over the audible as a modality for truth, Gandhi also lent it olfactory form, as a fragrance which drew the potential convert to itself involuntarily. In other words, he conceived of neither the visible nor the audible as pure forms, since one could include the sense of smell and another the written word as an amalgam of sight and sound. It was the interpretive and so mediating function of language itself that he distrusted, one for which silence served as an antonym.

The unmediated visibility that Gandhi prized as a modality of truth was nothing more than a making visible of silence in persuasion. A metamorphosis or conversion, to use religious terms, in which silence lost its autonomy and was mediated by sight as a negative form. And while this logic seems to countermand Gandhi's emphasis on unmediated relations, it does conform to his propensity for negative forms more generally, of which non-violence, non-possession and non-cooperation are the most famous. Unlike the kind of mediation that characterized the colonial State, which produced rival interests as positive forms requiring arbitration, silence mediated by sight renounced all positivity and could only be known by its absence as something that was both inaudible and invisible.

Silence allowed for unmediated relations because of its doubly negated form. Unlike the ability to speak or reason, which constituted one of the classical definitions of the human species, silence did not depend on the logic either of shared capacities or the biological similarities that in Gandhi's view served only to fragment humanity into various kinds of hierarchies. Indeed, the imperative to unify the human race through language and reason not only ended by dehumanizing those among its members who were seen as being unreasonable and beyond persuasion, it also drew an absolute separation between one species and another. It was silence or the inability to communicate through language, then, which made moral relations between humans and animals possible.

The context for Gandhi's reflections on inter-species relations was provided in his time by the violent controversies between Hindus and Muslims over cow-slaughter. Grappling with these conflicts, Gandhi sought to expand and reinterpret the Hindu injunction to protect cattle not only to human but all animal life. He saw in cow-protection humanity's effort to go beyond itself, and in a 1921 article in his journal, *Young India*, emphasized the unilateral and voiceless character of this demand: 'The appeal of the lower order of creation is all the more forcible because it is speechless.' (Gandhi 1921b, 6). Without either identifying animal with human life, or requiring the kind of contractual reciprocity in their relations that was strangely expected among human beings, Gandhi based them on the very absence of similarity and similitude.

As with his views on conversion, which we have seen turn out to be about the problem of liberal persuasion more generally, Gandhi's understanding of cow-protection was also about the liberal values of reciprocity and contract. In his view, of course, such values were made possible by the colonial State as a neutral third party, there to mediate between its subjects construed as political interests. But as we have seen, Gandhi thought these relations to be unworkable and deeply violent in the hierarchies they set up. He was fascinated by what moral and so political relations might look like if they were not founded in what he thought was the transient and unequal agreement of a contract. The controversies over cow-slaughter allowed Gandhi to imagine relationships unmediated by language in another way.

In a 1924 article in *Young India,* he came close to attributing language to the cow: 'The cow is the purest type of sub-human life. She pleads before us on behalf of the whole of the sub-human species for justice to it at the hands of man, the first among all that lives. She seems to speak to us through her eyes: "you are not appointed over us to kill us and eat our flesh or otherwise ill-treat us, but to be our friend and guardian."' (Gandhi 1924, 6). Yet, crucial here is the fact that this appeal is not only voiceless, but unknowable and thus calls for the unilateral interpretation and moral judgment of human beings. Inevitable in the relations between species, Gandhi thought that relations among human beings, too, should be marked by an acknowledgment of their fundamental incommunicability and therefore silence. The similarity and difference of this position with Carlyle's should be evident.

What does all of this have to do with the link between

silence and freedom with which I began this essay? Let us recall that its 19th-century critics had linked the ruination of parliamentary democracy to its abandonment of ideals like truth, justice and goodness. It was the externality of such ideals to the rehearsed speech of party politics that was crucial in limiting the latter's reach. The individual's freedom, in other words, was premised upon these ideals, which alone made political judgement in the public interest possible. They could be instrumentally deployed by parties backed by ascribed social identities, of course, but nevertheless represented ends in their own right rather than power as a means turned into an end in the form of limitless desire.

Gandhi also sought to reinforce the individual's moral agency in the face of this ruination. And he did so through the prescription of silence over speech. But rather than protecting the subject from outside influence and so reifying the individual as a purely autonomous being, silence here worked as a form of internal discipline that protected the outside world as well. It was meant, additionally, to open the individual up to the externality of truth, which in Gandhi's view was another name for God. And this implied that human beings were not brought together by any shared quality like speech and reason, nor a biological one like race or reproduction, but only in their openness to quite alien and metaphysical figures such as truth, justice and goodness.

To be workable, therefore, democracy required the existence of a subject outside or beyond its own loquacious logic. What became of words and voice in this vision? They were reduced to pure artifice and deprived of any authenticity in the revelation of a subject's inner truth. This did not stop communication, just as Gandhi did not cease to read and write during his days of silence, but it did displace and discipline speech as the privileged revelation of inner life. Words and language served as external constraints to test, limit and shore up this subject, whose truth Gandhi described in his autobiography as being founded on a presupposition: 'I have not seen Him, neither have I known Him. I have made the world's faith in God my own, and as my faith is ineffaceable, I regard that faith as amounting to experience. However, as it may be said that to describe faith as experience is to tamper with truth, it may perhaps be more correct to say that I have no word for characterizing my belief in God.' (Gandhi 2018, 441).

It is not that the knowledge or experience of God is so ineffable as to be beyond words, but that it functions wordlessly by virtue of its absence or negative form as a presupposition. God here represents nothing but the silence that for Gandhi destroys the self while opening it up to the externality of its own truth, and on this basis its relations with others as well. A revelation of emptiness rather than any concealment of being, silence made freedom possible in the very stop it put to the false and often violent mediations of speech, showing that social and even inter-species relations rested on a quite different foundation. And while his ideas might seem arcane, they are no more so than those of Rousseau's on the making of the general will as a statistical average. We have seen, indeed, that Gandhi applied them to the most concrete and quotidian problems, from conversion to cow-slaughter.

References

Carlyle, Thomas. 1843. *Past and Present*. London: Chapman and Hall.

Gandhi, M.K. 1921a. *Hind Swaraj or Indian Home Rule*. Madras: G.A. Natesan and Co.

Gandhi, M.K. 1921b. Hinduism. *Young India*. 6 October 1921.

Gandhi, M.K. 1924. Notes. *Young India*. 26 June 1924.

Gandhi, M.K. (1931) 1984. Conference at the Missionary Society in London, 8 October 1931. In *The Collected Works of Mahatma Gandhi* volume 48. New Delhi: Publications Division, Ministry of Information and Broadcasting.

Gandhi, M.K. 2018. *An Autobiography or the Story of My Experiments with Truth*. Translated by Mahadev Desai, introduced with notes by Tridip Suhrud. New Delhi: Penguin.

Mill, John Stuart. 1861. *Considerations on Representative Government*. London: Parker, Son, and Bourn.

Nandy, Ashis. 1988. *The Intimate Enemy: Loss and Recovery of Self Under Colonialism*. New Delhi: Oxford University Press.

Weil, Simone. 2013. *On the Abolition of All Political Parties*. Translated by Simon Leys. New York: New York Review of Books.

Part Two

CONVERSATIONS WITH CONTEMPORARIES

SELF AND ITS RELATION TO OTHERS

Gandhian Thinking in the 21st Century

Prem Anand Mishra

Living in the globalized and multicultural world of the 21st century is both an opportunity and a challenge. It is an opportunity as it gives us the exposure to know and understand different shades of people, culture, or community through direct and indirect means of contact; at the same time, it is a challenge as we have to confront individuals, groups, or communities at different levels because we think that they are not like us. Knowingly or unknowingly, a social phenomenon is in practice that creates social disharmony at different levels by making a binary opposition of us/them in the society in terms of race, ethnicity, faith and religion. This social phenomenon is occurring through a process which is called 'Othering' in contemporary social science literature. The process of otherness has created conflicts and violence at many levels—from local to global—and there are many sites of it ranging from personal to public life. Thus, there exists a problem of relation between the self and the other.

The problem of 'relation between the self and the other' has been addressed in many ways by the thinkers/philosophers of both Indian and Western traditions. Gandhi also faced this question of 'self' (from the individual self to the national self) and its relation to the 'other' (from other individuals to British civilization). He addressed this question both in theory and practice. This paper is focused on the theory part of his views on the relationship between self and others.

I

At the very outset, it might be asked: how does Gandhi view the relationship between the self and others? To explore the basis of the relation between self and other in Gandhi's worldview, first of all, we may recall Gandhi's concept of moksha. Gandhi argued that the main aim of the individual is to attain moksha (Gandhi 2015, xii). His notion of moksha is both philosophical and pragmatic in nature. Being a man of action, he had a more profound and practical understanding of moksha, thus, he defined his concept of moksha in very active and practical terms. He argues that one can attain moksha only through engaging with 'others'. For him, if attaining moksha is the chief aim of life, then, considering 'others' is part and parcel of achieving moksha. Thus, one cannot ignore 'others' as moksha is not something outside the realm of others. This might also be seen as Gandhi's contribution to the Hindu conception of moksha. As Bhikhu Parekh observes:

> Since self and Other were interdependent polarities, each creating and being in turn created by the other, moksha involved the complementary processes of dissolving the 'Other' by attaining total identification with all creation. Hindu religious tradition had stressed the former and Gandhi did not add much to it. The way he defined the latter and related the two contained novel insights and represented his great contribution (1989, 95).

Second, the basis of the relation between self and others in Gandhi's paradigm can also be explored in his analysis of human nature and the individual's place and his/her role in this universe. For him, the human being is a trinity of animality, humanity, and divinity. He argues that human behaviour is regulated by many factors such as moral standards, the sense of shame, conscience, and duty. For him, the basic manifestations of the ethical life are the sense of social and personal responsibility and the awareness that he/she is part of the whole and linked with others. The basis of this idea is 'unity of existence' and an 'underlying moral harmony' in the universe. Gandhi's insistence on 'the unity of existence' is derived from the metaphysical presuppositions of Satya in the Advaita school of Hindu philosophy. Further, his belief in Satya leads to the belief in an underlying moral harmony. Thus, the moral bond connecting all life implies an inescapable moral obligation to all our fellow human beings.

As Gandhi believed in the 'essential unity of God and man and for that matter of all lives' (CWMG 25, 389), it was natural for him to take the next step and claim a universal responsibility that binds us all through our common transcendence. He insisted, 'if one gains, all gain, if one falls, all fall; we can't stand by and watch' the suffering of our fellow humans as we are all involved in realizing our oneness through mutual service and uplift (CWMG 63, 240). Thus, humanity's moral solidarity and its corresponding responsibility is an ever-present fact for Gandhi.

Third, the basis of the relation between self and others in Gandhi's worldview can also be explored in his view on purushartha. He does not accept the view that an individual is essentially helpless in the face of the forces that influence him/her from within and outside. Invoking purushartha, he argues that the responsibility one feels is not merely an illusion. It is real and the choice one determines through consciousness is substantial and profound. We may argue now that the idea of purushartha, which Gandhi evokes, implies that the human being owes a responsibility which is not only moral but also a psychological and socio-political one.

Yet, it might be asked: what is the defining feature of responsibility in Gandhi's worldview? He seems to argue that responsibility is a state of conscious feeling of duty towards oneself and other/society. Further, for him, responsibility is not only a theoretical construct for philosophizing the role of the individual in this living world, but it also calls for an active awareness of the purpose of the actions performed and their corresponding consequences. Moreover, Gandhi's notion of responsibility deconstructs the binary of responsibility to oneself and responsibility to others. The reason: the individual is not separate from others. He is the same as the others. In his worldview, there are no others, there is only the self, or versions thereof. In fact, Gandhi's belief in our 'oneness with other', was fundamentally based on his perception of the divinity of humanity, as he claimed that individual is 'part and parcel of the whole' and 'cannot find [God] apart from the rest of humanity' (CWMG 63, 240). This intersubjective definition of the grounds of being is the foundation of Gandhi's notion of responsibility.

But what is the meaning of being responsible, in a practical sense, in Gandhi's worldview? In his worldview, to say that a person is responsible means that he/she is capable of correctly understanding the question of what is true/right in the political and social field. This correct understanding of true/right and acting accordingly forms the relative truth of Gandhi. In his worldview, it must be pointed out that only knowing one's responsibility is not enough, one must also act accordingly. Further, any responsibility, in his framework, is based on 'knowledge' and 'will to act' which are to be in the direction of absolute truth.

Gandhi's writings clearly point out that every human being has his responsibility to both himself and others or society. He argued that even a person who has left this society for his spiritual attainments like a mendicant or an anchorite or a monk or a sanyasi cannot escape from his social and moral responsibility. The reason is that such persons also owe a debt to their heritage and society and they must repay the debt. For him, this can be done only through discharging their social responsibility. In fact, for him, the spiritual aspirants have more and greater responsibility towards the society than the others as they have overcome the ego and self-interest, and fear. Thus, they can, and should, set an example in society. Once addressing Buddhist monks in Burma, he said:

> I do not for one moment grant that a *sanyasi* needs to be a recluse caring not for the world. A *sanyasi* is one who cares not for himself but cares all the time for others. He has renounced all selfishness. But he is full of selfless activity... Swaraj (self-rule) does not merely stand for National independence, but for the self-rule of the individual. A *sanyasi*, having attained Swaraj in his own person, is the fittest to show us the way (Varma 2001, 46).

Thus, in Gandhi's worldview self and other are related to each other with the notion of responsibility. In other words, Gandhi's notion of responsibility towards others emerges out of his views on the relationship between self and other. Now, let us discuss the nature of responsibility in Gandhi's worldview and the question as to how to act responsibly in the world.

II

To grasp the nature of responsibility in Gandhi's worldview, let us examine the grounds on which Gandhi fixes the responsibility of self towards others. Although we do not find any systematic writings by him on this subject, we may trace some philosophical concepts in his writings that provide us sufficient clues to reconstruct the basis of responsibility of self to others in his worldview.

In this context, one may refer to the notion of 'mutual love' in his writings by which he seems to argue that every human being is responsible to others. He argues that not only our own social life but even nature cannot survive without mutual love. He accepts that there exists a force of repulsion in nature as well as in our own social life, but finally it is the force of love that prevails. This is the reason humanity is progressing, otherwise it would have collapsed long ago. In this sense, mutual love or force of attraction is a fact of life and nature whether human beings consciously know it or not. Gandhi's writings also suggest that one must consciously understand the dynamics of mutual love and feel the responsibility to others to avoid his own destruction as well as the progression of humanity. He argues that we have to extend the field of mutual love from our own family to the nation which is the 'larger family'. To quote him,

> Though there is repulsion enough in Nature, she lives by attraction. Mutual love enables Nature to persist. Man does not live by destruction. Self-love compels regard for others. Nations cohere because there is mutual regard among individuals composing them. Someday we must extend the national law to the universe, even as we have extended the family law to form nations—a larger family (Gandhi 1969, 118).

Similarly, in Gandhi's writings, one may note his repeated notion that humanity is an 'undividable whole'. This undividable humanity is the philosophical basis on which Gandhi fixes individual responsibility. To unpack Gandhi's notion of 'undividable whole', we may take the help of a metaphor that Gandhi has used to describe the paradigm of undividable whole. The metaphor is about the relation between a drop of water and the ocean. He wrote, 'The ocean is composed of drops of water; each drop is an entity and yet it is a part of the whole; the one and the many. In this ocean of life, we are little drops. My doctrine means that I must identify myself with life... that I must share the majesty of life in the presence of God' (Roy 1985, 103). He further noted, 'Individuality is and is not even as each drop in the ocean is an individual and is not. It is not because apart from the ocean it has no existence. It is because the ocean has no existence if the drop has not, i.e., has no individuality. They are beautifully interdependent. And if this is true of the physical law, how much more so of the spiritual world!' (Roy 1985, 88).

Another metaphor is about the 'chain and the link'. He mentioned, 'And one discovery I have made is that, really speaking, there is no distinction between individual growth (read self) and corporate growth (other), the corporate growth is therefore entirely dependent upon individual growth and hence that beautiful proverb in the English language that a chain is no stronger than the weakest link' (CWMG 34, 505).

Certain points need to be considered here. First, Gandhi seems to argue that individual growth (self) is more important, and it is an essential condition of corporate growth (other). However, it does not mean the supremacy of the individual (self) over society since the individual cannot become a person if society is subordinated to the needs of the individual. As a matter of fact, in Gandhi's view, one of the important traits of the individual (self) is the person's willingness to sacrifice himself for the sake of society. Thus, what we note is that when a person is defined in terms of seeking authentic self-hood, the very conception of self incorporates others or society.

Second, as we may infer, Gandhi seems to argue that since human beings and other beings are linked in the manner of the chain, one has to realize that the strength of the chain depends on the condition of what may be the weakest link. Thus, the conscious concern for the weakest link or other links is demanded of the human being because unlike other animals the human being is capable of visualizing alternatives and acting in a manner that ignores or infringes the unalterable law of nature. It is only this concern that can ensure his long-range interest.

Both these paradigms and perceptions lead to a similar conclusion and throw significant light on how self and others are related to one another and why one should be responsible towards others. The necessary corollary of this idea is that no man can degrade or brutalize another without degrading and brutalizing himself. Again, no man can inflict psychic and moral damage on others without inflicting it on himself as well. Parekh argues that 'this was so in at least three ways' (1989, 89). First, to degrade others was to imply that a human being may be so treated and to lower the expected level of the moral minimum due to every human being from which all alike suffered. 'To slight a single human being is...to harm not only that human being but with him the whole world.' Second, to degrade and dehumanize others was to damage their pride, self-respect, and potential for good, and thus both to deny oneself and the world the benefits of their possible contributions and add to the collective moral, psychological and financial cost of repairing the damage they were likely to do themselves. Third, as a being endowed with moral sense and capacity for reflection, no man could degrade or maltreat others without hardening himself against their suffering and cries for help, building up an elaborate and distorted system of self-justification and coercive apparatus to put down and disconnect, and thus both coarsening his moral sensibility and lowering his own and the collective level of humanity. As Gandhi put it, 'No man takes another down a pit without descending into it himself and sinning into the bargain. Since humanity was indivisible and vital human interests were identical, every man was responsible to an extent for others and should be deeply concerned about how they lived' (Parekh 1989, 89-90).

Similar to the notion of undividable humanity, one may find the repeated expressions of 'oneness of mankind' in Gandhi's writings. Although this notion has been explained by him in different contexts, it can be interpreted in the sense of why one should be responsible to others. He wrote, 'Mankind is one, seeing that all are equally subject to the moral law. All men are equal in God's eyes. There are, of course, differences of race and status and the like, but the higher the status of a man, the greater is his responsibility' (Gandhi 1969, 118). Thus, Gandhi accepts the various differences among human beings but despite those differences, in his view, there is an underlying unity because they all are subject to the same moral law. Further, as noted above, in his view, the higher status of men carries greater responsibility.

Related to this, one often finds the idea of 'brotherhood and identity with all forms of life' in his writings by which it can be seen how he viewed one's responsibility to others. He wrote, 'I want to realize brotherhood or identity not merely with the beings called human, but I want to realize identity with all life, even with such things as crawl upon earth. I want, if I don't give you a shock, to realize identity with even the crawling things upon the earth, because we claim descent from the same God, and that being so, all life in whatever form it appears must be essentially one' (Gandhi 1969, 119). Here we note that Gandhi extends the individual's responsibility not only to the human being but to all forms of life, arguing that they are essentially one. Similarly, he describes the idea of 'kinship with all' in his writings. This kinship with all extends not only to human beings but to animals too. He notes that his kinship extends to 'horse and sheep, the lion and leopard, the snake and the scorpion' (Prabhu and Rao 2002, 424). The logic of 'brotherhood and identity with all forms of life' and 'kinship with all' is that, as Gandhi notes, 'every man and woman has unilateral obligation' as 'man is made in the image of God' (Prabhu and Rao 2002, 424).

Further, one may deduce the basis of responsibility of self to other, in Gandhi's worldview, by tracing out his notion of interdependence. In fact, the extension of self as a basis for 'identification with others' implies interdependence. Thus, he does not see that duty to self is separate from the other spheres of society. The reason is, as mentioned, the interdependence of the individual and the different spheres of society. He notes, 'Duties [responsibility] to self, to the family, to the country and to the world are not independent of one another. One cannot do good to the country by injuring himself or his family. Similarly, one cannot serve the country injuring the world at large' (Gandhi 1969, 120). He refines the notion of 'interdependence' in one of his writings more philosophically. He wrote,

> Interdependence is and ought to be as much the ideal of man as self-sufficiency. Man is a social being. Without interrelation with society, he cannot realize his oneness with the universe or suppress his egotism. His social interdependence enables him to test his faith and to prove himself on the touchstone of reality. If man were so placed or could so place himself as to be absolutely above all dependence on his fellow-beings he would become so proud and arrogant as to be a veritable burden and nuisance to the world. Dependence on society teaches him the lesson of humanity. That a man ought to be able to satisfy most of his essential needs himself is obvious, but it is no less obvious to me that when self-sufficiency is carried to the length of isolating oneself from society it almost amounts to sin. A man cannot become self-sufficient even in respect of all the various operations from the growing of cotton to the spinning of the yarn. He has at some stage or other to take the aid of the members of his family. And if one may take help from one's own family, why not from one's neighbours? Or otherwise what is the significance of the great saying, 'The world is my family'? (Gandhi 1969, 119-20).

Again, in Gandhi's writings, we note the 'idea of self-sacrifice' by which we may deduce the basis of responsibility of self to others. This is best illustrated by his notion and practice of Satyagraha. As a 'practical idealist', Gandhi knew that an individual can take some action, unknowingly or unwillingly, concerning others in such a way that may harm others. He also argues that if a person gets engaged in an unjust cause by mistake, he cannot escape from the responsibility. To safeguard against this, Gandhi argues that one must be ready to sacrifice oneself rather than sacrificing others. In his words, 'sacrifice of self is infinitely superior to sacrifice of others'. For this, he presents the idea of 'soul-force' and claims, 'if this kind of force is used in a cause that is unjust, only the person using it suffers. He does not make others suffer for his mistakes. Men have before now done many things which were subsequently found to have been wrong. No man can claim that he is absolutely in the right or that a particular thing is wrong because he thinks so, but it is wrong for him so long as that is his deliberate judgment. It is, therefore, meet that he should not do that which he knows to be wrong, and suffer the consequence whatever it may be. This is the key to the use of soul-force [satyagraha]' (Gandhi 2008, 54).

Related to the notion of sacrifice, there is an idea of 'dialogical empathy' in his worldview that pertains to responsibility. This is two-sided. The first side is the classical meaning of empathy; perceiving another person's experience through the person's eyes and appreciating that person's emotions under the condition of conflict. Dialogical empathy calls for understanding what is going on in the minds of one's opponents and recognizing their human side, including their fears and insecurities. It is the very opposite of demonizing one's enemy. On the other hand, dialogical empathy means trying to look at one's behaviour through the other's eyes, recognizing critically one's moments of distrust, fear, and anger. Thus, dialogical empathy has two components: first, empathizing with the other i.e. appreciating the other's perception, and second, comprehending the other's perception of one's own role in engagement. This, as we may note, is a move forward towards the question of responsibility. In fact, a degree of responsibility, as a moral experience, is involved in this process of dialogical empathy, no matter how individuals transform themselves as they move from a passive role in society to non-violent engagement with others.

Gandhi's notion of responsibility is not confined only

to structural analysis and intervention. It equally offers a philosophy of self-transformation of the individual. Thus, for him, the individual's major task is to make a sincere attempt to live according to the principles of truth and non-violence. Its fundamental tenets are therefore personal and moral but Gandhi cuts the binary of personal/public morality as well as responsibility and offers a whole set of responsibilities that include; resisting injustice, developing a spirit of service, selflessness, and sacrifice, emphasizing one's responsibilities rather than rights, self-discipline, simplicity of lifestyle, and attempting to maintain truthful and non-violent relations with others. Thus, Gandhi's notion of responsibility embodies multi-dimensional responsibilities with multiple others.

An important form of responsibility is responsibility for the future, both near and distant. The immediate and near aspect of responsibility might again be noticed in his notion of Satyagraha. For him, in the given Indian colonial context, the near or immediate response was that an individual was to resist injustice, untruth, in conjunction with others or alone. He argues that such resistance should be non-violent if at all possible, yet, he does not exclude the use of violent means in certain circumstances. For example, preferring violence before injustice instead of cowardice and to remain a helpless witness, he stated categorically, 'Where there is only a choice between cowardice and violence I would advise violence' (Prabhu and Rao 2002, 142).

On the other hand, for distant responsibility, that has to be borne out by the individual and take appropriate methods and steps, he presents the vision of Ramrajya i.e. Kingdom of God. His vision of Ramrajya which means 'perfect non-violent society' is based on the 'sovereignty of the people based on pure moral authority' (Prabhu and Rao 2002, 326).

On the nature and possibility of Ramrajya, he once wrote, 'I do not know what it will be like in Heaven. I have no desire to know the distant scene. If the present is attractive enough, the future cannot be very unlike' (Prabhu and Rao 2002, 326).

As we may observe, his argument for responsibility places a heavy burden on human beings. From his perspective, 'we are not responsible for what we do but also what we tolerate' (Tercheak 1998, 194). This Gandhian responsibility 'implicates us in the actions of the institutions around us whether or not we derive some benefit from them' (Tercheak 1998, 195). From his perspective anyone who tolerates injustice nourishes and exonerates it. Moreover, he/she is escaping from his responsibility. For Gandhi, modern complexities confuse the issue of responsibility by assigning it to impersonal institutions where no one seems accountable or masking power and domination with the imperatives of efficiency or productivity. However, complexities, Gandhi claims, can never repeal personal responsibilities, at least if we want to continue to govern ourselves.

III

It might be argued, if the self has a responsibility towards others then what about individual freedom? This invites us to think of Gandhi's idea of freedom and its relation to responsibility. On this issue Jahanbegloo argues, 'Responsibility for Gandhi precedes freedom because it leads us towards a just treatment to others, the ideal presented by freedom should, in turn, re-inform one's neighbourliness towards the individual other. Moreover, the process of facilitating contact between opponents and overcoming evil requires an appreciation of each other's self-experience and experience of others' (2013, 85).

Gandhi does not view freedom in an absolute way but locates it in the context of others or society. He is not against individual freedom but wants to adjust it to the requirements of social progress. For him, to value human freedom only as the freedom to pursue one's self-interest lacks moral and spiritual depth and creates a life devoid of meaning and truth. On the other hand, he criticized the unrestricted individualism and called it 'the law of the beast of the jungle'. In fact, he wanted people to learn to strike the mean between individual freedom and social restraint. He wrote, 'I value individual freedom, but you must not forget that man is essentially a social being. He has risen to his present status by learning to adjust his individualism to the requirements of social progress. Unrestricted individualism is the law of the beast of the jungle. We have to learn to strike the mean between individual freedom and social restraint. Willing submission to social restraint for the sake of the well-being of the whole society enriches both the individual and the society of which one is a member' (Prabhu and Rao 2002, 312). Thus, freedom for Gandhi was not merely a right but a responsibility and duty. True freedom is not merely the freedom to do what one desires, but also the ability to ensure that what one chooses is the result of a sense of duty and self-knowledge. For him, this choice is not exercised as 'freedom from restraints' but as 'freedom through restraints'.

It is on these grounds that Gandhi equates freedom with his notion of Swaraj or self-rule or self-constraint. As Iyer observes, 'Gandhi equated freedom with self-rule because he wished to build into the concept of freedom the notion of obligation to others as well as to oneself while retaining the element of voluntariness that is the very basis of freedom. The notion of self-rule implies the voluntary internalization of our obligation to others which will be obstructed by our placing ourselves at the mercy of our selfish desires' (1973, 349). This states precisely what Gandhi intended and achieved. In fact, Gandhi deliberately disassociated Swaraj from the mere transfer of power and political independence in the literal sense. In his view, the moral claim to rule was nonsensical, even reckless, without a practical demonstration of Swaraj. He argued that Swaraj could come only through acceptance of considerable personal and political responsibility that involved enormous self-sacrifice and social service. No nationalist before Gandhi had embraced the responsibility of the colonized so unequivocally. As he wrote in *Hind Swaraj*, 'To blame the English is useless'; Gandhi's 'Editor' (speaking in the author's voice) declared to the Reader, 'they will either go or change their nature only when we reform ourselves... We shall become free only through suffering' (Gandhi 2008, 63-4). Indians must recognize this duty because 'Swaraj has to be experienced, by each one for himself' (Gandhi 2008, 39). It can be achieved only through a commitment to the cause of freedom, so 'it is our duty to say exactly what we think and face the consequences' (Gandhi 2008, 64).

Gandhi uses this theory of duty to shape his idea of rights: 'Having a right surely does not mean that I should exercise that right in utter disregard of my sense of proportion...The exercise of right depends on one's sense of duty. It is my duty to follow dharma...I do what I consider my duty' (CWMG 69, 208). This follows from his argument that 'real rights are a result of the performance of duty' (CWMG 10, 44). In short, freedom is not only freedom from coercion and domination, but also self-regulation through self-restraint. Thus, freedom or Swaraj was understood by Gandhi both in the sense of personal and political responsibility.

In the 21st century, where the 'other' is perceived as a 'threat', a rights-based approach is prevailing over duty, unrestricted individualism is shadowing moral restraints, and responsibility has been reduced to mechanical accountability, Gandhi's idea of the self and its relation to others through moral responsibility provides us a framework to re-design our individual and political worldview for the betterment of humanity.

References

Gandhi, M.K 1969. *All Men are Brothers.* Switzerland: Unesco unesdoc.unesco.org/images/0007/000710/071082eo.pdf

Gandhi, M.K. 2008. *Hind Swaraj or Indian Home Rule.* Ahmedabad: Navajivan.

Gandhi, M.K. 2015. *An Autobiography or My Experiments with Truth.* Ahmedabad: Navajivan.

Iyer, R. 1973. *The Moral and Political Thought of Mahatma Gandhi.* New York: Oxford University Press.

Parekh, B. 1989. *Gandhi's Political Philosophy.* London: Macmillan Press.

Prabhu R.K. and U.R. Rao. 2002. *The Mind of Mahatma.* Ahmedabad: Navajivan.

Ramin Jahanbegloo. 2013. *The Gandhian Moment*. London: Harvard University Press.

Roy, Ramashray. 1985. *Self and Society: A Study in Gandhian Thought.* New Delhi: Sage.

Tercheak, R.J. 1998. *Gandhi: Struggling for Autonomy*. New Delhi: Vistaar Publication.

The Collected Works of Mahatma Gandhi (CWMG). Vol. 1-100. New Delhi: Publication Division, Ministry of Information and

Broadcasting, Government of India. Retrieved from https://www.gandhiheritageportal.org/.

Varma, Ravindra. 2001. *The Spiritual Basis of Satyagraha*. Ahmedabad: Navajivan.

M.K. GANDHI THROUGH WESTERN LENSES

Romain Rolland's *Mahatma Gandhi: The Man Who Became One with the Universal Being*

Madhavi Nikam

Indian political psychologist, social theorist, and critic Ashis Nandy in his *The Intimate Enemy: Loss and Recovery of Self Under Colonialism* (1983) says that 'All interpretations of India are ultimately autobiographical' (80). There are several readings of Mohandas Karamchand Gandhi, including every dimension of his personality. From Joseph J. Doke, a Christian missionary in South Africa who wrote the first biography of Gandhi in 1909, there are several incisive readings and inquiries into his life from various perspectives and philosophical standpoints: Gandhi's personal image that led to the titles of Mahatma, Bapu, Father of the Nation, half-naked fakir, and the like; his political life and leadership that played a major role in India's independence from British rule. In the existing literature on Gandhi, there is a prevalent sense that most of these elements are necessary for understanding Gandhi. It is no wonder, then, that much of the prominent contemporary literature on the phenomenon of Gandhi continues to be largely anecdotal, historical, and biographical in character

Romain Rolland (1866–1944), a French writer, art historian and mystic, was the recipient of the Nobel Prize for Literature in 1915. Rolland, who had a pacifist bent of mind, was a great admirer of Gandhi. Influenced by Gandhi's philosophy of non-violence, his ideology and political acumen, he wrote a book on Gandhi in 1924 without ever having met him. The book turned out to be crucial for both Rolland himself and for Gandhi's reputation in Europe. Rolland happened to personally meet M.K. Gandhi in 1931 when the latter was in London for the Round Table Conference. Throughout his life Rolland maintained his interest in India and Indian spirituality. Rolland is also the first to clearly indicate a kind of reconciliation between Gandhi and Indian Communists which was otherwise doubted by many thinkers and philosophers. He exhibits the impact of Stalin and Lenin while analyzing Gandhi through his biography. He accepts in his letter to Surendranath Tagore in 1933 that it is the need of the hour to combine Gandhian philosophy and Lenin's communism for the betterment of society, so that the two may come together at this hour to overthrow the old world and found a new order.

Rolland expressed his desire of approximating two personalities together several times during his writings. In the same communication he observes that planned non-violence and well-organized radical violence should be associated armies. Coordination of both should act against the common foes of humanity, such as war, totalitarianism, imperialism, etc. Rolland, the visionary, must have felt the need to bring two ideologies together with the view of protecting weaker sections of society. And it was the philosophy of combining two extreme opposite forces of non-violence (Ahimsa) and violence to bring positive results in the society. That way

Rolland was trying to incorporate the new order into the old one. Rolland had first heard of Gandhi through his friend D.K. Roy who mentioned Gandhi as a 'magnetic lawyer' who was influenced by Tolstoy in his diary on 23rd August 1920. It was also written that Gandhi 'preaches passive resistance to them and turns them away from violence' (Rolland, 3). Rolland had believed that non-resistance would be detrimental to his own nation, given the politically unstable climate of Europe then. He argued in favour of pacifism since Europe was then moving into a stage of great insecurity. His work was a cudgel against fascism, and the passivity of the Vichy government. Rolland describes Gandhi in his book, *Romain Rolland and Gandhi Correspondence: Letters, Diary Extracts, Articles, etc* (1976) as follows:

> Gandhi is small, insignificant-looking, except when he begins to speak, and of unruffled patience. There is nothing severe in his manners; he laughs like a child and adores children. His asceticism is extreme...Gandhi's principle is that life is a preparation for suffering martyrdom and death, and the results he has obtained in Bengal are surprising. (13)

Rolland writes that his book on Gandhi ruffled the feathers of the Orientalists who fretted that someone outside their circle had something to say. However, Gandhi approved of and appreciated Rolland's perspective on his life and work. Mahadev Desai, Gandhi's associate, quotes Gandhi as he writes: 'Romain Rolland is at this point not only a poet, he is a seer with the vision of the truth' (Rolland 1976, 18).

Before Rolland promoted Gandhi by mixing anti-imperialism, the pacifist ideology, and the saintliness of his life, Gandhi was known in Europe and America merely as an Indian lawyer. Rolland's critique of expansionism and Europe's destructive propensities during the Great War, and in the colonized regions of Asia and Africa was an ambitious task. Rolland writes, 'Under the mask of civilization, or of a brutal national idealism, the politics of the great States methodically practice fraud and violence, theft and degradation (rather, extermination) of the so-called inferior peoples' (Fisher 2017, 15). Throughout the period of war, Rolland protested against Europe's imperialism. He predicted that Europe's imperialistic aggression would be confronted with anti-imperialistic antagonism. Rolland recommended an intermediary path between the imperialistic and anti-imperialistic forces of East and West. Progressive intellectuals of Europe and developing countries could have a dialogue using their hearts and geniuses to work towards amicable and peaceful solutions to imperialistic perpetration. Gandhi's political ideology offered one humane solution to the development of imperialist and anti-imperialist aggression. The Gandhian path moved toward international cooperation, redress of the grievances of colonized nations, and a negotiating mechanism to satisfy the mutual needs of the imperialist powers and the countries seeking liberation. Rolland's anti-imperialism was thoroughly Gandhian. His condemnation of imperialism was often harsh but the remedies he suggested always left the possibilities open for negotiation between East and West. Rolland's intention was to bypass the massive disturbances and random violence of struggles of national liberation and the efforts to suppress them. The real work of forming a durable society could begin only after the struggles subsided.

Rolland was fully aware of the different ways of Gandhi and the Communists but he thought that combining them was the only way of bringing change in Indian society. He knew the enmity and abhorrence of the Communists for Gandhi and he recounts, too, in his diary in January 1928 that the Moscow Communists or those who followed their line were showing two faces. On the one hand, they treated Gandhi as an enemy and proclaimed the bankruptcy of non-violence in India, on the other, they disguised Gandhi as a Bolshevik and put about unlikely rumours of an imminent visit to Moscow. He believed that the concept of free society could only be realized by the acceptance of Communist violence in the Indian context and therefore he stressed on the need to unify Gandhian ideology and Communist philosophy for the establishment of utopian society in a country like India.

The Marxist and Leninist theoreticians often raise their eyebrows at the flexible attitude of Rolland towards Communist violence and Gandhian non-violence as they believe that world history records major changes in society usually through violent activities and not by non-violent means. Hiren Mukherjee in his book, *Gandhi: A Study* observes,

> It would be so much more welcome if non-violence could work, but historical change, of the basic sort especially, does not come as wish-fulfilment, however ardent and largely shared that wish might be. More often than not, if history is our guide, such change involves violence. (1979, 34)

Rolland, therefore, requested Gandhi to add Communist violence to his ideology of non-violence so that the results would come quickly and be permanent. Stating a number of examples from the past, he tried to convince Gandhi that the European people, like a majority of Indians, are not of a religious mentality to follow the path of non-violence and non-cooperation, rather they believe in bravery and a sort of violence in almost everything. Therefore, he thought that Gandhi could not force them to follow non-violence against their wishes, he could only be pursuant in convincing them. To quote him from his book, *Romain Rolland and Gandhi Correspondence* in this regard:

> The violence of the Communists in Russia was due to the armed intervention of great powers and he also refused to label Russian Communist ideology as materialist, since it had given rise to the most heroic of sacrifices, even though it did not imply non-violence (1976, 170).

For Gandhi, Swaraj in itself was not an end. *Hind Swaraj* (1909) was a book written by Gandhi after his return from England, after discussions with the British liberal intellectuals and Indian freedom fighters operating from London through radical means. He expressed the idea of Swaraj in his aforementioned book. For Gandhi, Swaraj is a mental state, not physical or political emancipation from England. He believed that if Indians adopted the materialistic goals of Western Civilization, and its modes of production and production relations for the sake of independence, then there was no reason for political independence in the first place. He states that such independence can be attained even under the British regime.

Gandhi hailed from an orthodox Hindu family and hence understood the philosophical roots of the religion he belonged to. He devoutly followed these tenets in his own behaviour. However, as a mass leader, he had to tone down his principles a bit for the sake of his followers. He was often titled 'a saint and a politician', but there was nothing scriptural or otherworldly about his main political ethics. He mainly learned this not from religion, but from observing his father Karamchand Uttamchand Gandhi in his work as Diwan of Porbandar, Rajkot, and Wankaner.

Famous Indian writer Munshi Premchand shares a striking similarity with Mahatma Gandhi especially on the grounds of their humanism. Both Gandhi and Premchand had high ideals in their life. Their precepts of love for truth and simple living, back to villages, cooperation in place of class struggle, communal harmony, sympathy for the Dalit, gender equality, fearlessness, morality, and non-violent non-cooperation were in common. Both were against the formula 'Art for art's sake'. Gandhi and Premchand tried to articulate this from the perspectives of the common man and tried to think as he thought, shared his feelings, his hopes, fears, dreams and aspirations. Both in their thoughts and emotions and their identity, their oneness with the common man was complete. Both Gandhi and Premchand were the models for the masses of India. Perhaps this is the key to their immense appeal.

Mahatma Gandhi was deeply influenced by Henry David Thoreau's preaching about non-violent resistance. To resist things that were wrong, to resist immoral government action by simply refusing to cooperate was the Gandhian way, based on Thoreau's ideology. Thoreau's thoughts were also adopted by Gandhi in developing his concept of Satyagraha or Truth Force. Civil rights leader Martin Luther King adapted Gandhi's idea of civil disobedience to the civil rights movement in the United States. Martin Luther King drew inspiration from Gandhi's preaching of non-violence. King was inspired by the teachings and philosophy of the Mahatma. The United States has a number of statues, busts and memorials to Mahatma Gandhi. According to Martin Luther King, Mahatma Gandhi was the first person in the world to elevate the love ethic of Jesus beyond just interaction between individuals to a massive social force. While describing his interpretation of the non-violence that seeks to win over an adversary to friendship, rather than to demean or defeat him. King asserts that he developed the method for his social reform using Gandhian principles as the model. King said when he visited India in 1959 that he might go to other countries as a tourist, but to India he went as a pilgrim.

Throughout his correspondence with Gandhi he never thought that Gandhi moved from his firm stand of non-violence for even a second. He was stubborn and firm in his ideology of non-violence; he convinced Rolland in turn that his method of non-violence was more permanent and enduring than the violent means of the Communists. His various attempts to convince Gandhi of his point of view proved futile; he mentions at one point in his correspondence that 'there are many things in the universe which I am forced to accept without approving them—starting perhaps with life itself, since destiny forces us to live by killing other forms of life' (1976, 443).

Conclusively, Rolland brings to the notice of the Communists that Gandhi was a very stubborn person, a shrewd political activist who was always firm about his views and ideas and was always ready to experiment with things to test their truth. While talking about Gandhi's views on modern technology, Rolland writes:

> Gandhi...in no way condemns machinery and industrial techniques, in so far as they bring help and relief to humanity, his quarrel is merely with their murderous excesses and the morbid myth of economic over-production. When you look at India, you find a very special situation (Rolland 459-60).

The political philosophy of Gandhi seemed to be the only solution to the imperialism and imperialist aggression of the interwar period in the East and the West. He genuinely felt that the democratic and conciliatory ways of fighting were more suitable for the Soviet model. He, therefore, propagated the philosophy of non-violence as the only way to break the iron net of imperialism. The Gandhian way is a way of cooperation, redressing the agonies of the colonized nations and facilitating a dialogue to cater to the mutual needs of the imperialist powers and countries seeking liberation. Rolland seems to fail on all grounds in convincing him that armed resistance could bring a change in the situation. Through his correspondence with Gandhi, Rolland seems neither convinced of the methods of Communism nor approves the non-violence of Gandhi completely. Finally, Rolland came to the conclusion that the ideas and philosophy of Gandhi, long contemplated and time-tested, were not to be changed by anything because Gandhi showed great belief in bringing about economic equality by the means of non-violence.

References

Brown, Judith Margaret. 1991. *Gandhi: Prisoner of Hope*. New Haven: Yale University Press.

Chadha, Yogesh. 1997. *Rediscovering Gandhi*. London: Random House.

Doke, Joseph J. 2005. *Gandhi: A Patriot in South Africa*. New Delhi: Publications Division, Ministry of Information & Broadcasting.

Fisher, David. 2017. *Romain Rolland and the Politics of the Intellectual Engagement*. London: Routledge.

Gandhi, Mohandas Karamchand. 1927. *Autobiography, Or My Experiments with Truth*. ; Ahmedabad: Navajivan Publishing House.

Haksar, Vinit. 2017. *Gandhi and Liberalism: Satyagraha and the Conquest of Evil*. India: Routledge.

King, Martin Luther. 1960. *Pilgrimage to Non-violence.* Chicago: Fellowship Publications.

Lindley, Mark, Y. P. Anand, and Humanist Chaplaincy. 1995. *Gandhi and Humanism.* Humanist Chaplaincy, Harvard University.

Marcin, Raymond B. Gandhi and Justice. 2004. *Logos: A Journal of Catholic Thought and Culture* 7 (3): 17–30.

Mukherjee, Hirendranath. 1979. *Gandhiji: A Study.* People's Publishing House.

Nanda, Bal Ram. 1958. *Mahatma Gandhi.* Boston, Massachusetts: Beacon Press.

Nandy, Ashis. 1989. *The Intimate Enemy.* Oxford: Oxford University Press.

Rolland, Romain and Mohandas Karamchand Gandhi. 1976. Romain Rolland and Gandhi Correspondence. New Delhi: Ministry of Information and Broadcasting.

GANDHI AS REFLECTED IN TAGORE'S BIOGRAPHICAL SKETCHES

Udaya Narayana Singh

Prof. Sabyasachi Bhattacharya's work (1997) titled *The Mahatma and the Poet: Letters and Debates between Gandhi and Tagore 1915-1941,* has given us a set of refreshing ideas on what the two, both born around the same time in the 1860s, thought about the future of India. The work contains both public discussions and personal communications, starting with Gandhi's arrival in India in 1913. The narrative was periodized (1915-22, 1923-28, 1929-33 and 1934-41) to understand their different perceptions better, and in particular, Tagore's farsighted condemnation of state-sponsored 'Nationalism' in all forms. Tagore viewed the widely acclaimed 'non-cooperation' as a negative impulse that would in no way be able to rejuvenate our polity and its dwindling economy. It would instead contribute to our sense of intolerance that would ultimately destroy our democratic aspirations. Although both desired to see 'a true independence, a reliance upon spiritual force, a fearless courage in the face of temporal power, and withal a deep and burning charity for all men' as Bhattacharya put it, it was unacceptable for the followers of Gandhi to accept Tagore's criticism of Satyagraha or Non-cooperation.

The manner in which the agitation against the division of Bengal in and around 1905 became politically divisive, because of which Tagore had stopped participating in real-life political agitation, was at the back of his mind when Gandhi gave the call to boycott all British institutions. Tagore thought that boycotting of schools by students would lead to an anarchy from which recovery would not be easy. For Tagore, non-cooperation was an unduly simplistic response to a complex problem of how to shun the alien rulers' governance. In response to this, Gandhi is supposed to have stated:

> I, therefore, think that the Poet has been unnecessarily alarmed at the negative aspect of Non-cooperation. We had lost the power of saying 'no'. It had become disloyal, almost sacrilegious to say 'no' to the Government. This deliberate refusal to cooperate is like the necessary weeding process that a cultivator has to resort before he sows. Weeding is as necessary to agriculture as sowing. Indeed, even whilst the crops are growing, the weeding fork, as every husbandman knows, is an instrument almost of daily use. The nation's Non-cooperation is an invitation to the Government to cooperate with it on its own terms as is every nation's right and every good government's duty. Non-cooperation is the nation's notice that it is no longer satisfied to be in tutelage.[11]

In Gandhi's own autobiography (1927), *The Story of My Experiments with Truth*, Chapter 127, 'Shantiniketan' describes the initial phase of his arrival and learning the intricacies of politics in India under G.K. Gokhale. When he was returning to

[11] https://www.news18.com/news/buzz/rabindranath-tagores-conversations-with-mahatma-gandhi-on-nationalism-is-a-debate-we-all-need-to-read-1836397.html

Pune from Shantiniketan, after hearing about Gokhale's death, Gandhi described his conversation with Andrews: 'Andrews accompanied me up to Burdwan. "Do you think," he asked me, "that a time will come for *Satyagraha* in India? And if so, have you any idea when it will come?" "It is difficult to say," said I. "For one year I am to do nothing. For Gokhale took from me a promise that I should travel in India for gaining experience, and express no opinion on public questions until I have finished the period of probation. Even after the year is over, I will be in no hurry to speak and pronounce opinions. And so, I do not suppose there will be any occasion for *Satyagraha* for five years or so." I may note in this connection that Gokhale used to laugh at some of my ideas in *Hind Swaraj* (Indian Home Rule) and say: "After you have stayed a year in India, your views will correct themselves."' Thus, it was not only Tagore who was sceptical of Gandhi's ideas.

Looking back at the effect of Non-cooperation, Martin Luther King, Jr. had made an interesting comment in his own autobiography on the effect of this peaceful instrument that was ingeniously discovered by Gandhi: 'Gandhi was able to mobilize and galvanize more people in his life time than any other people in the history of this world. And just with a little love and understanding, goodwill and refusal to cooperate with an evil law, he was able to break the backbone of the British empire. More than 390 million people achieved their freedom, and they achieved it non-violently.' (Carson 2001, 129)

The symbolism in Gandhi's inimitable style of protestation, especially in the context of destroying foreign clothes and in promoting the charkha or spinning wheel, mainly to tell the world that economic domination imposed by the imperial powers would not be tolerated, did not impress Tagore who thought that clothes should be distributed among the needy instead, as the poor in the country lived in great misery. Tagore wrote a sarcastic essay in *Modern Review*, a Calcutta-based magazine of great repute, titled 'The Cult of the Charkha'. There are often great misunderstandings and misreading in Tagore's texts which make us believe that he was perhaps against Gandhian principles and methods. One such example can be seen in the following editorial comment on Tagore's 1916 novel, *The Home and the World* (*Ghare Baire*), set in the times of the Swadeshi Movement in 1905, by Alam and Chakravarty (2011, 612): '*Ghare Baire*, Tagore's best-known novel, is set during the Swadeshi Movement of 1905, when Indian women stepped out of seclusion to participate in the nationalist struggle. Through the intertwined lives of the visionary but politically ineffective landowner Nikhil, the flamboyant, militant nationalist Sandip, and Nikhil's wife Bimala, torn by her divided loyalties, the sophisticated, multi-voiced narrative lays bare the troubled interface between the confines of home and the turbulent world outside.' Here, we may note that Georg Lukacs (1922/1983) criticized the novel for presenting 'a contemptible caricature of Gandhi,' forgetting that the narrative is set in a period that precedes Gandhi's rise. But Bertolt Brecht recognized this as a 'wonderful book, strong and gentle,' about the limitations of nationalism (Brecht 1980, 55).

While the Swadeshi movement during Gandhi's Satyagraha period was aimed against the system imposed by the British, and not against all that was Western, Tagore rather believed in the power of Western thought and science, and that it had tremendous healing and emancipatory influence. Celebration of individual choice and freedom was a hallmark of Tagore's arguments on what kind of future the leadership of our times would like to achieve. That Tagore did not appreciate fasting as a method of protestation thought to be unique in the Gandhian era is also a well-known fact now, as Tagore thought this self-mortification as purification would not lead us anywhere. Fasting for political purposes was something that Tagore was sceptical about. He was also critical of Gandhi for what many believed was his irrational declaration that the Great Bihar Earthquake was God's punishment for our sin in upholding untouchability. Krishna Kripalani (1980, 391-92) suggests that Tagore's 1932 play, *Chandalika* that was based on a Buddhist legend, explored selfishness and vanity, and juxtaposed solipsism with selfless love, which was inspired by Mahatma Gandhi's long fast against the British government's decision to separate the 'untouchables' of the country from the rest of the electorate through the Communal Award.

In March-April 1919, Gandhiji launched a nationwide campaign of passive resistance to protest the repressive act designed by Sir Sydney Arthur Taylor Rowlatt, known as the Rowlatt Act, which was basically to take emergency measures of preventive indefinite detention, incarceration without trial and judicial review to curb a perceived threat from revolutionary nationalist organizations. The success of Gandhi's hartal (public strike) in Delhi on 30th March and in Punjab on 6th April of that year led to the massacre by the British of nearly 400 unarmed protesters and the wounding of another 2,000 in Amritsar's Jallianwala Bagh on 13th April 1919. British repression in the Punjab continued, even after Gandhi called off the campaign on 18th April 1919. When he failed to muster support from politicians, Tagore felt compelled to register a lone protest. On 31st May, he wrote a letter to Lord Chelmsford, the then Viceroy, rejecting his knighthood. The letter was published on 2nd June, and it aroused the consciousness of the Western world against the atrocious rule of the so-called civilized British government. In 1921, after much thought, Tagore decided to oppose Gandhi's Non-cooperation Movement against the British government, for which he faced strong criticism from all quarters, and even from Bengal.

Many view these incidents as Tagore's disrespect for Gandhian ideas, methods and principles. However, if we look at the biographical sketches of Mohandas Gandhi in Tagore's writings that are spread in different essays and chapters, the impression would be otherwise. In his opening essay on মহাত্‌মা গান্‌ধী (Mahatma Gandhi), Tagore begins by making a comment on a new kind of tribe that emerged in the initial phase of political movements in our country, in the following words: 'পোলিটিশয্‌ান ব'লে একটা জাত আছে তাদের আদশর্‌ বড়ো আদশের্‌র সঙ্‌েগ মেলে না। তারা অজসর্‌ মিথয্‌া বলতে পারে; তারা এত হিংসর্‌ যে নিজেদের দেশকে সব্‌াতন্‌তর্‌য্‌ দেবার অছিলায় অনয্‌ দেশ অধিকার করার লোভ তয্‌াগ করতে পারে না। পাশ্‌চাতয্‌ দেশে দেখি, এক দিকে তারা দেশের জনেয্‌ পর্‌াণ দিতে পেরেছে, অনয্‌ দিকে আবার দেশের নাম করে দুনর্‌ীতির পর্‌শর্‌য় দিয়েছে।' (There is a caste called 'the Politician'. Their aims never match with bigger ideals one may have. They can tell innumerable lies. They are so ferocious that they never hesitate to occupy another country in the garb of protecting their own. In the West, I have seen, while they are able to dedicate their lives, they have also tolerated corruptions in the name of national interest) (Translation by the author).

In fact, Tagore opens the discussion on Mahatma Gandhi by saying, 'India has a complete geographical image and identity' (In Bengali: 'Bharatbarsher ekti sampurna bhougolik murti ache'). The 'totality' of India that begins from the East and spreads up to the West, or one that starts from the Himalayas in the North and reaches down to Kanyakumari in the South creates a picture that was attempted to be internalized as a whole even in ancient times, especially in the epic, the Mahabharata that tried collecting whatever lay scattered in so many parts and spread over such a long time. The other way of knowing this complete India lay in its tradition of pilgrimage. Ordinary people tried covering the entire spread of the space by moving from one religious place to another, as if to bind the whole region by a network of bhakti or devotion. In fact, India was so large an entity that it was not possible to internalize it as a whole. What modern surveys and cartographies could do to bring about a geographical idea of India was not easily available in earlier days. Tagore thought that in one sense that was good because anything gained easily never leaves a great impression in our mind. So, all the difficulties one had to bear in conducting a pilgrimage were rewarding because only in that way one could get to know the totality of India.

Then Tagore laments that we were so much trapped in the regionalist trends and tendencies that it required someone like Mahatma Gandhi, along with Ranade, Surendranath (Banerjee) and (Gopalkrishna) Gokhale to appear in the public sphere to take India forward or to know her in a great fashion. He thinks that insertion of the text of the *Gita* in the middle of the Mahabharata and situating this philosophical theoretical text in the middle of a battleground, in a great argumentative country such as ours, shows that 'কুরুকে্ষতের্র কেন্দর্স্থলে এই-যে খানিকটা দাশর্নিক ভাবে আলোচনা, এটাকে কাবেয্র দিক থেকে অসংগত বলা যেতে পারে; এমনও বলা যেতে পারে যে, মূল মহাভারতে এটা ছিল না। পরে যিনি বসিয়েছেন তিনি জানতেন যে, উদার কাবয্পরিধির মধেয্, ভারতের চিত্‌তভূমির মাঝখানে এই তত্‌তব্কথার অবতারণা করার পর্য়োজন ছিল।' (This dialogue in the middle of the battlefield, Kurukshetra, may seem slightly inappropriate for the kavya, or poetic text; One can even say that this portion was not there in the original Mahabharata. Whoever interpolated and inserted this part later knew that in the Indian mind, there was a need to introduce this theoretical discussion there). This interpolation acted as a binding force then.

But as time went by, our belief-system and culture became infested with division and narrowness. We forgot to regard or accept great heroes with all their positive and negative features—something that our epics had taught us. In fact, that was also the reason that these texts assumed a very important place in our religious practices. When the external force and alien culture tore our fabric of unity apart and penetrated into our homes, it was like a flood that swept us away. Our kingdoms and principalities tried putting up resistance on a piecemeal basis, resulting in hopeless defeats. We lived together but we could never get united in this country—'আমরা একতর্ ছিলুম, অথচ এক হই নি।' (We were together, but were never united). It required many centuries to learn our lessons, and meanwhile, the battle-cry never subsided in the Bengal, Maratha and Rajputana regions. 'যত বড়ো দেশ ঠিক তত বড়ো ঐকয্ হল না; দুভর্াগেয্র ভিতর দিয়ে আমরা অভিজ্এতা লাভ করলেম বহু শতাব্‌দী পরে।' (Our unity did not match up to the size of our country; We gained this experience after facing many centuries of misfortune). One after another came the Portuguese, the Dutch, the French and the British. We began to give away our own collections and riches to the foreign powers. And whatever little remained with us was grabbed by the greedy Mahanths and Pandas. Many decided to escape in the name of looking for their personal salvation as hermits and Sanyasis who never did anything for the common folk as the latter, they thought, were consuming the opium of this ordinary worldly life almost like 'possessed' (Mohagrasta) people.

Meanwhile, there had begun in Europe a move to establish

one's own political and cultural identity, thanks to Mazzini and Garibaldi in Italy, who taught us what independence could achieve for a culture. Even on American soil, the independence movement had its own achievements. Many sacrificed their lives to bring in this liberty and to protest against the dividing tactics of the alien rulers: 'বিভাগ সৃষ্িট করে পরস্পরকে যে অপমান করা হয়, সেটার বিরুদ্েধ পাশ্চাতেয্ আজও বিদের্াহ চলছে।' In India, we have learned the value of independence from Western contemporary history. This is where Mahatma Gandhi played an important role in binding the whole nation together. He was not among those who would think that one could achieve anything politically by appeasing the alien rulers or by falsely posing themselves against the external forces. It was in this context that Tagore made that comment on the 'tribe' of Politicians. The petty party politics, mixed with the false claims of patriotism and added prevarication—all these were contributed by others in public life when Gandhi emerged as a leader with a great difference. Firstly, he was against the strategy of using 'untruth' for political gains. Tagore thought the Mahatma was praiseworthy because he had the foresight and patience to experiment with Truth. When the history of the world is dominated by bloodshed in the countries and communities that sought independence, how freedom and liberty could be achieved by the masses without violence was a great experiment that defined Gandhi. Tagore said: 'পৃথিবীতে সব্াধীনতা এবং সব্াতন্তর্য্ লাভের ইতিহাস রক্তধারায় পঙ্িকল, অপহরণ ও দসুয্বৃত্তির দব্ারা কলঙ্িকত। কিন্তু পরস্পরকে হনন না করে, হতয্াকাণে্ডর আশর্য় না নিয়েও যে সব্াধীনতা লাভ করা যেতে পারে, তিনি তার পথ দেখিয়েছেন।' (In the world, the history of the move for gaining freedom and independence is replete with bloodshed, plunder and loot which had all marred it. But he has shown the way that one could gain independence even without killing each other, or not perpetrating mass-scale murders).

Tagore raised this issue of how politicians and statesmen were performing various sorts of vicious and sadistic activities in the name of national interest. He believed people did not hesitate to plunder or kill and even employ their sciences to perpetrate violence now. But the generals do not make a nation; it is the culture and tradition of the people that define them. One does not remember such politicians as much as those like the Mahatma who worked to uplift the downtrodden. Even in the so-called 'Holy war' (Dharma yuddha) or 'Moral war' (Naitika yuddha) there is a terrible 'cruelty' (Nisthurata). There is an education even in these experiments, based on which the Christian theology taught us to clothe the most deprived people, and feed the most hungry people যে সকলের চেয়ে দরিদ্র তাকে বস্ত্র দিতে হবে, যে নিরন্ন তাকে অন্ন দিতে হবে; (One who is the poorest, he will have to be given clothes to wear, and the hungry must get food that is due). Tagore thought (and he said) that Mahatma-ji was able to meet a European sage and devout Christian, Leo Tolstoy, from whom he had picked up this lesson of Non-violence. Tolstoy strove to explain to all that human rights must be protected at any cost (নিয়ত প্রচেষ্টা ছিল মানবের ন্যায্য অধিকারকে বাধামুক্ত করা; He constantly struggled to remove the obstacles for all legitimate human rights). Gandhiji did not have to learn about this doctrine from any missionary or religious practitioner but from a great author with a sensitive mind. Even from the medieval Muslim saints we had received this gift because Dadu, Kabir and Rajjab had propagated this idea that whatever is pure and free, and is the best gift of one's soul, that belongs to all mankind, and not to a closed-door religious establishment. 'যা নির্মল, যা মুক্ত, যা আত্মার শ্রেষ্ঠ সামগ্রী, তা রুদ্ধদ্বার মন্দিরে কৃত্রিম অধিকারীবিশেষের জন্যে পাহারা-দেওয়া নয়; তা নির্বিচারে সর্ব মানবেরই সম্পদ;' (Whatever is pure, free, and the best gift of one's soul, does not require a strict vigil to be guarded in the closed-door temple to make them safe for the artificial ruling elites, as that is a property of mankind as a whole).

In every age that is what happens because of those noble men or 'Mahatman' who are ready to learn from all religions, the history of all regions and from ethics as the best gifts of nature—and Mahatma Gandhi was no exception. Tagore, therefore, concluded this biographical sketch by saying:

> মহাত্মা নমর্ অহিংসনীতি গর্হণ করেছেন, আর চতুদির্কে তাঁর জয় বিস্তীণর্ হচে্ছ। তিনি যে নীতি তাঁর সমস্ত জীবন দিয়ে পর্মাণ করেছেন, সম্পূণর্ পারি বা না পারি, সে নীতি আমাদেয় সব্ীকার করতেই হবে। আমাদের অন্তরে ও আচরণে রিপু ও পাপের সংগর্াম আছে, তা সত্তেব্ও পুণেয্র তপসয্ার দীক্ষা নিতে হবে সতয্বর্ত মহাত্মার নিকটে।... (শানি্তনিকেতন, ১৬ আশিব্ন ১৩৪৩)

(Mahatma has adopted the gentle principle of Non-violence, and one can see that this has contributed to his all-around success everywhere. The principle which he has stuck to by devoting his whole life, we must accept it, whether we can take it and implement it completely or not. In our own heart and behaviour, there is a constant battle of natural instincts and indulgence. And yet, we have to take the lesson of virtue by following the doctrine of Mahatma Gandhi).

In another sketch of Gandhi, written and published in the October of 1937 (Agrahayan of 1344 Bengali year), also called 'Gandhi-ji', Tagore comments that the whole ashram in Shantiniketan would celebrate Gandhiji's birthday when the stirrings it created did not allow anyone to forget what it was the ashram was commemorating. There are those men who are rarely born and therefore they do not belong to any particular time, and Gandhi was one such rare and eternal personality. If one wants to understand him only in the context of the present age, that would diminish him. But that would force us to overlook his personality that had the traits of eternity.

We often look at great men or their greatness only in so much as he or she could meet our immediate demands and expectations ('Ashu prayojan'). But when we consider such people on a bigger canvas, the inner contradictions and indeterminacies they may have within themselves are wiped away by their divinity. What is accidental and temporary is never highlighted. In fact, that is the justification of seeing and celebrating our great living legends. Tagore said that in the future times, there might not be the 'national contradictions' and the condition of strife that existed then and perhaps the popular demands would have been met. And yet, even after the liberty that India might achieve soon, it would be important to see which historical emergence and whose self-expression would survive in the national memory. We would not look at Gandhiji as an instrument of achievement of political sovereignty. We would rather try to appreciate the firm mental power of the man and his resolve that aroused the inner strength and consciousness of a whole nation. The huge boulder (জগদ্দল পাথর) that lay on our hearts and minds has been knocked off by his astute move, and as if there has been a rejuvenation of our political selves. It was like gaining a new life for us all. All fear, hesitation, and attempts to seek benevolence of the rulers, and the lack of confidence are all vanished, as if through his magic wand.

The whole nation had accepted subservience for long. It was an 'accepted' truth, as if the foreign rulers were superior in knowledge, governance structure and physical prowess. But how their apparent shine could be dimmed by our inner strength, internal understanding, or by our own knowledge, tradition and dedication to service was demonstrated by Gandhi. The ordinary folk were as if mesmerized by the British who were considered superior in culture, education, knowledge and politics. A few political leaders like Lokamanya Tilak had attempted to prove this wrong by arousing the self-esteem among our people but the success that Gandhiji had in making us arise and awake in our daily lives and in our respective fields of work was unparalleled. He made us realize that we had ourselves written the destiny of our defeat by showing our weaknesses. The business empire of the British was built on our lack of courage and acumen, and we became a mere peg in their huge network of commerce and trade. Mahatma showed the ills of this 'self-defeating' tendency, 'Atmakrita-paraabhav'.

All the recent moves of the British rulers to come to terms with the political leadership in India resulted from the massive uprising that Gandhiji led in the most unconventional manner. It was due to his vision that we could now demand our rightful place on the world stage. Whether it was his sharp argumentative skills in the round table conferences here or in England, or his symbolic protestations by using spinning wheels (Charkha) or the indigenous cloth manufacturing (Khaddar), or in promoting the non-conventional energy sources, or alternative medicine—all these were strategies that unnerved the Western powers with an evil eye towards India (Tagore 1937, 1938). Tagore knew that there was scope for disagreement or debate on what Gandhi said or did in these matters, and that he himself had admitted his mistakes on so many occasions, but what one must admire is his courage and conviction. In yet another essay penned by Tagore (1931a), he had commented on the Mahatma's frequent use of fasting as a moral and political instrument in the following manner: 'তাঁর উপবাস, সে তো অনুষ্ঠান নয়, সে একটি বাণী, চরম ভাষার বাণী।' (His fast is not an event, it is a statement—in a language of the ultima)! His experience of visiting Gandhiji in Yerawada prison in Pune (in September 1932) to ensure that he agreed to break his fast to join back in normal life is worth reading elsewhere (Tagore 1932b). The telegraphic messages exchanged by the two are also worth looking at.

The indefatigable spirit ('Aparaajeya sankalpa-shakti') must be a thing to admire. How he was able to stay calm even in the wave of nation-wide maddening stirrings is a thing to admire. It is the foundation of his huge personal strength that one must admire, thought Tagore. Lastly, Gandhiji also taught us not to blindly follow the old tradition where they hurt a large section of humanity or the living world. His fight against the blind faith that had deprived a large section eternally assumed a different meaning in his lifetime. This is because he knew that our real freedom would come when we would not be servile to our intolerant and negative traditions—'জাতিভেদ, ধমর্বিরোধ, মূঢ় সংস্কারের আবতের্ যত দিন আমরা চালিত হতে থাকব ততদিন কার সাধয্ আমাদের মুকি্ত দেয়' (As long as we would be driven by the forces of casteism, religious disharmony, and blind prejudices, how could anybody grant us liberation)? It would be more important to fight and win over our internal enemy, and not only wage a war against the external forces.

References

Alam, Fakrul & Radha Chakravarty, eds. 2011. *The Essential Tagore.* Visva-Bharati & Harvard University Press.

Bhattacharya, Sabyasachi. 1997. *The Mahatma and the Poet: Letters and Debates between Gandhi and Tagore 1915-1941.* New Delhi: National Book Trust.

Brecht, Bertolt. 1980. *Bertolt Brecht Diaries,* 1920-22. Edited by Herta Ramthun. London: Routledge.

Carson, Claybourne, ed. 2001. *The Autobiography of Martin Luther King, Jr.* New York: Grand Central Publishing.

Das Gupta, Uma, ed. & tr. 2006. *Rabindranath Tagore: My Life in My Words.* New Delhi: Penguin/Viking.

Gandhi, M.K. 1927. *The Story of My Experiments with Truth,* Vol. 1. Translated from the Gujarati by Mahadev Desai, સત્યના પ્રયોગો અથવા આત્મકથા. London: Penguin Books; Ahmedabad: Navajivan Publishing House.

Kripalani, Krishna K. 1980. *Rabindranath Tagore: A Biography.* Kolkata: Visva-Bharati.

Lukács, George. 1922. Tagore's Gandhi Novel—Review of Rabindranath Tagore: *The Home and the World.* Berlin periodical, *Die rote Fahne.* Also reprinted in 1983: *George Lukács, Essays and Reviews,* Merlin Press. (Retrieved from https://www.marxists.org/archive/lukacs/works/1922/tagore.htm)

Tagore, Rabindranath. 1912. *Jibansmriti* (My Reminiscences). Translated by Surendranath Tagore. Kolkata: Macmillan.

____ (1931a). 'Chautha Ashwin' (Shantiniketan, 4th Ashwin, 1338 Bangabda), *Bichitra,* Kartik, 1339b.

____ (1931b). 'Rashiyar Chithi: To Surendranath Kar' (Moscow, 25th Baishakh, 1338b).

____ (1932a). 'Mahatma-jir Punyabrata' (Shantiniketan, Kartik, 1339 Bangabda), *Prabasi.*

____(1932b). 'Brata Udjapan' (Shantiniketan, Kartik, 1339 Bangabda).

____ (1932c). 'Mahatma-jir Anashan' (Lecture, Shantiniketan, 20th May).

____ (1937). 'Mahatma Gandhi' (Shantiniketan, 16th Ashwin, 1343 Bangabda), *Prabasi*.

____ (1938). 'Gandhiji' (Shantiniketan, Agrahayan, 1344 Bangabda), *Prabasi*.

____ (1940a). *Chhelebela* (Boyhood Days). Kolkata.

____ (1940b) 'Gandhi Maharaj'. *Prabasi*, Phalgun, 1340b.

____ (1943) *Atmaparichay* (Self-Recognition). Kolkata.

____ (1947) *Mahatma Gandhi* (A collection of all biographical sketches and comments of Tagore on Gandhi published in different literary magazines and newspapers). 29th Magh, 1354 Bangabda, Kolkata.

GANDHI'S EXPERIMENTS AND AMBEDKAR'S EXPERIENCES

The Ethics and Perils of Being a Mahatma

Aakash Singh Rathore

Introduction

This paper reads Gandhi's autobiography (*The Story of My Experiments with Truth*) along two discrete but interwoven trajectories: one, internally, in relation to the manner in which his thought more generally is grounded in a deeply visceral orientation. This internal reading homes in on the nature of Gandhi's specific experiments, which, though fascinating, seem to be beset with incoherencies and inconsistencies, as will become apparent in subsequent sections below. The specificity and significance of these visceral experiments are also largely ignored in academic Gandhian scholarship, which tends to represent Gandhi's thought—true to *mahatmahood*—as turned toward upward transcendence rather than toward downward somatization.

Second, Gandhi's experiments will be scrutinized externally in relation to B.R. Ambedkar's own experiences (partly recounted in his autobiographical fragment, *Waiting for a Visa*), which helps us to uncover an even more problematic self-indulgence deep in Gandhi's praxis. We leave untouched the debate over whether Gandhi eventually learned the dangers and drawbacks of his thought and practice from years of engagement with Ambedkar, as several scholars claim. Instead, the paper tarries upon open exploration of the ethics and the perils of *mahatmahood* in the light of Gandhi's experiments and Ambedkar's experiences.

Milk and the Mahatma

We all know of Gandhi as the man who brought down an empire through non-violent civil disobedience. Those of us academics and scholars who work in political philosophy also tie up his trans-continental political activity with his eccentric anti-modernism, as seen in writings such as *Hind Swaraj*. And those who study moral philosophy or epistemology or the philosophy of religion routinely explore his idiosyncratic reinterpretation and application of Jain and other traditional religious ideas such as Anekāntavāda (epistemic pluralism of sorts) and Ahimsa, in relation to his concept of truth, or rather, Truth. In other words, everyone who studies Gandhi seriously recognizes the horizontally interconnected nature of his thinking; that is, the organic lateral interrelations of all of his ideas, whether political, moral, epistemological, and religious.

Insofar as there is a vertical element recognized in Gandhian scholarship, it tends to take shape as the subsumption of everything this-worldly under the transcendent, to God, which is to say, to Truth. This well-established and well-worn path of seeing the orientation of salvation and self-overcoming as being in the upward direction is reinforced even by current a-theistic (if not atheistic) trends to offer a more philosophically rigourous presentation of Gandhi, of Gandhi as (quasi-analytic) philosopher.

It was actually not too long ago that scholars debated whether Gandhi could be regarded as a (political) philosopher at all. Less than twenty years ago, Columbia University professor Akeel Bilgrami published a splendid and widely-read article that served to justify viewing Gandhi as a philosopher. Bilgrami suggested that Gandhi's political strategies were so integrated with abstract epistemological and methodological commitments that his thought took on the quality of bona fide philosophy, albeit not, obviously, academic philosophy.

Bilgrami's efforts met with seemingly universal approbation. There has been no shortage of torchbearers on the topic, an endless schedule of seminars devoted to reading Gandhi as a philosopher, and numerous research theses and doctoral dissertations composed on Gandhi's thought within academic philosophy programmes both in Indian universities and abroad.

Putting to one side, for the moment, what *scholars* say about Gandhi's philosophy, I want to turn toward his own self-representation, partly because of just how enormously divergent these two viewpoints are. The vantage point of Gandhi's self-representation means pulling back the academic-minded readers of Gandhi from the flight to the transcendental. For, a close reading of Gandhi's autobiography reveals that the distinctive vertical element in Gandhi's thought is not 'up there', so to say; it is not a transcendental flight. If there is any especially distinctive verticality involved in the preponderantly horizontal interwoven matrix of Gandhi's philosophical praxis, it is not up toward mentality or way up in the direction of transcendence, but rather a deep-down process of somatization. It is in the descent of ideals and lofty thought down into blood and guts and semen and excreta—for Gandhi, it is the body that serves as the ultimate battle-ground where all is lost or won.

It is interesting to note an inverse parallel between Gandhi and the great German philosopher Friedrich Nietzsche here. Nietzsche had once declared his highest ideal to be a 'Roman Caesar with the soul of Christ' (Nietzsche 1968, 983); ironically, there is a bizarre acceptance-through-inversion of Nietzschean somatization-as-overcoming in Gandhi's notion of Satyagraha, sometimes translated by Gandhi as 'soul-force'. For here, with Gandhi, we have something of a Christ with the soul (force) of a Roman Caesar.

What *The Story of My Experiments with Truth* brings home quite well is that the sharp distinctions drawn between Gandhi's political action, Satyagraha, Ahimsa, Swaraj, and his work on social reform, removal of untouchability, Swadesh, and his obsession with health, diet, exercise, hygiene, and celibacy, are merely academic distinctions. Being academic, they suffer from the broader typical defects of academic research and scholarship. That is, they discount the priority of the body, take flight from the flesh, and ignore the grounding of so-called higher themes (mind, spirit, truth) in their organic embodiment. To take just one example, throughout his autobiography, Gandhi writes at length of civil disobedience, of non-cooperation, of swaraj, of political action of all kinds, but only once does he declare what was for him 'one of the greatest experiments of my life' (Gandhi 2015, 252). What do you think it was?

It was to not drink milk!

And indeed, one surprise after another, what we come finally to learn in the closing pages of the book is that

Gandhi's discomfort with the title Mahatma, the great-soul, which he had mentioned several times throughout the book but without an in-depth explanation, turns out to derive from his persistent worry that he cannot possibly be great-of-soul when he can scarcely resist the temptation of—milk.

For us, perhaps, there is not the slightest doubt that Gandhi was a Mahatma, even in spite of his numerous and in some cases, disastrous flaws. The reader would probably agree that the only two people worth attending to who denied that he was a Mahatma were Dr. Ambedkar and Gandhi himself. Ambedkar suffered terribly from one of Gandhi's disastrous blunders. Feeling deeply betrayed by Gandhi over the Poona Pact episode and the insincerity of the Indian National Congress with respect to the abolition of untouchability in all of its invidious forms, Dr. Ambedkar stated in 1956: 'He was never a Mahatma and I refuse to call him Mahatma' (Ambedkar 1955). Let's further understand Dr. Ambedkar's position.

Ambedkar's Gandhi

> I know Gandhi better than his disciples. They came to him as devotees and saw only the *Mahatma*. I was an opponent, and I saw the *bare man* in him. He showed me his fangs. (Ambedkar 1955)

Gandhi's relationship with other epoch-makers of his time, whether allies like Jawaharlal Nehru, friends like Rabindranath Tagore, or antagonistic rivals like Mohammed Ali Jinnah, was never straightforward, uncomplicated, or free of turbulence. Among the most controversial relationships was that between Gandhi and Dr. B.R. Ambedkar. Scrutinizing the relationship between Gandhi and Ambedkar is of crucial importance to a proper understanding of both of these pioneering figures, in spite of their notorious rivalry. As Upendra Baxi has argued, 'our understanding of leading historic figures like Gandhi or Nehru is bound to remain incomplete, both in the sense of biography and history, in the absence of the grasp of their relations with Ambedkar' (Baxi 1995, 123-4).

The rivalry between Gandhi and Ambedkar lives on through polemics in street-corner debates, newspaper columns, blogs, books, documentary films, and so on, often with aggressive insults parlayed between the pro-Ambedkar, anti-Gandhi group and the pro-Gandhi, anti-Ambedkar group. And indeed, the numerous differences between Gandhi and Ambedkar during their own lifetimes are always evoked in support of the currently-sustained enmity between their followers.

Ramachandra Guha has well capsulated many of these salient differences between Gandhi and Ambedkar:

> Gandhi wished to save Hinduism by abolishing untouchability, whereas Ambedkar saw a solution for his people outside the fold of the dominant religion of the Indian people. Gandhi was a rural romantic, who wished to make the self-governing village the bedrock of free India; Ambedkar an admirer of city life and modern technology who dismissed the Indian village as a den of iniquity. Gandhi was a crypto-anarchist who favoured non-violent protest while being suspicious of the state; Ambedkar a steadfast constitutionalist, who worked within the state and sought solutions to social problems with the aid of the state (Guha 2010, 33).

But what Guha has captured here would seem to be the bases for a perfectly amicable dispute. The Gandhi-Ambedkar dispute was far from cordial. It was, at times, an existential battle, a life-or-death struggle.

The 1932 Poona Pact remained a thorn in the side of Dr. Ambedkar until the end of his life, and the details of its unfolding continue to irk Dalits and Ambedkarites right up to the present day, and for very good reason. Gandhi's hunger fast in defiance of communal voting rights that the British had awarded to the untouchables presented Ambedkar with an agonizing dilemma. Ambedkar had to choose between letting Gandhi starve to death in order to permit the untouchable communities to retain essential voting privileges within democratic elections or, on the other hand, giving in to Gandhi's demand of undivided general elections for the untouchables, thereby undermining their political representation, but saving Gandhi's life.

Ambedkar gave in to Gandhi, the Poona Pact was signed, and Gandhi broke his fast.

After this event, Ambedkar understandably became increasingly bitter toward Gandhi's movement and his biopolitical methods.

Many historians view this unfortunate event as the paradigmatic conflict between Gandhi and Ambedkar. Actually, the situation is far more complicated. In an interview conducted for BBC Radio in 1955, Ambedkar, nearing the end of his life, spoke candidly about Gandhi, withholding none of the acrimony that had accumulated over the years since his coerced submission to Gandhi decades before. In reply to the interviewer's question, 'So, you would say Gandhi was an orthodox Hindu?' Ambedkar answered:

> Yes, he was absolutely an orthodox Hindu. He was never a reformer. He has no dynamics in him, you see. All this talk

> about untouchability was just for the purpose of making the untouchables drawn into the Congress; that was one thing. And secondly, he wanted that the untouchables would not oppose his movement of *Swaraj*. I don't think beyond that he had any motive of uplift (Ambedkar 1955).

In the same interview, Ambedkar characterized Gandhi as a cunning politician, rather than as a Mahatma. He suggested that Gandhi's decisions and declarations relating to the untouchables were based on calculated politics rather than on an appreciation of the inherent injustices of the caste system and the urgent humanitarian need to address it. As far as Ambedkar saw it, Gandhi's deeper motivation was to pack the numbers of Hindus by including the numerous scheduled castes within this section, as against independent communities like Sikhs and Muslims.

For his part, Gandhi sought without success to continue to lure Ambedkar into his own fold. In a letter from Gandhi to Ambedkar (dated 6th August 1944), Gandhi wrote:

> I know to my cost that you and I hold different views on this very important question [i.e. untouchability]. And I know, too, that on broad politics of the country we see things from different angles. I would love to find a meeting ground between us on both the questions. I know your great ability and I would love to own you as a colleague and co-worker. But I must admit my failure to come nearer to you. If you can show me a way to a common meeting ground between us I would like to see it. Meanwhile, I must reconcile myself to the present unfortunate difference (Gandhi 1958, 272).

As is apparent from Ambedkar's 1955 assessment, the 'present unfortunate difference' to which Gandhi had to reconcile himself was not itself reconciled in any subsequent events. The politics of the era pitted Gandhi and Ambedkar as antagonists on too many issues, and on issues so crucial to their persons and personalities that the bridging of their divide remained impossible.

Ambedkar firmly believed that Gandhi remained attached to an idealized version of the varna system, a system against which Ambedkar was inalterably and profoundly opposed, and, indeed, intent on completely 'annihilating'. Ambedkar's systematic polemic writings against Gandhi, including *Mr Gandhi and the Emancipation of the Untouchables* and *What Congress and Gandhi Have Done to the Untouchables,* are full of numerous citations of Gandhi on the question of varna, quoted with venomous disdain and contempt by the egalitarian Ambedkar. He sketches the progression of Gandhi's ideas on the subject from his early South Africa days to the end of his life, attempting to show that Gandhi's subtle differentiation between caste and varna amounts to mere rhetoric.

Moreover, in starkest possible contrast to Gandhi's romanticist nostalgia for a pre-modern organization of human social and political economy, Ambedkar was an irrepressible pro-enlightenment modernist. Gandhi and Ambedkar remained fixed in these fundamental beliefs. Thus, although Gandhi and Ambedkar both understood themselves to be champions of the emancipation of the untouchables, their conceptions *from what* and *into what* the untouchables were being emancipated were radically and fundamentally at variance.

Despite this, many scholars believe that Gandhi's ideas came closer to Ambedkar toward the last decade of his life. Harold G. Coward argues forcefully that because 'of continually having to contend with Ambedkar's critique' Gandhi's ideas on the political activity of the untouchables and indeed his ideas on varna changed from the 1940s onwards. Coward makes a special point to mention Gandhi's support for appointing Ambedkar to chair the Constituent Assembly's constitutional drafting committee, even in the face of opposition, as well as sundry remarks of Gandhi, such as appointing a 'chaste and brave Bhangi girl' as president of the new India.

These and similar arguments about Gandhi's changing position toward the end of his life raise perhaps a reasonable doubt about the issue of varnashrama constituting one of the principle bedrocks for the irreconcilability of Gandhi and Ambedkar. But one cannot fail to mention that Ambedkar himself was unconvinced of this argument, and perhaps he deserves the last word on whether his understanding of Gandhi's later position was more reconcilable with his own.

In fairness, it should be noted that a larger share of Gandhians have indeed come over to Ambedkar's position on the need to annihilate caste in order to establish egalitarian justice, and at least in this respect, the contemporary Gandhian and Ambedkarite camps have far less justification for mutual antagonism.

Ambedkar himself remained unconvinced of any change in Gandhi's position, despite the evidence that certain scholars have proffered to show that Gandhi moved closer to Ambedkar's position in the last years of his life. Hence Dr. Ambedkar's 1956 assessment: 'He was never a Mahatma and I refuse to call him Mahatma. He doesn't deserve that title. Not even from the point of view of his morality' (Ambedkar 1955).

What is especially intriguing and noteworthy is that there is evidence in Gandhi's autobiography that he himself would have agreed with Ambedkar's assessment.

Gandhian Experiments

In the Introduction to his autobiography, Gandhi notes that it is his experiments in the political field that have won him the title of Mahatma, a title he does not value, and one that has deeply pained him as well. But, to not value the title and to not deserve it are quite different. Gandhi is clear, only on the final page of his autobiography, why it is not a title that he deserves: 'To attain perfect purity one has to become absolutely passion-free in thought, speech, and action. I know that I have not in me yet the triple purity. That is why the world's praise fails to move me, indeed it very often stings me' (Gandhi 2015, 451). But Gandhi sets the standard unnaturally high while also, I believe, endeavouring in earnest to achieve it, despite the many well-known human episodes of backsliding.

All these endeavours of his are what he calls 'experiments', and I think we would do well to turn our attention to the nature and number of Gandhi's experiments. I find these endlessly fascinating and compelling, and I should probably disclose that for the last few years, I have been practising several of them myself, especially the somatic ones, those related to dietetics and exercise, in an effort to see what intellectual or spiritual effects these might have. This is why, despite the fact that he never offers either sophisticated argumentation or scientific evidence, I nevertheless exuberantly endorse Gandhi's view-point, which he magisterially pronounces to have arisen simply from his own conviction:

> I know it is argued that the soul has nothing to do with what one eats or drinks, as the soul neither eats nor drinks; that it is not what you put inside from without, but what you express outwardly from within, that matters. I shall

> content myself with merely declaring my firm conviction that restraint in diet both as to quantity and quality is as essential as restraint in thought and speech (Gandhi 2015, 252).

Some argumentation would probably have helped. Especially when you contemplate this motley list of experiences that can be culled out from his autobiography, each one of which Gandhi locked himself on to as an 'experiment', but for us with seemingly no coherent centre to unify them: eating meat; listening patiently to Christian missionaries; implementing the proverb 'return good for evil'; learning to dance; cooking English food; physical exercise; walking instead of using transportation; taking lodgers; using idle kids for labour; learning the violin; not educating children in the 'three Rs'; eating uncooked food; washing his own shirt collars; living a life of ease and comfort; hydropathy and earth treatments; giving up milk; writing an autobiography; living with white people; treating a broken arm; giving up salt; satyagraha; fasting; celibacy; attempting to discover a true system of pedagogy; mixing morally good children with morally bankrupt ones to see who influences whom; eating only raw vegetables; 'medical experiments'; 'ethical experiments'; swaraj; ahimsa.

I have enumerated here only those specific events that Gandhi explicitly refers to as an experiment in his book. There are numerous other quite experimental things that he did, but chose not to refer to explicitly as experiments. Consider, for example, his invitation to a family of 'untouchables' to live in the Satyagraha Ashram in 1915. He referred to this as a 'test' rather than an experiment—what is the difference exactly? He does not bother to say. For this reason, perusing this list of Gandhi's explicitly entitled 'experiments' might remind the reader of Jorge Luis Borges' story about the wonderful Chinese encyclopaedia, *The Celestial Emporium of Benevolent Knowledge,* that gives a taxonomy of all the known animals:

> Those that belong to the Emperor; embalmed ones; those that are trained; suckling pigs; mermaids; fabulous ones; stray dogs; those included in the present classification; those that tremble as if they were mad; innumerable ones; those drawn with a very fine camelhair brush; et cetera; those that have just broken a flower vase; those that from a long way off look like flies. (Borges 1999, 231).

Especially splendid is 'those included in the present classification'. And indeed, if you look back somewhere in the middle of the list of Gandhian experiments, you find something similar: 'writing an autobiography'. As Gandhi puts it, 'I am not writing the autobiography to please critics. Writing is itself one of the experiments with truth' (Gandhi 2015, 258).

One thing all Gandhian experiments seem to have in common is that they are exercises in 'translating into practice anything that appealed to the intellect' (Gandhi 2015, 273). They are embodiments of ideals, literally: in-body-ments. A thought, idea, or principle that could not be put into practice was not a thought, idea, or principle worth having. This, I think, is one of the most powerful and admirable aspects of Gandhi's life and work. To distil it into a well-known Americanism, 'you have to walk the talk'. But let us be clear. This is not all about choice. It is not just a question of wanting to translate thought into practice and choosing to do, or not to do, so. There is also a causally determined, irrepressible expression of body in all our actions, of flesh in spirit.

Hence the compelling nature of the very first experiment that Gandhi mentions in his autobiography, from when he was just a child, the experiment of eating meat:

> I wished to be strong and daring and wanted my countrymen also to be such, so that we might defeat the English and make India free. The word 'Swaraj' I had not yet heard. But I knew what freedom meant (Gandhi 2015, 35).

In reference to this experiment as well as to the idea of swaraj, Gandhi cites this telling ditty,

> Behold the mighty Englishman
> He rules the Indian small,
> Because being a meat-eater
> He is five cubits tall. (2015, 34)

Although obviously Gandhi's thoughts on swaraj evolve most profoundly as he matures, one thing never changes throughout his life: swaraj remains always about embodiment; the realization of the ideal in the flesh; in one's own body, and in the body politic. Overcoming political slavery is secondary to the primary bodily base, mastering the self, not being passion's slave.

For Gandhi, self-mastery is deeper than and prior to politics. Its experiments occur in the areas of dietetics, health, exercise, and celibacy. Note that: celibacy and not sexuality. Brahmacharya qualified as an experiment; his five experiences with prostitutes, on the other hand, were mere shameful whoring. This might be the atavism of traditional moralism or, worse, the grip of orthodox ideas upon him. But I suppose, more charitably, that it is due to the essential and organic interrelation of the body-centred experiments with the principles of Ahimsa and Truth. For example, back again to the subject of milk, Gandhi writes,

> My experiments in dietetics are dear to me as a part of my researches in Ahimsa...But my use of goat's milk today troubles me not from the viewpoint of dietetic Ahimsa so much as from that of Truth (408).

However, to be sure, there may also be an element of simple conservatism that dictates what may or may not qualify as a bona fide experiment. Or more than conservatism, a discernible puritanism—a particularly Christian puritanism to boot. It is, after all, abundantly clear that Gandhi's understanding of his own religious tradition, of its scriptures, strictures, theology, and more, was heavily filtered through protestant Christian teaching, language, symbolism, and worldview. This took every possible manner of manifestation, from the Semitization of Hinduism in line with the likes of Vinayak Savarkar and innumerable others of the era (including elevating the *Gita* to the status of the 'Hindu Bible'), to the reframing of the meaning of Hindu religiosity in such Christian terms as 'God-fearing', or referring to God as 'one's maker', and so on and so forth, to the extremely puritan articulation of the body as the locus of 'sin', and the flesh as 'evil' and 'the devil's abode'. Therefore, any attempt to understand the theories and practices of somatizing, of embodying, in Gandhi's life and work must first puncture through, must excavate and distinguish, the layers of the puritan Christian language and worldview that, willy-nilly, was sedimented in his thoughts and enveloped him.

In spite of all that language and expression, what I have been trying to suggest is that for Gandhi, at least the Gandhi of *The Story of My Experiments with Truth*, the realization of that truth is through, and only through, its embodiment. The body is the metric, the measure of what has or has not been achieved on the road to truth. This helps to account for a number of the more nebulous and disjointed statements that Gandhi made, as well as the Celestial Emporium-style nature of his list of experiments; their wild disjunctures find unity when each event is refracted through the prism of the flesh. It also helps to shed some light on his enigmatic declaration, so contrary to his equally frequent theological account of a conscious Christian anthropomorphic Creator, that there is no other God than Truth, that God is otherwise empty of all content, character, and consciousness. Every other aspect of God is incarnate, in us.

Remaining sensitive to the central role of the body in Gandhi's thought, it becomes rather easier to accept his many neglected and otherwise cognitively inassimilable declamations on dietetics and health that never fail to baffle academic scholars. This is, however, not to blithely suggest that it is easy to understand what Gandhi was trying to say. He was so conflictedly and inescapably immersed in a theology that at the same time deified fleshly incarnation and demonized the human body as such, that Gandhi was bound to posit a battery of contradictory ideas.

Ambedkar's Experiences versus Gandhi's Experiments

In Dr. Ambedkar's own autobiographical writing, *Waiting for a Visa,* he recounted experiences from his youth that gradually awoke him to the indignities imposed upon him due to his prescribed social status in the Hindu social order:

> I knew that I was an untouchable and that untouchables were subjected to certain indignities and discriminations. For instance, I knew that in the school I could not sit in the midst of my class students according to my rank but

> that I was to sit in a corner by myself. I knew that in the school I was to have a separate piece of gunny cloth for me to squat on in the class room and the servant employed to clean the school would not touch the gunny cloth used by me (Ambedkar 1993).

Reading Ambedkar's life narrative, one gets a sense of the urgency for direct and immediate action against the deleterious effects of caste. Not so for Gandhi, or at least for Dr. Ambedkar's Gandhi. Dr. Ambedkar argued that the social and moral consequences of caste separation espoused by Gandhi in his ideal theory of varna were degrading to those condemned hereditarily, in that ideal system, to serve the other varnas: 'It educates them into slaves and creates all the psychological complex which follows from a slave mentality. There is, on the one hand, tyranny, vanity, pride, arrogance, greed, selfishness' in the varnas, hereditarily entitled to service from others; 'and, on the other hand, insecurity, poverty, degradation, loss of liberty' as well as loss of self-reliance, loss of independence and loss of 'dignity and self-respect' for those condemned merely to serve. Dr. Ambedkar brought to summation his appraisal of the social, political and psychological consequences of Gandhi's ideal theory of varna with these damning words: 'Democratic society cannot be indifferent to such consequences. But Gandhism does not mind these consequences in the least' (Ambedkar 1991).

In short, not only were Gandhian experiments internally incoherent and haphazard, when read externally against lived experiences such as those of Dr. Ambedkar, they were also self-indulgent, blind to the social realities that they toyed with, and ultimately supportive of a social system that degraded and humiliated a large portion of the population.

Conclusion

As mentioned, the debate remains open as to whether Gandhi came late in life to agree with these assessments of Ambedkar with respect to the degrading consequences of his views on varna. With respect to haphazardness, however, Gandhi did try hard to present a coherent set of propositions to enlighten the thoughts he was embodying through practice. There is a formula that serves as something of a key to his mapping of all the variegated experiments and is presented on his autobiography's closing pages. There it is reiterated, first of all, that there is no other God than Truth. And then, to take it further, that the only realization of Truth is Ahimsa. But the realization of Ahimsa, in turn, relies upon self-purification: 'Without self-purification the observance of the law of Ahimsa must remain an empty dream' (Gandhi 2015, 450).

This clear somatological declension that begins by equating God to Truth, Truth to Ahimsa, and then the preconditioning of Ahimsa on self-purification, is immediately obfuscated by the way it is given in a puritanical-theological re-expression by Gandhi as, 'God can never be realized by one who is not pure of heart' (Gandhi 2015, 450).

This self-purification is, as we have already seen earlier when discussing Gandhi's title of 'Mahatma', a triple purity in thought, speech, and action. This is something Gandhi points out that he has yet to achieve. How is it to be achieved? Gandhi tells us that it can only be achieved through non-attachment.

Now, the precise method of achieving this required non-attachment upon which the entire edifice of the formula 'self-purification-for-Ahimsa-for-Truth-which-is-God' is built, is summarized by Gandhi with an economy of expression found nowhere else in this long-winding and multidimensional autobiography. He states it so simply—but who on earth knows what it means?

We close with the stark, naked brevity of Gandhi's method: 'I must reduce myself to zero' (Gandhi 2015, 451).

References

Ambedkar, B.R. 1955. BBC Interview, https://www.youtube.com/watch?v=omGcgEstVIE.

Ambedkar, B.R. 1991. *Babasaheb Ambedkar: Writings and Speeches.* Vol. 9. Bombay Education Department, Government of India.

Ambedkar, B.R. 1993. Waiting for a Visa. *Babasaheb Ambedkar: Writings and Speeches.* Vol. 12. Bombay Education Department, Government of India.

Baxi, Upendra. 1995. Justice as Emancipation. In *Crisis and Change and Contemporary India,* ed. Upendra Baxi and Bhikhu Parekh. New Delhi: Sage.

Borges, Jorge Luis. 1999. John Wilkins' Analytical Language. *Selected Nonfictions.* Harmondsworth: Penguin.

Gandhi, M.K. 1958. *The Collected Works of Mahatma Gandhi.* New Delhi: Publications Division, Government of India.

Gandhi, M.K. 2015. *Autobiography: The Story of My Experiments with Truth.* Boston: Beacon Press.

Guha, Ramachandra. 2010. Gandhi's Ambedkar. In *Indian Political Thought: A Reader,* ed. Aakash Singh Rathore and Silika Mohapatra. London: Routledge.

Nietzsche, Friedrich. 1968. *The Will to Power.* New York: Vintage.

GANDHI AND BOSE

Nikhil Katara

The relationship between Gandhi and Subhas Chandra Bose is an important one for various reasons. The two are often quoted, and remembered for their support towards the cause of the Indian freedom struggle, though they are also accepted to be different from each other as far as ideological principles are concerned. Gandhi, with an interest in fighting for freedom through non-violent means, is often considered to be at odds with Bose, who was willing to adopt military means to fight for India's freedom struggle. The conversation regarding Bose and Gandhi has been appropriated, and misappropriated, in the course of India's history multiple times, and the reasons for the same have been many, but what would be a good starting point for this argument for us would be to explore the ideologies of Bose and Gandhi individually first.

Bose was a radical thinker, but to form a vision towards the national goal, he needed time to reflect. That time was offered to him by the Behrampore and Mandalay jails, where he put down his observations in the form of reflections in a jail notebook.

On a national movement, he wrote that Bengal needed a real national movement which is neither political, nor jingoistic. He meant a movement that affected many spheres of social and political lives and many sections of the community. He focussed specifically on the creative spirit and laid emphasis on the fields of poetry, music, painting, sculpture, and other fields of religious and commercial life. He wanted to remove inequality from society as such. His idealism extended towards the business community as well. Culturally he wanted to generate poets, historians, philosophers and economists who had the creative spirit to make India stand up and have an identity for itself in the fields of science and culture (Bose 2016, 42).

In his jail reflections Subhas developed a new ethical code for India. He drew up a nine-point code which gave emphasis on honour and self-respect, love for the country, thoughts on sannyasa, importance of brahmacharya and the ethical value of people's lives based on civic and national duty. He gave importance to the nature of truth in this code and equated it to beauty (Bose 2016, 53).

Mohandas Gandhi on the other hand was an ardent believer in the use of ahimsa as the basis of his search for truth. He explains it in his autobiography, *The Story of My Experiments with Truth*. 'I am realizing every day that the search is in vain unless it is founded on ahimsa as the basis. It is quite proper to resist and attack a system, but to resist and attack its author is tantamount to resisting and attacking oneself. For we are all tarred with the same brush, and are children of one and the same Creator, and as such the divine powers within us are infinite. To slight a single human being is to slight those divine powers, and thus to harm not only that being but with him the whole world' (Gandhi, n.d.).

The nature of truth was a matter of consideration, and he ruminated initially that 'God is Truth' and later revised it to 'Truth is God'. In *The Story of My Experiments with Truth* Gandhi explains that his uniform experience convinced him that there is no other God than Truth. He emphasized the fact that truth can only be attained by a complete realization of Ahimsa and by no other means (Gandhi, n.d.).

It can be observed that both Bose and Gandhi were principled men who spent time developing their philosophy that fuelled their fight for the national freedom struggle. For Gandhi, ahimsa became the primary political tool to attain this, but for Bose the same was one among many tools. This was one of the points on which they disagreed. In 'The National Struggle' Subhas noted that a single incident at Chauri Chaura was used to strangle a national movement. He criticized Gandhi to not consult representatives from different provinces before calling off the civil disobedience movement (Bose 2016, 64).

Gandhi, in a letter to Sarat Chandra Bose on 9th April 1926, wrote, 'I know there is an alternative to the Charkha and that is rowdyism, but I am useless at it and what is more, I have no faith in it. And as a practical man, I know that our rowdyism is nothing compared to the rowdyism of the government. I have therefore burnt my boats and staked my all on the Charkha. I invite you and all who are troubled by the knowledge of the many woes of the nation to join me in the effort. Believe me it requires all the skill, all the discipline, all the organising power that we can summon to its aid' (Bose 2016, 70).

While these were points on which they disagreed, they did have a healthy respect for each other. In a broadcast by Subhas Chandra Bose on 16th July 1945, Subhas was noted to say that he was no outsider to the Congress and that he had always given the Congress his best. He classified the Congress as an integral component of himself and he only spoke out against it when he observed gross errors in the conduct of the Congress working committee (Prasad 2008, 77).

Maulana Azad, in his autobiography, *India Wins Freedom*, observed that Bose's escape to Germany had an impression on Gandhi. There were various actions of Bose that Gandhi didn't agree with, but Gandhi admired Subhas Bose for the way in which he escaped from India (Bose 2016, 150).

In a telephonic interview with Madhuri Bose, grand-niece of Subhas Chandra Bose, she was noted as saying, 'Both Netaji and Mahatma Gandhi firmly believed that all the people of India, irrespective of caste, religion and gender should be able to live together in peace and harmony.' Meanwhile Sugata Bose, who is a historian and grand-nephew of Subhas Chandra Bose, mentioned that many differences between Gandhi and Bose are highly exaggerated and he notes that their relationship was marked by mutual appreciation and a sense of admiration for each other (Jha 2019).

This echoes the fact that it was Bose who gave Gandhi the title 'Father of the Nation'. In his last radio address from Burma in 1944, Bose said, 'Father of our Nation! In this holy war for India's liberation, we ask for your blessings and good wishes.' And so it can be concluded, that while there were differences in the approach of how Bose and Gandhi would have liked to fight for India's freedom, they both respected each other, and wanted a secular India, free from British control (Dutta 2020).

References

Bose, Madhuri. 2016. The Road to Mandalay. In *The Bose Brothers and Indian Independence: An Insider's Account,* 36-61. New Delhi: Sage Publications.

Bose, Madhuri. 2016. Bose Brothers and Gandhi. In *The Bose Brothers and Indian Independence: An Insider's Account,* 116-154. New Delhi: Sage Publications.

Bose, Madhuri. 2016. Swaraj Beckons, Swaraj Denied. In *The Bose Brothers and Indian Independence: An Insider's Account,* 62-115. New Delhi: Sage Publications.

Gandhi, Mohandas. n.d. *The Story of My Experiments with Truth.* Accessed November 5, 2020. https://www.mkgandhi.org/ebks/An-Autobiography.pdf

Jha, Satish. 2019. Differences between Gandhi & Bose highly exaggerated. *Deccan Herald,* October 1. https://www.deccanherald.com/national/differences-between-gandhi-bose-highly-exaggerated-754950.html

Dutta, Prabhakar. 2020. Subhas Chandra Bose, Mahatma Gandhi and Nehru: Admirers or adversaries? A myth buster. *India Today,* January 23. https://www.indiatoday.in/news-analysis/story/subhas-chandra-bose-mahatma-gandhi-nehru-admirers-or-adversaries-myth-buster-1639417-2020-01-23

Prasad, Bimal, ed. 2008. Towards Freedom: Documents on the Movement for Independence in India 1945. New Delhi: Oxford University Press.

SOME REMARKS ON GANDHI'S AND TAGORE'S PHILOSOPHIES OF LOVE

Indrani Bhattacharjee

This paper engages with the conceptions of love professed by two highly original Indian thinkers at around the same time in very different circumstances. In December 1908, the poet Rabindranath Tagore began writing a series of philosophical and spiritual reflections that went on to become the text of Shantiniketan, a mostly untranslated set of addresses, exhortations and essays on chiefly philosophical themes. The work was undertaken in the same year that the poet suffered a personal tragedy, the loss of his youngest son. The death of this child marked the height of a long spell of grief and bereavement in Tagore's life, and the beginning of a period of tremendous creativity. The English *Gitanjali* was published in 1912, ushering in several years of extraordinary international acclaim. The serial publication of Shantiniketan (hereinafter, *SN*) was concluded in 1916.

Mohandas Gandhi wrote the Gujarati text of *Hind Swaraj* on board a ship from England to South Africa in November 1909, over a ten-day-long period of creative ferment. An

English translation by his own hand followed in 1910; its title page, reproduced in the Critical Edition (Sharma and Suhrud, 2010, hereinafter *HS*), bearing the curious and characteristic notation 'No Rights Reserved.' The text is unadorned, urgent, bold and often impassioned in tone. Gandhi himself regarded it 'as his seed text' (*HS*, xi), by which I understand the primary locus of his philosophy of life, which included his political ideas. From a Tagorean perspective, *HS* is that authentic creation that expresses the creative personality of its author—the result of the author's giving himself to the object created. An awareness of such authorial commitment would appear to have liberated him from laying claim upon the work thus produced.

SN is also a seed text in one sense. Within it one can discern the contours of Tagore's unique assimilation of the Advaita of the *Upaniṣads*, ideas lifted from the earliest texts of Indian Buddhism, various expressions of medieval Indian spirituality and ethics, and the aesthetics associated with classical Indian literature. Tagore presented his philosophical thinking in English at various points in the final three decades of his life, beginning with *Sādhanā: The Realization of Life* (1913), and quite often what he said in such writings and addresses was expressed with more sophistication and economy than in *SN*. However, at no point does one see him depart very radically from what he professed in his first lengthy work of philosophical prose. In this essay, we will focus on some of the earliest essays in what was published as Volume I of *SN* (Tagore 1988), all of which was written in the period between December 1908 and December 1909.

The present essay is an attempt to focus, in a partially decontextualized way, on the conceptions of love developed by both authors in these texts. In *HS*, the matter is discussed by way of reflecting upon the meaning of satyāgraha, and the relationship of 'self-suffering' with love for one's fellow-being. Bhikhu Parekh (1989, 2001) uses the term 'suffering love' to characterize the notion that is examined here. Since the argument below makes fairly liberal use of Parekh's own understanding of Gandhi's view, some parts of the view ascribed to Gandhi are later developments of, but more or less consistent with, the 'seed' ideas presented in *HS*. This was unavoidable given the brevity of the discussion of love in *HS*. A second caveat is in order. No attempt has been made to undertake the onerous task of tracing and explicating the many elaborations of Tagore's conception of love by way of his literary works, in part because this author is not qualified to undertake such an examination.

The present project is rather more limited. Both Gandhi and Tagore unequivocally affirm that love (prem in both *SN* and the Hindi rendering of *HS*) and renunciation (tyāg in Tagore's Bengali) or what Parekh calls 'detachment' on Gandhi's behalf are conceptually interdependent. Yet, the implications that each draws from this concerning the nature of love differ in important ways. What follows is an exploration of these differences, together with outline accounts of the self, understood both as a metaphysical construct and as being-in-the-world, that are associated with these views. It is suggested below that given the following reading of Gandhi's remarks in *HS*, satyāgraha ought to be understood as creative work of a particular sort—the kind of creative work that does not bring into existence something that did not exist before, but rather the kind that strives to nurture and *thus* bring to light something of value. In Gandhi's understanding, what are thus brought to light are aspects of our shared humanity. A robust defence of satyāgraha as care[12]—in the sense used by ethicists of care—seems possible, but that would go beyond the brief of this paper.

I. *Hind Swaraj*: Love as 'Soul-force'

Let us begin by attending to a couple of remarks in Chapters 16 and 17 of the text of *HS*. In Chapter 16, Gandhi compares two kinds of resistance or 'force' that groups may offer in support of a petition to rulers. The first of these involves a threat of violence if not violence itself, in case the group's demands are not met. Since he cannot find moral arguments to justify the use of violence, he approves a second variety of force in such situations, which manifests as a declaration to the rulers that 'You can govern us only so long as we remain *the governed; we shall no longer have any dealing with you*' (*HS*, 70; emphasis in original). This he goes on to label in three ways, namely, as 'love-force' (*dayābal*), 'soul-force' (*ātmabal*), and 'passive resistance' (satyāgraha), cautioning the reader about the somewhat inaccurate nature of the third label.

At first the term 'soul' may strike one as odd; for all practical purposes, the term *ātmān* used as a prefix can be translated as 'self' in English, and into its cognates in most

---

[12] Tagore saw clearly that Gandhi's mission involved care-work. The binary of manly/effeminate being alien to his way of thinking, it was natural for him to ascribe an inspirational and wise maternal role to Gandhi—perhaps akin to that of Vidulā in the Mahabharata—in a letter written on the eve of the Jallianwala Bagh massacre. 'And you have come to your motherhood,' he wrote, 'to remind [India] of her mission, to lead her in the true path of conquest, to purge her present-day politics of its feebleness which imagines that it has gained its purpose when it struts in the borrowed feathers of diplomatic dishonesty' (Bhattacharya 1997, p. 56).

Indian languages (e.g., *ātmanirbhara*). There also exists a standard use of the term in Advaita Vedānta, to be found in at least one juncture in the *Bhagavadgītā,*[13] a text with which Gandhi was intimately acquainted. Why does Gandhi go with 'soul' instead? It would seem that this use is consistent with Gandhi's constant focus on the spiritual nature of human beings, which he saw as providing the ontological basis for moral motivation in general (Parekh 2001, 93).

The equation of soul-force with love-force is the next thing that needs tackling. Chapter 17 of *HS* begins with Gandhi quoting the poet Tulsidas, upholding the second line of the verse quoted (translated 'Therefore, we should not abandon pity so long as we shall live') as 'scientific truth' (*HS*, 72; *śāstra vacan* in both Gujarati and the Hindi translation). Gandhi's gloss on this line from Tulsi is presented in the next sentence: 'The force of love [dayābal] is the same as the force of the soul or truth.' Sharma and Suhrud explain in a

---

[13] *uddhared ātmanātmānaṁ nātmānam avasādayet/ ātmaiva hyātmano bandhuh ātmaiva ripurātmanah//bandhurātmātmanah tasya yenātmaivātmanā jitah/ anātmanastu śatrutve vartetātmaiva śatruvat//* VI: 5-6.

Radhakrishnan's translation of the text (which, incidentally, is dedicated to 'Mahātmā Gāndhi') preserves the distinction between two senses of the term in the following way:

> Let a man lift himself by himself; let him not degrade himself; for the Self alone is the friend of the self and the Self alone is the enemy of the self. For him who has conquered his (lower) self by the (higher) Self his Self is a friend but for him who has not conquered his (higher) Self, his very Self will act in enmity, like an enemy (1963, 189-190).

'The (higher) Self' here refers to the metaphysical unity called either ātmān or brahman by Advaitins, depending on the scope of the term. 'The (lower) self' is simply 'the empirical self' or jīva in this context. See Parekh (1989, 91-93) for his discussion of Gandhi's rendition of the relationship between the empirical self and ātmān.

footnote that the Gujarati term dayābal is used by Gandhi to express a 'disposition suffused with the Christian idea of love.' We shall return to this a little later. The jump from 'love-force' to 'soul-force' is explained by reference to the overarching Advaitic philosophy to which Gandhi subscribed. Parekh (1989, 90) explains Gandhi's rendition of non-dualism in terms of three precepts or 'principles':

(i) 'The *unity of man*';
(ii) 'The *unity of life,*' which has implications for the relations that human beings enter into with one another and the natural world, and;
(iii) 'The *unity of creation*' expressed and experienced as harmony, which has implications for human conduct in the world.

Precept (ii) delineates the realm of moral action, whereas (iii) gestures toward spiritual discipline, manifested in, for example, the attitude of trusteeship that a wealthy person bears towards her property, or in the attempt to bring about harmonious relations through dialogue aided by love-force. Precept (i) states a fundamental ethical implication of non-dualism, and is therefore taken by Gandhi as unquestionably true. Parekh points out that the three precepts above describe the scope of the non-dualist ontology at different levels of conceptualization.

It helps to read Gandhi's equation of self-force and love-force in the light of non-dualism, as rendered in terms of precepts (i) and (ii). Any act by an individual human being has consequences for the unitary fabric (where 'act' stands for any expression of the person's individuality or *soul,* as Gandhi calls it), since all persons are always already tied together in a single spiritual (*ātmika*) bond—*sūtre maṇigaṇā iva,* like precious stones on a thread, as the *Bhagavadgītā* (VII: 7; Radhakrishnan 1963, 215) would have it. Gandhi argues that the existence of a spiritual bond, and thus of love between persons favourably placed in relation to one another is the natural way of things. This implies that occasional rifts between such persons are either aberrations or something worse—large wrinkles willed by individuals into a fundamental cosmic unity. This thought appears to him in a flash of insight, reflected in ordinary facts about human relationships.

Thousands, indeed tens of thousands, depend on their existence on a very active working of [love-] force. Little quarrels of millions of families in their daily lives disappear before the exercise of this force... History is really a record of every interruption of the even working of the force of love or of the soul. Two brothers quarrel; *one of them repents and reawakens the love that was lying dormant in him;* the two again begin to live in peace; nobody takes note of this. But two brothers, through the intervention of solicitors or some other reason, take up arms or go to law—which is another form of exhibition of brute force—their doings would be immediately noticed in the press, they would be the talk of the neighbourhood, and would probably go down to history. And what is true of families *and communities is also true of nations...* History, then, is a record of an *interruption of the course of nature* (*HS,* 72-73; emphases in original).

Gandhi's fulminations against the professions of medicine and lawyering (*HS,* Chapters 12 and 13) are best understood in the light of his conviction of the non-dualist thesis: both in his view involve disregarding, obscuring or profiting off violations of the precepts above. For example, lawyers live off disputes rather than their resolution on grounds of truth: truth becomes hostage to the manner in which judicial proceedings are organized, thus making genuine reconciliation impossible.[14]

The notion that the work of love-force is constant, though often interrupted by the opposing flow of human self-interest, dictates Gandhi's ideas concerning rightful conduct (dharma) of human beings. A person's humanity is expressed in other-regarding behaviour, and respectful, non-disruptive, non-violent conduct towards all existence. Satyāgraha is the performance of such conduct in a manner that highlights the agent's self-sacrifice in her attempt to align her actions, and thus herself, with the 'natural' order or cosmic harmony. As a political act, it involves undertaking personal suffering instead of retaliating against injustice with violence. Without the satyāgrahī's/passive resister's readiness to undertake suffering, her expression of dissent would likely fail to jolt the other into recognizing the common chain of being or humanity that binds them together. The underlying metaphysical truth of non-dualism is obscured by the visible diversities among people. It isn't likely to be grasped in the emotionally fraught circumstances of enacted political dissent. Thus the satyāgrahī must internalize this truth in her daily

[14] The reader would be justified in her sense of outrage, given that one continues to hear of judgments in Indian courts suggesting that a rapist marry the person raped, and injustices against historically wronged groups go unpunished. However, as Parekh explains, it is neither just love nor mere suffering that produces effective satyāgraha (thus indicating the soundness of the principles on which it is established). Suffering could well be accompanied by anger and reproof, in which case it has no value either morally or when understood as a political stratagem. Expressions of love, on the other hand, need not rely on a political campaign. For Gandhi, '[L]ove spiritualized suffering, which in itself had only a psychological value; suffering gave love its psychological energy and moral power' (2001, 70-71). The best analogue for suffering love may be the passion and suffering of Christ on the cross.

conduct as a matter of spiritual discipline. Her readiness as well as commitment to satyāgraha is tested in the course of political action, when, in the face of obvious injustice, she must engage in a dramatization of the essential human unity.

It will be seen that the satyāgrahī's act of dissent is both an expression of self-force (i.e., her commitment to the humanistic principle derived from the thesis of non-dualism) and love-force (i.e., her love for the other, expressed as overt acceptance of suffering in an attempt to make whole the *ātmika*/human bond between them). Parekh (1989, 149) emphasizes that satyāgraha is 'a 'surgery of the soul' made necessary by the opponent's refusal to talk or to do so in a spirit of humility, sincerity and good-will'. It is clear that the practice of satyāgraha makes possible expansion of the self through regard for the other—a dimension of love that few would deny. It is a *humanistic* moral practice, since at its core is a commitment to valuing humanity in both oneself and the other.

One should note in passing, however, that such a rendering of love makes it elusive *as an affect*. What Gandhi's view of love skirts completely is the valuing of the other for her characteristics or virtues, that is to say, valuing a concrete other. One has a glimpse of such love in Emerson's account of friendship between persons, and in the self-affirming regard for Jesus, not as a deity or King, but in 'the style of friendship to a good and noble heart,' the sort of regard that makes room for 'sallies of admiration and love' (Emerson 2000, 69)[15] from fellow humans. Emerson's creative rendition of the imitation of Christ through a friendly appreciation of Jesus provides an especially useful counterpoint to the view discussed above.

---

[15] From 'An Address', the extraordinary, iconoclastic address that Emerson made at the Harvard Divinity School in 1838.

This is because, like Gandhi, Emerson is a great advocate of self-reliance in thought and action, and does not fail to affirm the self in love (or friendship). But his conception of love captures its affective dimension: Emerson expressly speaks of acknowledging the other's being for all that it is worth in the subject's eyes, making possible an exchange or dialectic between two persons that results in mutual growth. The example of Christ is useful for a second reason. In the context of satyāgraha the gesture of love is made from a moral high ground, since, among other things, the dissenter seeks to remind the oppressor of her own humanity, and its presence in others, including those that she oppresses. There is no place in the account for coming to discover lacunae in oneself as a result of *loving* or *being friends with* someone one recognizes as being one's moral equal, or superior.[16]

Parekh (1989, 147; 2001, 64-65) argues in effect that the Gandhian principle of non-violence ought to be understood against the backdrop of Gandhi's subscription to the Jaina principle of anekāntavāda, the view that no individual epistemic agent is infallible with respect to knowledge of a given fact, because it is possible for each person to be presented with different aspects of truth. Thus satyāgraha becomes both a means to acknowledge one's fallibility as a knower, and to address the strong emotions that result from not understanding the other's perspective on truth, *as well as* a ploy to open up space for reasoned dialogue so that reconciliation may become possible. If this is true, then it does not seem *in principle* correct to say that Gandhi's view of love in the *HS* does not account for spiritual or moral growth of both dissenter and (former) oppressor. Even if we allow this objection, however, we are left with a view of love that does

[16] Outside the context of conflict, that is.

not offer a more substantive conception of the loved one, beyond the generalities that she shares in our humanity, and, like us, is an epistemic and moral agent.

In one sense, this problem with Gandhi's account is inevitable, since he selects the vantage-point of conflict-resolution to think about love. Hence, the model of love that he comes up with is one of *love in spite of discord*. His account is skewed in the direction of the satyāgrahī—on what she could or must do to sew up the rent in the fabric of humanity. It would appear that the satyāgrahī's focus is squarely on averting the present crisis, and once it is averted, on bolstering her spirit until presented with another round of dissent, dialogue and affective political gesture. These are difficulties resulting from the programmatic nature of the project: because the emphasis is laid squarely on love as a moral and political *solution* rather than a human requirement/affect/aspiration, there results a certain limitation in the view.[17]

II. *Shantiniketan*, Book I: Love as Longing to Give Oneself[18]

The shortcomings of satyāgraha as a political strategy have been dwelt on at length in a number of places (e.g., Parekh

---

[17] It must be acknowledged that the view that this paper takes of 'Gandhi's view of love' is also restricted. It ignores his later writings, and looks past, for example, the affective dimension of Gandhi's personal friendship with Tagore. The only justification that can be offered in defence is that this is an attempt to provide an initial sketch of the view based on the claims about love put forward in *Hind Swaraj*, a famously rough-hewn work.

[18] *SN* is organized into sets of essays and addresses. I have used the format [RR#, title: book: numbered essay: page number] to cite the work. The essays are not numbered in the original, but since the number of essays/ addresses in each book range between three and twenty, this should not pose a problem for the reader.

1989, 153-64; Mukherjee 2016, 69 ff.), and will not be discussed here. The purpose of this piece is to set up a juxtaposition between two renderings of the non-dualistic philosophy of Advaita Vedānta, both of which are concerned, among other things, with the subject-matters of personal morality, ethics and spirituality, and yet are quite different from one another in terms of where they place their emphases, and why they do so. We shall now attempt to set up a dialogue between the two conceptions of love that they yield.

Before we delve into Tagore's notion of love, a few words on Tagore's rendition of the Advaitic principle are in order. Tagore helps himself to the notion of God while remaining convinced of the unity of all that exists, of ekamevādvitīyaṃ, as we will see below. Since God as an object of love or as a constant companion cannot be quality-less brahman, Tagore associates ordered experiences of the physical and social worlds, and life itself, with a personal God. The same deity is presented to experience both as ruler of the world and fate (bidhātā), and as an intimate presence or companion (bandhu) (RR7, *SN:* III: 3: 9), the latter presentation answering to Gandhi's dweller-within (antaryāmī) or lord of truth (satyanārayaṇa) (Suhrud 2018, 4; 16-17; 22-27). As an artist, Tagore sees his work as God-given, but also as a source of joy, since, like God's creation, artistic creation is the labour of love: it is born, like the universe itself, when the self gives itself in artistic expression.[19] As he would go on to argue in

---

[19] In the lyrics of the song *tumi sandhyār meghamālā* is contained the idea that the materials for the artist's creation are, among other things, her joys and sorrows. The words *jagater ānandajagye āmār nimantraṇ*—translated by Amit Chaudhuri as 'To the festival of creation I have an invitation' (Alam and Chakravarty 2011, xvii)—in a familiar song and poem from *Gītāñjalī*, speak of the artist contributing to divine work—jagya being the

his 1930 Hibbert Lectures, an artist has a mandate to 'dwell within the indefinite margin of life in him which affords a boundless background for his dreams and creations' and to '[explore] ages of creation to find himself in perfection' (Tagore 1996b, 138). The allusions here to what Tagore calls *the human surplus*—energies in human beings much more in excess of what is necessary to fulfil the material needs of oneself and others, the source of artistic creativity, as well as acts of great courage, endurance, and often, whimsy—and to the notion of perfection (an English term for which he does not provide an exact equivalent in Bengali)[20] cannot be found in his early philosophy. But the quoted passage suggests that the work of an artist is not, or *not only* for her own satisfaction, despite appearances and claims to the contrary, but for the expression of novel possibilities for humanity's ongoing quest for perfection.

A theme that runs through *SN* Book I is that of the significance of a sense of lack in human life. At this stage, Tagore renders this sense of lack as a yearning for the knowledge and proximity of God. But as he unfurls and develops the thought over the next few entries,[21] one comes to understand that, for Tagore, 'love for God' means entering into the world, or 'realizing oneself' in it (Tagore 1996a, 315 ff.)

Bengali cognate of the Sanskrit yajña—by helping along the continuous unfolding of the human potential. One could give many more illustrations from Tagore's literary works, but perhaps these will suffice.

[20] The closest is pūrṇatā, translated as fullness. The allusion is almost certainly to the prefatory verse of *Īśā Upaniṣad*.

[21] *SN*, Book 1, consists of entries written between the 17th day of Agrahāyaṇa and the 3rd of Poụsa, 1315, Bengali Era (December 2–18, 1908). I have tried above to outline some themes running through the twelve pieces that comprise this set. Translations from this work are mine.

through work (karma) as well as through relationships forged with the world of things and people (prem). Thus the sense of lack turns out to be a phenomenological datum for the self hived off from the world, yet, reaching out towards it through a cloud of obscurity. What follows in this section is an account of how Tagore builds a case for this claim, together with a characterization of the *eros* that he thinks all-important for any expression of humanity.

Tagore sets out the ultimate purpose of spiritual seeking in terms of the Upaniṣadic text *te sarvagaṃ sarvatah prāpya dhīrā yuktātmānaṃ sarvamevāviśanti*—'the wise (*dhīrāh*), having received from all directions that which is suffused through everything,[22] are united with themselves, and enter everywhere' (RR7, *SN:* I: 4: 527).[23] How does one gain such universal passage into the world? 'When the self is released from all sin (pāp) and from the wrappings (*ābaraṇa*) of all habitual dispositions, it unites with all selves everywhere, and only then does it enter everywhere.' By *ābaraṇa* Tagore means the layers of belief, desire and habit that weave themselves around the self through unreflective and self-regarding behaviour. He notes that '...the passing day, through various tasks, thoughts and tendencies, wraps layer upon layer around

[22] In *SN*, Tagore sometimes uses bhūmā (literally, the universally existing, or in his translation, 'the All'—see Sādhanā (in Tagore 1996a, passim), a term from the Upaniṣads, to convey the idea of brahman. Certain other terms, such as nikhil, satya and *ānanda*, appear to do double-duty for both the advaitic unity and manifested brahman.

[23] Here is a transcendentalist parallel: 'More and more the surges of everlasting nature enter into me, and I become public and human in my regards and actions' ('The Over-Soul,' in Emerson 2000, 250). For Emerson, Tagore *and* Gandhi, no manner of personal growth is possible without opening oneself to the world.

us, erecting a screen (*ābaraṇa*) between my self (*ātmān*) and the world[.]' We take the self hemmed-in by this screen to be the real thing, and ultimately become powerless to resist being trapped inside this carapace (RR7, *SN:* I: 1: 523). Such sapping of the will is the effect of being in consistently bad epistemic states: it is because one takes what is illusory to be the real thing that one is trapped within the boundaries of an imagined self.[24] Consequently, one fails to have *authentic encounters* with the world, and for that reason is denied *authentic knowledge* of the self.

By pāp Tagore means something deeper and more pernicious than the tendencies that lead people to violate social norms of decency or good behaviour. Pāp is any and all tendencies deep-rooted in the self that bar the way to spiritual growth and/or authentic being in the world (RR7, *SN:* I: 5). Prima facie, these are tendencies to build up the self within the carapace—let us call this the ego—which are activated whenever we strive to amass what we take to be our worldly entitlements.[25] Tagore characterizes these as pāp because we choose to indulge or gratify them *instead of* heeding the call to transcend the boundaries of the ego in the quest for authentic love and knowledge.

---

[24] 'I am the master of my home; I am the householder in this household (saṁsār)... This home, this household is filled with me—so many legal deeds, documents, monetary arrangements, and disputes! But where is God? Etc.' (RR7, *SN*: I: 2: 524). Compare *Bhagavadgītā*, XVI: 13; 15 (Radhakrishnan, 1963, 338).

[25] Or as Emerson describes them, what we think we have 'gotten,' in the face of the unyielding nature of the world, in which all things are characterized by 'evanescence and lubricity,' slipping through the hands when one clutches them hardest ('Experience,' Emerson 2000, 309 ff.). Compare Tagore's description of our experience of objects in the world as a series of deaths (RR7, *SN*: I: 12: 540).

What is it like to authentically be in the world? Tagore explains by way of an example. He describes having a dream set in his childhood featuring his late mother. In the dream, his mother is seated in her room while he passes by, walking purposefully along the adjoining verandah. Suddenly it occurs to him that she is present in her room, in his life. This thought causes him to run back to her room, where she greets him warmly. Tagore continues:

> I began to think—I live in Mother's house, I walk past her door ten times over—doubtless she is present, but things continue as though she is not. What seems to be lost? She has not closed the kitchen-storeroom, she continues to serve food, her palm-leaf fan keeps me cool as I sleep. It is just that she does not hold my hand and say, 'You've come!' All things exist—food, water, wealth and other people—but where is that voice, that touch! *When the mind awakens fully, it wants only that, and when it does not get that which it wants, [one] seeks it in rooms furnished with various things; then one can on no account enjoy one's food and water* (RR7, *SN:* I: 3: 526; emphasis added).

Being in the world in this way involves being in *ātmika* connection with other people, as well as with physical nature.[26] It is not mere dissatisfaction with one's circumstances that

[26] 'When I experience this tree before us profoundly as a form of that [unitary] being, my entire being is filled with joy (ānanda). Since I do not see it thus, I see it with my eyes, and pass it by having determined that I have no use for it... We also do not see human beings by means of the *ātmān*; we see them through our senses, through reasoning, through the lens of our selfish ends, our world (saṁsār) and our dispositions (saṁskār); we see them as a member of the family, or a useful person, or an unrelated person, or a member of some class of persons or other' (RR7, SN: I: 4: 527).

makes us seek authentic encounters with the other. Any such dissatisfaction is the flip-side of an overwhelming desire to know oneself shorn of the trappings of worldly life.[27] This desire is satisfied when we break through our egotistical demands of the world and unite with the other. We saw in the previous section that union with the other is a straightforward ethical implication of the Advaitic thesis. But for Tagore, the pretext for union is not, and does not need to be, a situation of disagreement, conflict or oppression. The genetic story of the authentic encounter or union of selves that Tagore gives traces it to a desire intrinsic to human nature. This is the desire for self-transcendence, that is to say, in the first instance, a desire to escape the limitations of the ego that one finds oneself saddled with, thanks to unreflective or self-centred modes of living.

One of Tagore's favourite Upaniṣadic texts is Yājñavalkya's admonition to Maitreyī that all that the self desires in the world is for the sake of the self (RR7, *SN:* VI: 7: 619; Tagore 1996a, 291). This passage says, among other things, that because the father sees himself in the son (i.e., sees their individual selves as united in *ātmān*) that he loves the son. The love for *ātmān* being paramount, one inexorably seeks *ātmika* union with the other. This is not to say that human beings understand the desire for *ātmīya*, or intimately related others, quite in this way. In Yajñavalkya's view, their desire to know, love and be loved by others is an

[27] In *SN*, Book I, this desire is presented as a pull towards brahman in the final analysis. See his comments on ẹsāsya paramāgatih, etc. at II: 12: 558-560. Since brahman is no different from *ātmān*, it is also a pull towards one's authentic being. It would seem that the latter is phenomenologically prior to the former.

unconscious groping for *ātmān*. Taking a leaf out of that playbook, Tagore argues that all love is a presentation of the authentic quest for self-knowledge and encounter with the self. It is just that the quest for the self cannot proceed without the active collaboration of *the world* (which includes other persons) in bringing about the desired union. Thus love results in *both* knowledge of the other and one's own self. This yields the possibility that relatively more perfect instances of *ātmika* union involve mutual spiritual growth.[28]

We have already touched on Tagore's view that it is possible also to authentically engage with nature: to know things in nature as one's *ātmīya* is to infuse the self with awareness and knowledge of their being, and to receive aesthetic stimulation and joy from them. This is not as mysterious as it probably sounds. Children, who are as yet unencumbered by a powerful ego, relate to physical nature with nearly as much ease as they do with their parents, siblings, and friends.[29] The idea isn't that adult humans must be like children, but that they need to train their cognitive and affective faculties to be free of the numerous biases and unhelpful attitudes that the mind imposes upon them in order to enjoy authentic being-with-nature. Once again, this would not be a simple matter of shedding the attitudes

---

[28] Compare Bourgeault's account of the Fifth Way in Christian spiritual practice (see Bourgeault, 2010, 115-119). Paraphrasing Boris Mouravieff, she comments on the efficacy of the path of conscious love: 'Functioning as foils and mirrors for each other, the partners can work their way together through inner logjams that might have taken years to navigate individually.' The reader might recall a similar theme in Emerson's account of friendship with a morally equal or superior individual.

[29] See Tagore 1996b, 156-157.

in question, but would involve conscious practice (sādhanā) over a period of time.[30]

Tagore describes awakening to the world in this manner as the birth of the individual consciousness into world-consciousness (*jībacaitanyer biśvacaitanye janma*)—as becoming twice-born (dvija). 'Spirituality,' says he, 'does not give us anything more; it rids us of our apathy, our numbness. Only when this occurs do we receive consciousness with consciousness, *ātmān* with *ātmān*' (RR7, *SN:* I: 4: 527). As indicated above, it takes sustained practice to develop habits of mind that resist the building on of layers of egotistical beliefs and attitudes (RR7, *SN:* I: 7: 531-32). Mentally shedding the vestments of the ego makes possible unobstructed union with the beloved. On the phenomenological side, a precondition for such union is the experience of longing for union. The longing for union with the other, for love, is thus identical with a desire to rid oneself of the ego. The latter is what Tagore describes as the desire to give oneself up for the sake of a greater gain (*ātmān*, as presented in the object of one's love). It is, if you like, the yajña of the ego at the altar of love.[31]

30 An analogy might help. An ecologist friend of this author once described the lantana, a notoriously invasive and rather ugly species of shrub, as 'an amazing plant'. This is a hard-earned, educated appreciation for the plant that he would not have come by 'naturally'.

31 Radhakrishnan's note on *Bhagavadgītā* IV: 25 reads: 'Ś[aṁkara] interprets yajña in the second half of the verse as *ātmān*. 'Others offer the self as self into the fire of Brahman' (Radhakrishnan 1963, 166). Though Tagore had studied Śaṁkara, he would have been strongly opposed to the excision of love from an account of union of *ātmān* with *ātmān*.

III. Overlaps and Distinctions

The foregoing discussion of Tagore's ideas about spiritual growth and practice may seem somewhat out of place, given that Gandhi's view of spiritual practice has not been discussed in similar detail. The reader will recall that only precepts (i) and (ii) in Parekh's list were taken into consideration in paraphrasing Gandhi's account of love-force in *Hind Swaraj*. It may be possible to compensate for this by means of a discussion of Parekh's summary of Gandhi's view of love, which, though not present in quite this form in *HS*, fleshes it out considerably, making it possible to have a better sense of Gandhi's view as it is brought into closer engagement with Indian philosophical and religious thought.

> Gandhi argued that love was the only way of identifying oneself with other living beings. It implied opening up oneself to their presence, relieving them of their otherness and making them part of oneself. As love deepened the distance between the two decreased, and at its highest love culminated in total identification. Universal love was the only way to attain identification with all living beings. It involved infinite openness, breaking down all the barriers between the self and others, letting them flow into one's being and suffuse one's thoughts and feelings with the deepest concern for their well-being (Parekh 1989, 96).

So far, it is hard to detect any differences between this account of love and the account that Tagore begins to develop in *SN* Book I. Parekh goes on to explain that this notion of love (i.e., prem) was relatively new to the Hindu way of thinking—perhaps he has in mind its earliest expositions in medieval Bhakti poetry in various Indian languages—and that Hindu philosophical tradition (and presumably, the monastic traditions that produced arts of living out of it) was scornful of the notion of love, because love tended to produce attachment, and block spiritual progress. Gandhi had adopted detachment as a moral and spiritual ideal for himself, but then he also felt profound admiration for Jesus Christ. Therefore, he attempted to effect a reconciliation of the opposing ideals.

> He attempted to resolve the tension by redefining both love and detachment... [H]e seems to have thought that love was not an emotion but an objective concern for others' well-being, not a subjective feeling but a sentiment or spirit of good will. As for detachment it did not mean indifference but absence of attachment, not lack of interest but of self-interest. Gandhi thought that *when so understood love and detachment were not only compatible but interdependent*...To help others because one could not *bear* to see them suffer or because helping them had become a powerful *craving* or desire was not an expression of love but a form of self-assertion, even of self-indulgence. True love must be totally self-less...in the profound sense of not involving the self in any form at all... Gandhi thought that God's love for the world was of this kind; deep and warm yet non-emotional, serene and detached (Parekh 1989, 97; emphasis added).

The example of God is followed by the example of a surgeon operating on a patient in distress: her conduct was expressive of good-will, reassurance and concern, but it was also calm, because she was, and needed to be, detached, and non-emotional. In the second example we note an emphasis on love expressed as a critical intervention; presumably God's love for humanity, as Gandhi imagined it, is not delimited in the same way. Parekh argues that Gandhi's attempt at reconciling the twin ideals of love and detachment remained unsuccessful and far from convincing. Gandhi felt the clash of these ideals within his own being, since his practice of detachment could not be harmonized with the intense love that he felt for his countrymen.[32]

Tagore reconciled the same two ideals using his take on themes in the Gaudīya Vaisṇava tradition of thought and spiritual practice. In *SN*, he evinces great admiration for its figurehead, Chaitanya,[33] as well as for several poets of the *Ṛg Veda* and the *Upaniṣads*, the Buddha, and Christ—according to him, all individuals who embodied the ideal of love expressed by the bit of *Upaniṣadic* text quoted at the start of Section II. Tagore rejected the idea that detachment equalled freedom from the bonds of love, where 'bonds' implies a manner of commitment to the other different from what Gandhi ascribes to the surgeon, or indeed to God. In order to make this point, Tagore, too, redefined detachment: he thought that moral and spiritual practice were about erosion of the ego and a growing openness to, and deeper commitment to the world. To this he added the idea that in fact human beings do not desire the sort of freedom that empties that state of all affect. He thought that genuine freedom serves the end of spiritual (i.e., *ātmika*) gain, and thus it is only an extrinsic good.[34] Detachment is sought not so that the self may suffer loss through erosion of the ego, but for a greater gain, however obscurely one might glimpse the object to be gained.

---

[32] Tagore expresses this nearly unbearable sense of concern in a scene in the novel *Gorā*. The subject of that experience is the titular character, moved by the sight of simple country-folk vying with each other to get on a boat, unreasonably fearful that it would leave them behind.

[33] See, for example, Tagore 1996b, 142. Chaitanya is not mentioned by name, presumably because Tagore was speaking before a British audience who would not have known of him.

[34] This implies that Tagore did not think too highly of mukti or mokśa.

Popular discourse on human love contains the homily that love makes one vulnerable before the other. This is of course why 'love hurts' when making oneself vulnerable does not result in the greater gain of the union that was expected. Yet, people seek love. This is not 'irrational behaviour' on their part; Tagore would say that people seek love in order to find (or 'realize') themselves in the other, to seek freedom from the boundaries of their worldly selves. This would be the implication for human love, of passages such as these:

> If you say that through renunciation (tyāg) you will be free of the object renounced, our mind does not support what you say; if you say that by renouncing you will gain the thing renounced more fully, that too does not fully resonate with our mind. If you say that through renunciation love shall be found, then the mind cannot come up with a word in response—if it pays careful heed to what was said, then it is obliged to say, 'That would be a relief' (RR7, *SN*, I: 9: 538).

The sentences that follow express precisely the same view that Gandhi held, namely, that while love is a condition for renouncing or letting go, there can be no love without renunciation. This is how Tagore sees the matter. As a condition for renunciation, love is the *motive-force* that pushes the self out of its protective casing and puts it on the path of unrelenting solitude (for example, in the case of the world-renouncing dervish or saṁnyāsī, or such sportspersons and artists as 'live for the game'),[35] peril (the adventurer,

[35] In each of these cases, the possibility of falling to 'the last temptation' looms large: as T.S. Eliot defined it in *Murder in The Cathedral*, the last temptation is the temptation 'to do the right thing for the wrong reason.' It is perhaps too easy to do for the love of one's own self what one ought to do for the game.

the revolutionary, or the lover who takes a leap of faith by placing her trust in the other), suffering (in the case of a jilted lover, and certainly Christ, the 'lamb of God') and perhaps even ridicule (lovers again, Chaitanya being beaten by the mob, Jesus at the hands of the Romans). On the one hand, without *eros*, one cannot give up the comfort of one's habits of thought or usual modes of being—one cannot stop feeding the ego.[36] On the other hand, without renunciation of the ego, love cannot find fulfilment.

Let us turn for a moment to the outline view of suffering love that Gandhi provides in *HS*. The satyāgrahī, Gandhi tells us, is a person of courage because she opens herself up to any suffering that the oppressor might decide to subject her to. Such an act of courage is only possible when she is free of the usual encumbrances of the mind. '*Control over mind is alone necessary, and, when that is attained, man is free like the king of the forest, etc.*' (*HS*, 77; emphasis in original). This reinforces the need for personal spiritual discipline, so that one may become free of one's lower self to embody the courage that satyāgraha requires. Satyāgraha, the reader will recall, involves suffering love. Suffering must be undertaken freely, for one cannot suffer for love *while unfree*. But then, for Gandhi, one suffers for love (if one may so put it,) *in order to* realign the self and the other, thus making whole the moral fabric (dharma) of God's world as well as reaffirming the fundamental metaphysical unity of brahman.

---

[36] The theme of 'emptying' the self (*kenosis*) is present in Christianity. Against the backdrop of Paul's description of Jesus's sādhanā in those terms, and Ward Bauman's description of the death of Jesus 'as the result of personal dying to the self, as he himself taught it,' Bourgeault talks about kenosis practised by lovers as part of the Fifth Way. See Bourgeault (2010, 126 ff; 148-160).

Tagore also argues that to seek love via renunciation is to act freely. This is because breaking through the ego is perhaps the only 'freedom from' that the self *qua* spirit experiences. (So far, Tagore's view is in agreement with Gandhi's: neither man thought in the 1900s that India's destiny would change for the better with independence from the colonial ruler.) But on the other hand, to seek fulfilment in love is to *bind oneself* to the object of love, albeit freely. The paradigm of such love is God's love for human beings. Unlike Gandhi's un-emotional God full of profound concern for humanity, Tagore's God is a lover. 'He[37] who renounces everything for us without there being a need to do so is of the nature of love... *ānandādhyeva khalvimāni bhūtāni jāyante ij*—all things are created from joy, and not from some sort of obligation to create' (RR7, *SN*: I: 9: 538). In an essay titled 'Śrābaṇasandhyā' (RR8, SN: XI: 5: 560-563), not creation, but the (occasional, seasonal) beauty of the world is described at some length as a divine gift of love. Quite like God, a person who enjoys genuine freedom from the self gains the world by entering into a loving relationship with the world; the reader will recall that this is the meaning that Tagore attaches to *te sarvagaṃ sarvatah prāpya dhīrā yuktātmānaṃ sarvamevāviśanti.*

As indicated above, Tagore thinks that the individual who seeks authentic encounter with the self through love opens herself to suffering, and indeed is aided in her quest by suffering (RR7, *SN*: I: 6: 529-530). Settling for, for example, peace in one's quest to know the self can end up undermining the quest, says Tagore; it can lead us to draw a limit to the project of self-transcendence where essentially there is none

[37] Tagore's God does not have a gender, or rather can present as both father and mother, among other things. Such are the vagaries of translation.

(RR7, *SN*: I: 11: 537).[38] But then the only justification for taking on suffering is the prize at the end—the promise of self-transcendence, or what is the same thing, the bonds of love that one enters into freely.

IV. Concluding Remarks

What the present paper offers is a sketch of the relationship between certain concepts that appear together in the same logical neighbourhood—love, renunciation/detachment, suffering and freedom—in the thought of Gandhi in *Hind Swaraj* and Tagore in the first Book of Shantiniketan. The foregoing discussion establishes that the account of love that each thinker professes is distinguished by what it suggests about the contribution of love to the constitution of the self, and the role that it plays in influencing the view that the individual self comes to have of its relation to the world. Gandhi extols the expression of love resulting from ongoing work on the self, with the consequences of contact with the other acting as ingredients for further work on the self: ultimately, the practice of loving in contexts of satyāgraha promises to compound the moral benefits for everyone affected, and bringing about interpersonal harmony. Tagore sees the self as acquiring definition through its engagement with the other, emphasizing the expression of love as an authentic commitment to the other, expressed

[38] The poem and song *āpnāke ei jānā āmār phurābe nā* (roughly, My Knowing of Myself Shall Not End) seems to partially express this idea. See also Emerson, 'Circles,' in Emerson 2000, 253. Tagore's view that love contains both peace and lack of peace (aśānti) has rather troubling implications for the popular ideal of 'happy marriage' and related notions. Or better, it opens up the question of what happiness in a relationship really is.

as mutual growth along various dimensions. The two also differ with respect to their understanding of both freedom and detachment/renunciation, and their relationship to love.

There is much work to be done in terms of drawing inferences from this preliminary exercise, carefully studying the later views of both thinkers and working out their developed philosophies of love. The matter of Tagore's interpretation of Vedic texts as, among other things, making pronouncements on love, requires careful study. That Tagore's view does not align with the scholarly view of those texts seems rather beside the point given the way in which he opens up those texts to independent interpretation using the great number of perspectives that are harmonized within his thought. By illustrating the manner in which he makes *ātmīyas* of them, he exemplifies Emerson's idea of the text as a friend, rather than a remote entity holding its secrets apart from those who would seek to variously assimilate them. In view of such facts as these, this paper marks the beginning of a project rather than a comprehensive account of the subject-matter it explores.

References

Alam, F. and Chakravarty, R. eds. 2011. *The Essential Tagore*. Cambridge: The Belknap Press, Harvard University Press.

Bhattacharya, S. ed. 1997. *The Mahatma and The Poet: Letters and Debates between Gandhi and Tagore, 1915-1941*. New Delhi: National Book Trust, India.

Bourgeault, C. 2010. *The Meaning of Mary Magdalene: Discovering the Woman at The Heart of Christianity*. Boulder, CO: Shambhala.

Emerson, R.W. 2000. *The Essential Writings of Ralph Waldo Emerson*. M. Oliver (ed.). New York: The Modern Library.

Mukherjee, G. 2016. *Gandhi and Tagore: Politics, Truth and Conscience.* London: Routledge.

Parekh, B. 1989. *Gandhi's Political Philosophy: A Critical Examination.* London: Macmillan.

Parekh, B. 2001. *Gandhi: A Very Short Introduction.* Oxford: Oxford University Press.

Radhakrishnan, S. 1963. *Bhagavadgītā.* (Sanskrit text, translation and notes.) London: George Allen and Unwin. (This edition states the author's name simply as 'Radhakrishnan'.)

Sharma, S. and Suhrud, T. 2010. *MK Gandhi's Hind Swaraj: A Critical Edition.* (HS) Hyderabad: Orient Blackswan.

Suhrud, T. 2018. Editor's Introduction to M.K. Gandhi, *An Autobiography or The Story of My Experiments with Truth,* Critical Edition, M. Desai (trans.). Gurgaon: Penguin Random House India.

Tagore, R. 1988a. Shantiniketan, 1-10. *Rabindra Rachanābali,* (125th anniversary edition, 1395 Bengali Era), Vol. 7. Kolkata: Visva-Bharati. (RR7)

Tagore, R. 1988b. Shantiniketan, 11-17. *Rabindra Rachanābali,* (125th anniversary edition, 1395 Bengali Era), Vol. 8. Kolkata: Visva-Bharati. (RR8)

Tagore, R. 1996a. *The English Writings of Rabindranath Tagore, Vol. 2.* New Delhi: Sahitya Akademi.

Tagore, R. 1996b. *The English Writings of Rabindranath Tagore, Vol. 3.* New Delhi: Sahitya Akademi.

ABOUT THE CONTRIBUTORS

Indrani Bhattacharjee is Assistant Professor of Philosophy at the Jindal School of Liberal Arts and Humanities, O.P. Jindal Global University, Sonipat. She has doctoral degrees in philosophy from Jadavpur University and the University of Massachusetts, Amherst. She has taught for close to nine years at Azim Premji University, and for shorter stints at Tufts and Bridgewater State University in the United States. While her writing and teaching are strongly influenced by her training in analytic philosophy, Indrani is also interested in exploring veins of philosophical enquiry that actively combine dialectical thought with the deliverances of a synoptic and/or poetic vision and imagination. Her research and teaching interests include the philosophy of the Later Wittgenstein, philosophy of education, epistemology and Indian aesthetics. Her dominant research interest at this time is the early philosophical thought of Rabindranath Tagore (circa 1908-1916), a topic on which she is writing a book. In this book, she explores the sources of Tagore's humanism and cosmopolitanism through his essays in Bengali and English.

Meher Bhoot is Associate Professor and Head at the Department of German, University of Mumbai. Her areas of specialization are German Literature with a focus on Literature of the German Minorities, Postcolonial Studies and Culture Studies and her areas of interest are European Cultural History and European History of Art. She is an active member of the German Institute's Partnership with the Universities of Göttingen and Freiburg in Germany.

Under the aegis of this partnership she has been a Guest Professor at the Department of Intercultural German Studies, University of Göttingen, Germany in 2017. She is a DAAD Fellow since 2004 and has also been a recipient of the Rotary Cultural and Ambassadorial Scholarship (1997-98). She is also the Member Secretary of the Women's Development Cell, University of Mumbai since 2018 and member of the Internal Committee at the University of Mumbai. Apart from articles published, some of her co-edited volumes include *Revisiting Günter Grass, Voices from India and Germany, Interkulturelle Momente, Einfach menschlich.* She has also co-edited the textbooks for the short courses for teaching Marathi to non-native speakers. They are titled *Communicative Marathi for Nurses* and *Communicative Marathi for Rickshaw and Taxi Drivers.*

Faisal Devji is Professor of Indian History and Fellow of St. Antony's College at the University of Oxford. He is the author of four books, including *The Impossible Indian: Gandhi and the Temptation of Violence* (Harvard 2012).

Siby K. George is Professor of Philosophy at the Department of Humanities and Social Sciences, Indian Institute of Technology Bombay. His areas of research interest are phenomenology and poststructuralism. His publications include *Heidegger and Development in the Global South* (Springer, 2015), and the co-edited volumes *Cultural Ontology of the Self in Pain* (Springer 2016) and *Teaching in Unequal Societies* (Bloomsbury 2020).

Shweta Sachdeva Jha teaches English at Miranda House, University of Delhi. Her research interests are interdisciplinary and range from English and Urdu fiction, Children's Picture Books to Women's History and Literary Theory. She was awarded the Felix Scholarship to study for her PhD at the Department of History, School of Oriental and African Studies, University of London. Her publications on the history of the *tawa'if* include articles in journals and the chapter, '*Tawa'if* as Poet and Patron: Rethinking Women's Self Representation' in Anshu Malhotra and Siobhan

Lambert-Hurley eds. *Speaking of the Self: Gender, Performance and Autobiography in South Asia* (Duke University Press, 2015). Her most recent publications on Women's Fiction in Urdu include, 'Tracing Terror and the Uncanny in the Gothic Urdu Fiction of Hijab Imtiaz Ali' in Katarzyna Ancuta and Deimantas Valančiūnas eds. *South Asian Gothic: Haunted Cultures, Histories and Media* (University of Wales Press, 2021). Her work on children's picture books was funded by the Delhi University Innovations Grant (2015-16) on *Children's Picture Books in India: Rethinking History, Storytelling and Pedagogy*. Currently, she leads the Miranda House Archiving Project to compile a history of college women and their experiences. She has received the Avabai Wadia Fellowship from the Research Centre for Women's Studies, SNDT Women's University, Mumbai (2020-21) to work on this digital archive.

Nikhil Katara is the founder and artistic director at Readings in the Shed. He has co-written and directed the play, *The Bose Legacy Inked Through Letters*. As a writer he started his journey in 2011, with his own production titled *The Unveiling*, a science fiction drama. It won much appreciation for its scientific engagement and philosophical themes. To strengthen his critical thinking, he did his Masters degree in Philosophy at the University of Mumbai. He conducts a reading club where writers, philosophers and directors in the city of Mumbai critique literature on a weekly basis. He has written book reviews and opinion articles in the *One India One People* magazine and the *Free Press Journal*. He wrote the play, *Yatagarasu* which opened at Prithvi Theatre in June 2018. He has directed twenty performances at Readings in the Shed.

Rajesh Kharat is Founder Director, School of International Relations and Strategic Studies, University of Mumbai and Dean, Faculty of Humanities, University of Mumbai (on Deputation), and Professor and former Chairperson, Centre for South Asian Studies, School of International Studies, JNU, New Delhi. He has an MA in Political Science from the University of Poona, and has completed his M.Phil. and PhD from CSAS, SIS, JNU, New Delhi. He began his teaching career at the University of Mumbai in 1991 and taught at JNU for 30 years. He has published five books and more than 30 research articles in international and national journals and edited volumes on various themes of Contemporary South Asia.

Satishchandra Kumar is Professor and Head of the Department of Applied Psychology & Counselling Centre at the University of Mumbai. He is also the Coordinator of the Mahatma Gandhi Peace Centre. He is the recipient of the Summer Fellowship from the Albert Ellis Institute, New York. He was awarded the Research Fellowship by the Indian Council of Social Science Research (ICSSR), New Delhi. He has published in international peer-reviewed journals like *Journal of Personality and Social Psychology, Psychological Science, British Journal of Guidance and Counselling,* and also contributed to the Sage volume of *Eminent Indian Psychologists: 100 Years of Psychology in India.* He has published more than 40 research papers in national and international renowned journals, five books, and many students have done doctorate degrees under his guidance. His area of research interest is Industrial/Organizational Psychology which includes positive psychology, engagement at the workplace, stress and coping at the workplace. He is the reviewer on various international journals and books. He is also a member of many academic bodies and regularly advises corporates. He is also the co-editor of *Sambhashan,* the journal of the University of Mumbai.

Kanchana Mahadevan is Professor and Head at the Department of Philosophy, University of Mumbai. She teaches and researches in feminist philosophy, continental thought, critical theory and political philosophy. She also works in the interdisciplinary areas of aesthetics and film. Her book *Between Femininity and Feminism: Colonial and Postcolonial Perspectives on Care* examines the relevance of Western feminist philosophy in the Indian context, while bringing Western feminism into dialogue with its Indian counterpart. Her publications on Ambedkar explore his rearticulation of democracy from the Indian perspective. In her recently published research papers on care ethics, she has engaged with its critical potential in relation to health work and the cosmopolitan character of care. She is specifically interested in exploring the comparative and decolonizing dimensions of philosophy. She is currently working on a monograph on the relationship between the secular and the post-secular in the context of gender.

Margaret McLaren holds the George D. and Harriet W. Cornell Chair of Philosophy at Rollins College in Winter Park, Florida where she teaches philosophy and in the programme of Sexuality, Women and Gender Studies (SWAG). She received her MA and PhD in philosophy from Northwestern University. She is the author of *Feminism, Foucault, and Embodied Subjectivity* (State University of New York Press, 2002) and *Women's Activism, Feminism and Social Justice* (Oxford University Press, 2019) and the editor of *Decolonizing Feminism: Transnational Feminism and Globalisation* (Rowman and Littlefield, 2017). Her articles on gender issues, women and human rights, multiculturalism, Foucault, feminism, and virtue ethics have appeared in several journals, including *Social Theory & Practice, Journal of Developing Societies, Forum on Public Policy, Philosophy Today,* and *Hypatia*. She has also contributed to many anthologies including, *Feminism and the Final Foucault, Feminists Doing Ethics,* and *Florida Without Borders: Women at the Intersection of the Local and Global*. During the 2021-2022 academic year she is a Fulbright-Nehru Academic and Professional Excellence Fellow at Visva Bharati University, Shantiniketan.

Prem Anand Mishra is Dean and Head of Department, Faculty of Gandhian Studies at Gujarat Vidyapith, Ahmedabad, Gujarat (India) where he teaches Gandhian Political Philosophy and Peace Research. He is the author of seven books: *Gandhi's Philosophy of Action* (2020), *Gandhian Humanism and Theory of Social Harmony* (2019), *Debating Nationalism* (2018), *Position: Gandhi's Intervention in Contemporary Discourse* (2017), *Peace Research: Issues and Application*

(2015), *Gandhian Humanism in the Twenty First Century* (2015), and *Hind Swaraj: A Deconstructive Reading* (2012). He has also contributed to *Gandhi Marg, Journal of Gandhian Studies, The Indian Journal of Political Science, Anekant,* and *Indian Journal of Philosophy, Religion and Culture.*

Kirti Nakhare is an Assistant Professor in English, heading the Department of Business Communication, S.I.W.S. College of Commerce and Economics, Mumbai. She completed her doctoral research from the Department of English, University of Mumbai in December 2019. Her areas of interest include analysis of traditional versions of the epics, subaltern theory and comparative mythology. Her interest in comparative mythology spurred her on to successfully complete the post-graduate diploma in Comparative Mythology offered by the Department of Sanskrit, University of Mumbai. She successfully completed the online course on the Epics offered by the Oxford Centre of Hindu Studies. She has several publications to her credit and has presented papers at national and international conferences. Besides this, she participated in the OER project of University of Mumbai in association with CommonWealth Asia to create content on soft skills in 2010. She received the University of Mumbai's research grant for working on a Minor Research Project for the year 2010-11; a comparison between African and Indian Children's Literature was undertaken as part of the project. She created content for the African Literature Module of the UGC'S E-PG Pathshala project. She is a member of The Asiatic Society, Mumbai. Along with teaching, she is interested in travelling and is trained in Hindustani classical music.

Madhavi Nikam is Associate Professor at the PG Department of English, R.K. Talreja College, Ulhasnagar, Thane, Mumbai. She is a recognized research guide for PhD in English, University of Mumbai. Apart from being a member of the Senate of the University of Mumbai (from 2010-2015), she has been actively involved in academics and administration as well. Presently, as a member of the

Academic Council (2017-2022) of the University of Mumbai, she is representing the teaching fraternity. Dr. Nikam was the editor of two international journals, *Literary Insight* and *Contemporary Discourse*. Her contribution to research continues as the Secretary of Higher Education & Research Society, Navi Mumbai. She has organized many international and national conferences and seminars till date. Her work has been recognized with awards and accolades. She has published many research articles at national and international levels.

Indu Prakash Pandey is based in Schwalbach, Germany since 1967, and regularly spends several months in India. Born 1924 in Uttar Pradesh, he was jailed during the Quit India Movement of 1942. He completed his M.A. (Hindi) from the University of Allahabad and D.Lit. at the University of Utrecht, Netherlands. After serving as the Head of the Hindi department at Elphinstone College Mumbai for 14 years, he taught Hindi, Hindi Literature, Indian Culture and Philosophy at the South Asia Institute, Heidelberg (Germany) and the University of California, Berkeley (USA). Thereafter, he was sent on deputation by the Cultural Ministry of India for two years to teach Hindi at the University of Bucharest (Romania). He also held guest lectures on Hindi language and Literature at the University of Beijing (China). He taught at Johann Wolfgang Goethe-University Frankfurt (Germany) for 22 years. He has been a member of the Indian Central Board of Film Censors and the committee selecting the best film for the President's Award. He founded the Indian Cultural Institute in Frankfurt and was the long-serving head of the same. Dr. Pandey has published 25 books in Hindi, English and German as well as translations from Hindi into German. He has written a Hindi textbook for Romanian students and many books on Hindi Literature and Folklore.

Bhikhu Parekh graduated from the University of Mumbai and obtained his PhD from the London School of Economics in 1966. He has been teaching at the University of Hull since 1964 and is currently an Emeritus Professor at that university. He has been a Visiting Professor at several universities including McGill, Harvard, Institute of Advanced Study in Vienna, the University of Pennsylvania, and Universitat Pompeu Fabra in Barcelona. He delivered the Litowitz Lecture at Yale University in 2003, and was recently invited as Distinguished Visitor by the Cardozo Law School in New York. He was Vice-Chancellor of the University of Baroda from 1981-1984. He is the author of several widely acclaimed books in political philosophy, including *Rethinking Multiculturalism* published by Harvard University Press in 2000. He is a Fellow of the British Academy, and past president of the Academy of Learned Societies in the Social Sciences. Professor Parekh is also active in British political life. He was for five years Deputy Chairman of the Commission for Racial Equality, and chaired the Commission on the Future of Multi-Ethnic Britain, whose report (called the Parekh Report) was published in 2000. He received the BBC's Special Lifetime Achievement Award for Asians in November 1999, and was appointed to the House of Lords in March 2000. He received the Sir Isaiah Berlin Prize for Lifetime Contribution to Political Philosophy, and the Padma Bhushan from the president of India.

Aakash Singh Rathore is a Permanent Visiting Professor of Global Politics at LUISS University in Rome, Italy, and author of *Ambedkar's Preamble: A Secret History of the Constitution on India* (Penguin, 2020), and of the forthcoming book, *B.R. Ambedkar: A Biography*. Rathore was a Fellow of the Indian Institute for Advanced Study, Shimla and had earlier explored bodily self-representation in life writing, publishing *A Philosophy of Autobiography Body & Text* (Routledge, 2019). He is also editor of the five-volume box set, *B.R. Ambedkar: The Quest for Justice* (Oxford University Press, 2020). He tweets at @ASR_Metta.

Arushi Sharma is an Assistant Professor at the Department of English, University of Mumbai. She is guest faculty in the Department of English, IDOL, University of Mumbai. She also works as a trainer for functional proficiency and professional proficiency courses conducted by the Department of English, University of Mumbai. She has completed her M.Phil. from the Department of English, University of Jammu, J&K. Her research is on Native Americans as a post-colonial subject. She has presented papers at national and international conferences and has various publications to her credit. She has contributed in creating study material on American literature for SYBA students, IDOL, University of Mumbai. In addition to this, she is a poet too.

Uday Narayana Singh is an expert in Linguistics, Culture Studies, Translation and Creative Writing, and currently the Dean, Faculty of Arts, Amity University, Haryana and a Chair-Professor. He was the Director of CIIL, Mysore and Pro-Vice-Chancellor of Visva-Bharati, Shantiniketan. Singh set up the National Translation Mission and the Linguistic Data Consortium for the Government of India at Mysore and Centre for Applied Linguistics and Translation Studies (CALTS) at Hyderabad. He taught at Hyderabad (1987-2000), Visva-Bharati (2000-2009), University of Delhi (1985-87), South Gujarat (1981-85) and in MSU-Baroda (1979-81). With seven collections of poems in Maithili and Bangla, six books of literary essays, besides twelve plays in Maithili, he has translated/edited 16 books and published 250 research papers. He also designed and created 545 documentaries on language, literature and culture of Bangla, Tamil, Kannada and Marathi. A poet-invitee at the Frankfurt Book Fair (2006), London Book Fair (2009), and Leader of Cultural Delegation of Writers to China (2007), he has visited and lectured in Australia, Andorra, Bangladesh, Belgium, Caribbean Islands, France, Germany, Iceland, Italy, Nepal, Pakistan, Russia, Singapore, Spain, Sweden, Thailand, UK and the USA. He has received many awards and honours, including the coveted Sahitya Akademi Award in 2017 for poetry.